TAKING CHARGE OF OUR LIVES

Taking Charge of Our Lives

Living Responsibly in a Troubled World

American Friends Service Committee, San Francisco

Edited by Joan Bodner

1817

Harper & Row, Publishers, San Francisco

Cambridge, Hagerstown, New York, Philadelphia
London, Mexico City, São Paulo, Singapore, Sydney

Grateful acknowledgment is made for the use of the following material: "Unity" by Holly Near, © 1981 Hereford Music; used by permission. "The Woodcarrier" in Thomas Merton, *The Way of Chuang Tzu,* copyright © 1965 by the Abbey of Gethsemani; reprinted by permission of New Directions Publishing Corporation.

FIRST EDITION

Designer: Jim Mennick

Illustrator: Coby Everdell

Library of Congress Cataloging in Publication Data

Main entry under title:

TAKING CHARGE OF OUR LIVES

   Rev. ed of: Taking charge / Simple Living Collective, American Friends Service Committee, San Francisco. 1977.
   Bibliography: p.
   1. United States—Social conditions—1980-   —Addresses, essays, lectures.   2. United States—Social life and customs—1971-   —Addresses, essays, lectures.   3. Conduct of life—Addresses, essays, lectures.   4. Consumers—United States—Addresses, essays, lectures.   I. Bodner, Joan.   II. American Friends Service Committee. Northern California Regional Office.   III. Simple Living Collective. Taking charge.
HN65.T32   1984   306'.0973   83-48981
ISBN 0-06-250019-8

84 85 86 87 88   10 9 8 7 6 5 4 3 2 1

Contents

Preface

This book is unusual in the extent to which it represents the collected thoughts of many people as they have developed over a period of ten years.

In the spring of 1974, a study group met in Palo Alto, California, to discuss various problems: ecology; U.S. relations to Third World nations; U.S. domestic problems; visions of a better society; how to get from here to there. Meanwhile, a Simple Living Program was just getting under way in the Northern California Regional Office of the American Friends Service Committee in San Francisco. Several people became involved in both projects.

As the seminar participants considered what to do with the experience, knowledge, and close personal ties they had gained, someone suggested that they prepare a small packet of materials for people interested in simple living but unfamiliar with the subject. Five hundred copies of that initial packet vanished almost at once at the Pacific Yearly Meeting of the Society of Friends in August 1974, where it served as a focus for discussion and as a means of introducing the Simple Living Program to a wider audience. Additional orders came in so fast that the San Francisco AFSC staff could not keep up with the demand. This led to the revision and production of a privately printed book, which went through three printings. People who helped write (only) the early versions of the book include Bob Burnett, Barbara Fuller, Bill and Sherry Gross, Dan Gurney, Eric Sabelman, and Kelly Seifert. Dorie Wilsnack did the graphics for this early version.

As experience with working with these ideas grew, a group calling itself the Simple Living Collective came together to write a version that tripled the length and was published in June 1977 as the Bantam edition of *Taking Charge: Personal and Political Change Through Simple Living.* The Simple Living Collective included Lucy Anderson, Nancy Burnett, Beth Collison, David Hartsough, Jan Hartsough, Susan Lee, Alice Newton, John Shippee, Marie Simirenko, Alan Strain, Jack Stuart, and Coby Everdell (graphics). Each wrote an important portion of the book; all discussed together the entire manuscript. Chuck Fager edited the manuscript for the collective, as did Toni Burbank at Bantam, and Susan Gowan, Al Krebs, Carol Marsh, Joan Montesano, Bill Moyer, David Pingitore, Bill Leland, and Lee Swenson all contributed valuable ideas and advice.

During 1982, it was noticed that the AFSC's remaining supply of the 1977 book had dwindled to two or three boxes. Although the Simple Living Program no longer existed as such, it was felt that the concerns dealt with in *Taking Charge* were more important than ever. With the encouragement of editors John Loudon and Barbara Zukin at Harper & Row San Francisco, and of agent Michael Larsen, a contract was signed to produce a revised edition of *Taking Charge*. This book is the result.

Ten years of dealing with the ideas discussed in this book have brought new ideas and new ways of carrying out these ideas. As a result, perhaps 80 percent of the 1977 text has been revised, added to, or eliminated. Fewer but still major changes have been made in the "Queries," "What You Can Do," and "Sources of Further Information" sections that are part of each chapter. As overall editor, I take full responsibility for all errors, unforgiveable omissions, and unsupportable ideas that may have crept into the final manuscript. However, there are a lot of people who have made *Taking Charge of Our Lives* a good book.

First among these are the people who are in the book, telling their own stories and the stories of their groups and projects. Every direct or indirect quotation that is not accompanied by a footnote represents a personal conversation, often lengthy and usually with an interviewer the speaker had never heard from before. The trust and deep thought that those interviewed gave to these discussions is reflected in the quality of their comments.

The actual writing or revising was done as follows: "Introduction," "Consuming Ourselves/Creating Ourselves," "Consuming the World": John Shippee, Joan Bodner; "Food": Dick Strong, Jeri Edelston, Jan Hartsough, Mack Warner, Joan Bodner; "Children": Gwen Hunter, Joan Bodner; "Health": Lynn Vail, Joan Bodner; "Shelter" (new), "Community," "Aging and Elders" (new), "Work," "Energy," "Taking Charge of Our Lives" (new): Joan Bodner.

Of the people who helped in various ways, it is necessary to limit mention to the forty or so who devoted upwards of several hours of their time. Two of these get special thanks: Donald Bernstein, my spouse, who read, discussed, commented on, and corrected every word of the manuscript before it was seen by anyone else, all with almost infinite patience and usually at (for him) the most inconvenient times. He is responsible for both removing some of the worst parts of the manuscript and adding some of the best. Similarly, Jan Hartsough read, brainstormed, provided resource contacts, typed, copied, edited, criticized, cheered, and encouraged the entire project from beginning to end, mostly in her "spare time" from her already more-than-full-time AFSC staff job.

Three "readers" appointed by the AFSC's regional Executive Committee—Paul Niebanck, Arie Schuurman, and Madge Seaver—read, commented on, and discussed the completed draft with the editor in detail. Their knowledge and suggestions contributed many improvements to the final manuscript. David Hartsough, an AFSC staff member, read and commented on the majority of chapters. Carletta Jones reviewed the entire manuscript for the regional office from a Third World perspective, and her insights led to important changes. Barbara Graves of the regional office contributed her unique abilities to shepherding the manuscript through to its final form. In AFSC's national office, Margaret Bacon, Jim Lenhart, and Jane Motz also read the manuscript and made excellent suggestions.

A number of people contributed their special knowledge of particular subjects in offering ideas and/or reviewing chapter drafts. These include: "Consuming Ourselves/Creating Ourselves": David J. Cooper, Tom Hunter; "Food": Alice Newton; "Shelter": Chester Hartman, Jim Shoch, Fran Peavey; "Community": Renee Renaud, Joe Johnston; "Aging and Elders": Kathleen Lammers, Ethlyn Christensen, Mary Childs, Charlene Browne; "Work": Joyce Maupin, David J. Cooper, Kathleen McPherson; "Children": Judy Torgerson, Chris McCandless, Barbara Henrici Nixon; "Health": Joanne Madigan, Maribeth Riggs, Patty Gerund, Roger Cole; "Energy": Paul Framson, Jon Katz; "Consuming the World": David Chatfield; "Taking Charge of Our Lives": Fred Cook, John Shippee, David Chatfield, Stephanie Mills. Barbara Bates and Ben Kobashigawa typed most of the final draft, and Susan Rumsey and Kathy Reigstad at Harper & Row skillfully added some final touches.

JOAN BODNER
Spring 1984

Introduction

How can *I* make a difference—in my own life, in my community's life, in the world's life? How can I answer the challenge of living responsibly and, at the same time, find ways to challenge to greater responsibility those who misuse their economic, political, or personal power?

Many answers suggested in this book began their development in the "simple living" movement. That movement focuses on the need to simplify the number and kinds of material things that Americans[1] use if we are to stop consuming far more than our fair share of the world's limited resources. This approach is especially welcomed by many who have felt their important life decisions being overly controlled by what they would like to own instead of what they would like to *do*. The approach angers many who feel that "simplification" is not the answer to substandard urban housing, race and sex discrimination, or the lack of real community in our lives. In speaking of the challenges and rewards of living responsibly, we define each of these concerns as important parts of taking charge of our lives.

LIVING SIMPLY VS. LIVING POORLY

Interestingly, a simpler lifestyle, frugality, neighborliness, decentralization, and self-reliance are all part of the current establishment rhetoric. As such, they are often simply a cover-up for asking people to live poorly. Simple living is *not* a way of reconciling ourselves to economic and political policies that result in continued and growing poverty. What's the difference?

Living poorly is living without choices—and sometimes money has nothing to do with the issue. Living simply—that is, living responsibly—combines personal creativity with community efforts to create choices. Here are some examples:

Living Poorly Means . . .	_Living Responsibly Can Create . . ._
Inferior and non-nutritious food sold through stores that often charge more than they do in affluent areas.	Neighborhood food cooperatives, farmers markets, and cooperative urban gardens that operate on a non-profit basis.
Risk of eviction when rent or mortgage money isn't available, when a government agency plans a new highway, or as a result of rising prices and "gentrification." Risk of arson, if your building costs the landlord too much to maintain.	Neighborhood associations, urban and rural land trusts, and housing cooperatives responsive to and often owned by residents.
Almost total dependence on expensive experts or your own skills for repairs, maintenance work, or home improvements.	The opportunity to share and barter time and skills with neighbors and community members.
Fear of rape, robbery, burglary, murder, and other crimes of violence.	Neighborhood safety organizations where members of the community cooperate to minimize violence.
Isolation, hopelessness, and loneliness after "retirement."	Friendship, intellectual contact, and important roles to play in the community.
Fear of arbitrary and unexpected layoffs and firings.	Job protection through union membership, cooperatively run workplaces, and collectively owned businesses.
Dependence on impersonal, centralized agencies and expensive physicians for health care.	Locally controlled, responsive health-care facilities and personal knowledge about how to keep healthy.
Vulnerability to environmentally caused disease (black lung, cancer, emphysema) and to increased costs and dangers from environmental hazards (acid rain, chemical wastes, nuclear accidents).	Life in an environment that is free of the fear of unnatural diseases and disasters.
Unemployment, hopelessness, fear, drug use, and crime among young people.	Self-help housing, gardening, and skills-oriented projects that help young people do something for themselves, their neighborhoods, and their towns.
Garbage-filled streets, yards, and lives.	Recycling projects that clean up neighborhoods and yield profits for the community.
Dependence on centralized sources for heat, electricity, and other basic utilities.	Solar energy systems and other renewable, locally controlled energy sources.
Payment of high prices for advertising, profits, and transport of goods thousands of miles.	An emphasis on locally produced goods, services, and skills.

Living Poorly Means . . .	*Living Responsibly Can Create . . .*
Reductions in employment and social services due to militarism and unequal resource distribution.	A secure, nonviolent world where basic material needs are met for all without the threat or reality of war.

Living poorly deprives us of "conviviality" in our lives—the opportunity to live and work creatively with others, and to interact directly with our environment. Locally controlled institutions, cooperation, human-scale technologies, bicycles, gardens, preventive health care all are parts of what Ivan Illich calls "tools for conviviality."[2]

Participation in the work and decision-making of our institutions makes us more than mere customers, wage-earners, and clients. It is hard to feel we can take charge without the opportunity for participation and involvement in the institutions that shape our lives. We are poor when we do not have this control. We have begun to live responsibly when we have developed alternatives in which we both matter as people and can play an active part. Living responsibly differs from living poorly in the importance it gives to the growth and flowering of creativity and the human spirit.

Our vision might be thought of as creative stewardship over our lives, our material resources, our mental and spiritual endowments, our local communities, and our world.

CREATING AND CELEBRATING

Poverty of the spirit is a widespread problem at all economic levels. Alcoholism, drug use, suicide, and the popularity of the counseling professions are profound symptoms of this situation. The dominant culture urges us to fill our lives with video games, junk food, flashy cars, and cute items from "gift shops." Instead of relying on mass-produced toys, we need to re-learn how to share our personal insights, gifts, and capacities for celebration. For Susan Lee, an Independence Day celebration was such a learning experience:

In years past, my friends and I usually celebrated the Fourth of July by piling into cars with food, drinks, and fireworks. In a race with thousands of other people, we would head for the beach, driving over congested highways layered in smog, lined with franchised fast-food outlets, and dotted with traffic accidents. On arriving, we would compete with everyone else for enough space to enjoy ourselves. These ventures would be expensive, too, when we added up the cost of gasoline, paper supplies, food, fireworks, and the rest of the paraphernalia.

Last year a group of us decided to celebrate in a different, and for us more meaningful, way. We planned a party to celebrate "Interdependence Day," a recognition of our conviction that we as a people and as a nation are interdependent. We are members of one world family.

Those who came ranged in age from just under two to seventy-nine. Each

family brought food and an activity to share. With scraps of material she had on
hand, one woman delivered a quick course on designing and making patchwork.
Another family brought an old-fashioned, hand-operated ice-cream maker and
supervised the children while they turned the handle. Many quarts of ice cream
were made and eaten. One group sang madrigals, and others brought guitars.
People played games, shared gossip, and enjoyed one another's company. The
potluck dinner, spread across the buffet table, featured special dishes from each
household.

As darkness came, the group gathered around a huge bonfire that had been
built during the afternoon. The musicians brought out their guitars for a round
of folk songs, which evoked images of the forty-niners heading for California in
search of gold and the laborers who built the nation's railroads. We sang of other
peoples, too, who had similar pioneering histories. Later we shared our thoughts
about this country and what the celebration of Interdependence Day meant for
each of us. The evening ended as each person lit a candle and we all sang, "Let
There Be Peace on Earth." The beautiful lyrics, of how peace on earth must begin
with each of us, summed up the feelings we had in common. Celebrations like this
have special meaning for me, for they come from ourselves and our creativity.

Celebrations need not be confined to traditional holidays; they can acknowledge other meaningful events in our lives. Letting go of prefabricated, consumption-centered forms of creativity and allowing our
uniqueness to push through and express itself can be a very freeing
process. The gifts we give, the rituals and celebrations we join and create
—all these can deeply enrich our lives.

U.S. CONSUMPTION AND WORLD POVERTY

Our consumption levels have important implications for world peace
—now and as the supply of nonrenewable resources gets tighter during
the next several decades. If the world were a global village of one hundred people, five of them would be Americans. These five would have
over a third of the village's income, and the other ninety-five would
subsist on the rest. How could the wealthy five live in peace with their
neighbors? Surely they would be driven to arm themselves against the
other ninety-five—perhaps even to spend on military defense, as Americans do, about twice as much per person as the total income of two-thirds
of the villagers.

In a world economic context, living responsibly can be part of an
approach to curing a worldwide combination of overdevelopment and
underdevelopment that can be called "mal-development." The symptoms of overdevelopment—dependence on complex bureaucratic technologies and institutions, overconsumption, industrial pollution, and
interpersonal alienation—are most apparent in countries like our own.
The outward signs of underdevelopment are most apparent in poor
countries. However, both aspects of mal-development can be found in

How would our lives change if we were suddenly transformed into members of the victim group in the Third World?*

First, take out the furniture. Leave just a few old blankets, a kitchen table, and one wooden chair (the car went long ago—remember?).

Second, throw out the clothes. Each one may keep the oldest suit or dress, a shirt or blouse. The head of the family has the only pair of shoes.

Third, all kitchen appliances have already gone. Keep a box of matches, a small bag of flour, some sugar and salt, a handful of onions, a dish of dried beans. Rescue those moldy potatoes from the garbage can: those are tonight's meal.

Fourth, dismantle the bathroom, shut off the running water, take out the wiring and the lights and everything that runs by electricity.

Fifth, take away the house and move the family into the toolshed.

Sixth, by now all the other houses in the neighborhood have gone; instead there are shanties—for the fortunate ones.

Seventh, cancel all the newspapers and magazines. Throw out the books. You won't miss them—you are now illiterate. One radio is now left for the whole shantytown.

Eighth, no more postman, fireman, government services. The two-classroom school is three miles away, but only half the children go, anyway.

Ninth, no hospital, no doctor. The nearest clinic is now ten miles away with a midwife in charge. Get there by bus or by bicycle, if you're lucky enough to have one.

Tenth, throw out your bankbooks, stock certificates, pension plans, insurance policies, social security records. You have left a cash hoard of $5.

Eleventh, get out and start cultivating your three acres. Try hard to raise $300 in cash crops because your landlord wants two-thirds and your local moneylender 10 percent.

Twelfth, find some way for your children to bring in a little extra money so you have something to eat most days. But it won't be enough to keep bodies healthy, so lop off twenty-five to thirty years of life expectancy.

---

* Adapted from the FAO magazine, *Freedom from Hunger,* based on excerpts from *The Great Ascent* by Robert L. Heilbroner (New York: Harper & Row, 1963).

most nations of the world. Mexico City is often smoggier than Los Angeles, and underdevelopment can be found in several neighborhoods of every major city in the United States.

As long as mal-development continues, only a small proportion of the world's people can ever hope to have the health, education, and nourishment that the average middle-class American takes for granted. It is difficult for us to imagine the life of a "typical" Third World tenant farmer family, but the preceding box summary may be of assistance.

Important changes in these conditions are being made in many countries, and Chapter X discusses both the difficulties and the emerging solutions. The changes would proceed faster, however, if we were to insist that our governments, financial institutions and corporations stop acquiring the lion's share of poor nations' own resources to supply our consumption "habit." Ultimately, we need to restructure our consumption patterns so that a decent, nonviolent and secure life is available to the earth and to all its inhabitants. Peasants in El Salvador, urban workers in the Philippines, and blacks in South Africa should not have to feel compelled to take up arms in order to create a system where they can live decently. We in the industrialized nations need to stop endangering the peace of the world through the continued hoarding of an unfair share of its material goods.

BRINGING THE FUTURE INTO THE PRESENT

Despite the strength of the powers that benefit from the continuation of the many forms of living poorly, millions of people are individually and collectively creating a framework for a sustainable and liveable future. These alternatives may not seem like much—until you add them up. As this international network of people who are taking responsibility for their lives grows in strength, our own choices will help make the difference in whether the world turns away from an increasingly hazardous course.

The following chapters discuss many such choices that can be made by individuals and families, as well as examples from over one hundred different communities in our nation and the world. Since this book was written in San Francisco, a certain disproportion of the selections are of Northern California groups whose activities are better known to the writers. But the new values and communities that are developing as a challenge to the dominant system are growing up all around us. The wonder is that they remain as hard to see as they are—because many are not what we have been taught to think of as ways of making fundamental changes. Most of us can find living examples within ourselves or our families, on the next corner, down the block, or somewhere in our town. What can we do to encourage their growth and expansion?

USING THIS BOOK

This book is designed to explore a variety of ways that you can take charge. Each chapter starts with queries to help you draw out your own thoughts about a subject area. To give you the flavor of their range, here are some samples of these questions:

- Of the things that I own, which help me or my family or group to be more active, self-reliant, and involved with each other and others?
- Does my work have anything to do with fulfilling basic human needs, such as food, clothing, shelter, health, creative expression? How many of the people I know do work connected with these things?
- Can anything be done about the additives, preservatives, and pesticides in my food?
- How are decisions made that affect shelter in my community? Who decides where and what kind of new housing gets built? Who decides where and what kind of old housing is torn down? What is the basis of these decisions?
- Do I know how many people in my community are without shelter? Do I know who they are? Do I know what kind of shelter facilities my community provides? What are longer-range solutions?
- What communities am I already part of? How could more "community" be created within them?
- Is there a specific age at which I think other people (or myself) are no longer able to work? Learn new things? Have fun? Enjoy sexual relationships? What is that age and why do I feel this way? Do I think people much younger than I are too inexperienced or immature to make good judgments? On what do I base this opinion?
- Are certain kinds of jobs in my community done by people of one race or ethnic background?
- Do I feel guilty that I am economically unable to buy my children what "other children" have—clothing, toys, bigger allowance for amusements, summer camp? Do I discuss with my children how much money I get paid, how much some other people get paid, and why? Do I discuss with them the difference between economic values and human values, or do I think they are too young to understand? Do we listen to what children can tell us about these values?
- Is my work physically dangerous to me? To my unborn children? Does it endanger my mental stability? My ability to use nonwork time creatively and intelligently?
- Even if large quantities of energy were available at a reasonable price, would continued increases in our society's use of it benefit me and society?

- What relationship do militarism and military spending have to global resource use and distribution?
- Are we individually responsible for injustice that is built into the world economy?
- What institutions, organizations, and services exist in my area that support me in taking charge? What additional ones are needed? What can I do to support the ones we now have or to bring new ones into being?

The text of each chapter is followed by suggestions of "What You Can Do"—small to medium-sized projects for individuals and groups, supplementing examples mentioned in the text. Chapters conclude with lists of contacts and resources that can provide more information; Chapter XI's resources include many listings that deal with multiple issues (such as energy *and* food *and* shelter) as well as overall resources on living responsibly and on nonviolent social change.

In addition to individual reading and study, here are a few other approaches to using this book:

1. A study group of friends, neighbors, church or community organization members, or a high school or college class could spend one or two weeks discussing each chapter of interest. Some of the projects at the ends of the chapters are games and exercises for facilitating group discussion. This study can be enriched if group members take turns reading supplementary sources and reporting briefly on them to the group as a whole.
2. Individuals, groups, or subgroups could use a chapter as the basis for exploring a topic such as food or energy in depth.
3. A group could explore additional issues that are not discussed in depth here. These might include birth, death, law and security, or decision-making and value-clarifying techniques.

In beginning work on changing your life, you will probably want to start slowly with projects and activities that are challenging, but not overwhelming. Specific goal-setting, however preliminary, can be a way of focusing as well as getting beyond the panic that can come from the feeling that there are **hundreds** of things that are wrong with the world, all of which **must** be corrected by tomorrow! Goals should be achievable, and it is a good idea to be time-specific (for example, setting goals that are to be reached in one week, six months, one year, five years). Goals are a good source of self-affirmation when they are accomplished. In group goal-setting, write your thoughts on a large piece of paper and keep it for future reference.

The queries, analyses, and projects included in these chapters are meant as suggestions rather than prescriptions. Each individual's personal and social situation is a little different, and what is "living responsibly" for the authors and the editor of this book may not fit your own situation. We hope our readers will be inspired to go beyond our recommendations as part of the ongoing process of learning how to take charge of our lives.

NOTES

1. Throughout this book, the word *Americans* is used to describe residents of the United States. In doing so, we are well aware of the history that allows "Americans" to refer to themselves as such, excluding the remainder of the residents of North, Central, and South America. Because of this history, however, there is no other word in common usage that refers to United States residents collectively as a people.
2. Ivan Illich, *Tools for Conviviality* (New York: Harper & Row, 1973).

CHAPTER I

Consuming Ourselves/ Creating Ourselves

QUERIES

1. Do I enjoy my work? Does my work involve me as a whole human being—or do I leave at home my brain, skills, abilities, and interests?

2. What does it mean that a nation or an industry is "economically competitive"? Are there ways of working that make human sense that are not "economically competitive"?

3. How often do I buy things because my needs for love, friendship, celebration, job satisfaction, personal recognition, or cultural identity are not being met? How often have I bought someone something instead of showing my friendship or love more directly? Are "gifts" in my family or group things that we do, things that we are, things that we make, or things that we buy?

4. Of the things that I own, which help me or my family or group to be more active, self-reliant, and involved with each other and others?

5. Are my freedom of choice and my political and social values restricted by businesses and other institutions, the survival of which is dependent on high and growing levels of consumption? How?

6. To what extent are possessions and social status an important part of my self-image and that of my family? Are my feelings of self-worth based on the things I have and the "quality" of the neighborhood I live in—or on who I am as a human being? What educational, advertising, and social messages do I get that reinforce tendencies to evaluate myself and others in terms of possessions rather than of personal qualities? How could I change these messages? How could I change the messages I share with my neighbors?

7. Does my work have anything to do with fulfilling basic human needs, such as food, clothing, shelter, health, creative expression? How many of the people I know do work connected with these things?

8. How often do I acknowledge my personal gifts? How often do I hold

myself accountable for using them? To what extent do I use them in the service of others?

9. How much of what I spend on consumer goods goes for nonfunctional packaging, repair and replacement of poorly made items, nonrecyclable materials, advertising, corporate lobbying, market research? Do these contribute anything to quality or use value?

10. From what sources do I derive my ideas of "the good life"? Do I feel shame because I can't buy my children what is advertised on television or because I don't have time to clean the house like the people on television? Do I hesitate to invite people over because the furniture is old and dinner is beans instead of steak?

11. How much of what I buy consists of materials that are polluting or could be made more safely? How many of these products contain substances (often simply to make them "look good") that cause allergic reactions, diseases, and even cancer and birth defects?

The Wood Carrier

Khing, the master carver, made a bell stand
Of precious wood. When it was finished,
All who saw it were astounded. They said it must be
The work of spirits.
The Prince of Lu said to the master carver:
"What is your secret?"

Khing replied: "I am only a workman:
I have no secret. There is only this:
When I began to think about the work you commanded
I guarded my spirit, did not expend it
On trifles, that were not to the point.
I fasted in order to set
My heart at rest.
After three days fasting,
I had forgotten gain and success.
After five days
I had forgotten praise or criticism.
After seven days
I had forgotten my body
With all its limbs.

"By this time all thought of your Highness
And of the court had faded away.
All that might distract me from the work
Had vanished.
I was collected in the single thought
of the bell stand.

"Then I went to the forest
To see the trees in their own natural state.
When the right tree appeared before my eyes,

The bell stand also appeared in it, clearly, beyond doubt.
All I had to do was to put forth my hand
And begin.

"If I had not met this particular tree
There would have been
No bell stand at all.

"What happened?
My own collected thought
Encountered the hidden potential in the wood;
From this live encounter came the work
Which you ascribe to the spirits."

—THOMAS MERTON
Adapted from *The Way of Chang Tzu*[1]

How many of us have the opportunity in our everyday lives to create the result of our "own collected thought"? Most of our paid work consists of turning one screw, processing one type of document, fitting together prefabricated pieces, with speed more important than quality and few questions asked about what it is that we are actually making. The cash thus earned is then spent to consume other products made with as little love.

Theodore Roszak talks about two feelings people tend to strive for when they have the opportunity: responsibility *to* their work that it should be well done, intrinsically excellent by the highest standards of the craft or profession; and responsibility *for* their work that it should be well used, that it be of good and honorable service in the world.[2] That is, we want our work to have a quality that we can be proud of and we want to produce goods or services that are worth consuming.

It is very difficult to do work of quality today that we can truly feel responsible *to*. The history of industrialization has been a history of the destruction of the unity of thought and action, hand and mind,[3] in the name of increased production, efficiency, competitive advantage. While the early machine age gave workers relief from drudgery and tools that assisted the individual in doing finer work, the assembly line and time-and-motion study broke the production process into smaller and smaller pieces. The worker needed no longer to think—or to be paid for thinking—only to turn a screw, punch a card, process a document, wrap a Big Mac. This divorce of thinking and doing for almost one-half of one's waking life is as destructive to the basic nature of a human being as is the lack of food needed to sustain the body. Gandhi commented that

an improved plough is a good thing. But if by some chance one man could plough up, by some mechanical invention of his, the whole of the land of India and control all the agricultural produce and if the millions had no other occupation, they would starve, and being idle, they would become dunces, as many have already become.[4]

Most of the population of industrialized nations did not enthusiastically choose this method of production. When Ford Motor Company installed the first comprehensive conveyor assembly line in the years 1913–1914, it tried to pay the standard area rate of pay, $2.34 per day. But for the year of 1913, Ford had to hire 3.8 workers for each position, and by the end of the year, Ford had to hire 9.6 workers for each position: people were staying barely more than a month when they could get nonassembly line jobs that paid as well. By early in 1914, Ford had more than doubled wages to $5.00 per day and was finally able to keep a labor force.[5]

Money rewards have largely replaced what Buddhists call "right livelihood"; the opportunity to consume is substituted for knowledge that our work is of high quality and of good and honorable service. A fair share of the cash, a guaranteed annual income, or extensive social security benefits are important goals, but they do not address the human losses resulting from "mass production and bureaucratic processing which casts things and services into the world carrying no one's name, invested with no one's honor, bearing no one's style."[6]

Workers in some European countries and in branches of a few American corporations go beyond the standard union contract and participate democratically in decision-making concerning their schedules, hiring and firing, and even their relative pay. But "workers' control" has generally not gone as far as changing the conditions of work so that every person can use his or her brain in making decisions concerning the minute-to-minute work being done—at the short term expense of reducing production, taking more time, costing more money. Of course, the products that take more time to make may be more valuable to the consumer, because they are of better quality.

If we are also to be responsible *for* our work, workers' control means little if we cannot examine and choose *what* we produce, influencing the effects both its production and method of production have on our lives. Are we producing goods and services that make sense for people to consume? And even if the consumption makes sense, might some of these goods and services be better produced and consumed in the noncash economy of the home and community?

Why do we develop, manufacture, and use chemical food additives that leave us with questions about our health, when everyone old enough to remember agrees that food tasted better before they were used? Why are so many of us employed at keeping track of billings, investments, and financial ownership? Why do we waste labor, materials, and the opportunity for thinking work by designing and manufacturing consumer goods that cannot be repaired but only replaced? Why are so many employed at determining "eligibility" for various social services instead of every member of society having both the opportunity to do humanly important work and the right to enough material resources for a decent life?

In making an immediate, personal work choice, certain jobs are clearly not humanly useful, such as the production of nuclear weapons or the manufacture of other extremely harmful substances. Economic necessity is a poor moral argument for keeping such jobs, especially for those who are fully aware of the personal health risks that they (and their families) may be taking. But economic necessity is hard to get away from, and a great number of us are thus forced, at least in the short run, to keep jobs that have a negative or zero impact on ourselves and the world. There are also many positive jobs that would have a better impact if done quite differently.

We used to make most necessary products at home—clothing, furniture, toys, musical instruments, food, building materials. Now we buy them for cash. Increasing numbers of necessary services—food preservation and preparation, cleaning, child care, care of the chronically ill, game invention, social event organization—are also now primarily bought for cash. The situation created is circular: The actual and perceived need for cash forces more people from each household to spend more hours working outside their homes and communities. Therefore, as the need for cash increases, we have less and less time to do things for ourselves and with our families, friends, and neighbors. Because of the time commitments to work,

the ties of neighborhood, community, and friendship are reinterpreted on a narrower scale to exclude onerous responsibilities, [and] the care of humans for each other becomes increasingly institutionalized. . . . Thus understood, the massive growth of institutions stretching all the way from schools and hospitals on the one side to prisons and madhouses on the other represents not just the progress of medicine, education or crime prevention, but the clearing of the market place of all but the "economically active" and "functioning" members of society, generally at public expense and at a handsome profit to the manufacturing and service corporations who sometimes own and invariably supply these institutions.[7]

Also contributing to the breakdown of community is the very low skill level necessary to do many industrial society jobs. This allows companies to introduce and withdraw products and to open and close workplaces as is "economically efficient" without having to worry about spending years training a new labor force. The discharged labor force is forced to move or to commute to wherever the new jobs are available, making lasting ties to a community difficult.

HOW MUCH IS ENOUGH?

The prevailing assumption in our industrial society is that there are never enough products and services being produced and consumed. But is there always a positive benefit in increasing the quantity, whatever effect that increase may have on our time or ability to enjoy friendships, participate in our community's decisions, or walk among redwood trees instead of displaying this book on a redwood coffee table?

In our economic system, profits are made not only on necessary goods and services, but also on invented ones—ones we are convinced we need through advertising. For example, while the food growing, processing, and distribution industry has become centralized in the hands of fewer and fewer large companies, supermarkets carry over ten thousand different items, compared with about nine hundred in 1928.[8]

If we are unhappy at our work, we are encouraged to buy a new dress or a new model stereo system—and to discard the unfashionable or "technically obsolete" ones we already have. Everywhere we look, we are told that personal deficiencies can be overcome by using a particular brand of a product: cigarettes, makeup, coffee, laundry soap. Standards of material perfection for our homes and personal appearances are set that very few people really believe they meet. The indoctrination process starts early. In 1972, Joan Gussow, a professor of nutrition education, along with her colleague, Ruth Eshleman, and eight graduate students, studied the ads that appeared in twenty-nine hours of children's television. Of 388 commercials (one every three and one-half minutes), 319 were for food. They were distributed as follows:

Commercial	Percent
Breakfast cereals	38.5
Cookies, candy, gum, popcorn, snacks	17.0
Vitamins	15.0
Canned desserts, frozen dinners, drive-ins, peanut butter, oranges	9.0
Beverages and beverage mixes	8.0
Frozen waffles and poptarts	7.5
Canned pasta	5.0

Professor Gussow and her students found the accumulated impact of these ads "blatantly antinutrition." After watching thirty-three of them, one student had to be relieved for something akin to battle fatigue. The report concludes that "watching children's television if one likes and respects food—and children—is sickening."

"GIFTING": A PERVERSION OF GIVING

In few areas is the invented-need impact of advertising and the compulsive consumption it can promote more evident than in the transformation of giving into "gifting."

Gifting activity peaks during Christmas/Chanukah/winter solstice (hereafter referred to as Xmas) in the United States. Many of us run around for a month or so worrying and feeling guilty if we cannot find exactly the right things to buy for one another. Often we measure our worth by the extent of our involvement in Xmas gifting.

The main reason for the stress on Xmas gifting is profit. Many department stores and other retail outlets, as well as toy manufacturers and other industries, can survive without profits during the rest of the year if they come out far enough ahead in December. Their message to us is that the best way to show our love and appreciation for one another is to buy something.

Giving has been an important part of almost all human cultures. Giving and sharing have been the basis of the economic system in some traditional societies. In others, festivals in which gifts were given or goods were distributed were a means of insuring the survival of the community as a whole and compensating for inequalities in strength and skill. Among the Sioux Indians, high status was partly based on the ability and desire to provide for the old and helpless. During a hunt,

the council sent for certain young men who were being noticed by the people, and to these the chief said: "Good young men, my relatives, your work I know is good. What you do is good always. So today you will feed the helpless and the old and feeble. Maybe there is an old woman or an old man who has no son. Or there may be a woman who has little children but no man. You will know these and hunt only for them. Today you belong to the needy!" This made the young men very proud, for it was a great honor.[10]

Contrast a typical gift-giving in consumerist America:

The company gave me a fine Christmas bonus for staying with them another year, and together with our credit cards we really felt flush. We bought a lot of stuff. On Christmas Eve there were well chosen gifts for everyone, a roaring fire, eggnog, carols, family, and our tree centered on a pile of presents.

January twenty-eighth we got a bill from Master Charge and the next day from the Emporium, and Penney's, and Wards. Even Mobil got into the act. "Please remit the amount shown in the box above. Your minimum payment is $10." The Christmas spirit was gone and the bills were there to pay and I was wondering what was happening to us that we had to buy Christmas.[11]

Gifting has other unhealthy side effects. Fashionable weddings and those attending them are gauged by the values of the gifts given. Kids rate themselves against each other on the number of presents they receive for Xmas, Bar or Bas Mitzvahs, or their birthdays. Many people fear being unable to meet the gift expectations of others when they have financial problems or lose their jobs.

In our society, as among the Sioux, a holiday can be an occasion for giving material gifts where they are needed and welcome. Humans also need more than bare material necessities, and from time to time we may indeed think of or see "the perfect gift" for a friend or relative that we cannot create with our own talents and skills. If we can afford it, even at considerable personal sacrifice, the joy that it may give is well worth the money. But giving in this way comes from a different impulse than does advertising-inspired giving, or giving "to make a good impression."

One excellent source for taking back from the corporate "grinches who stole Christmas" is the *Alternative Celebrations Catalogue*. It contains many suggestions for new ways of celebrating various holidays and special events. Does your street or local park need a tree planted, instead of buying a Christmas tree? What are fun and inexpensive ways to create unique gifts instead of buying them? Do you have to give a material gift, or might the money be better donated to save an endangered species, to build an alternative institution, or to those with urgent material needs—in honor of your intended "recipient"? The *Catalogue* observes:

As for giving to a cause instead of to a person, this must be done with the person in mind. A young person who has always received something tangible may not be ready for a shift to money given for social purposes. But relatives with well-stocked homes and larders are often quite pleased to *not* receive some peculiar item they didn't want anyway. It all depends on the person. The purpose is giving that makes sense to the recipient as well as to the giver.[12]

IS "PERSONAL" CONSUMPTION A PUBLIC ISSUE?

While we may have relative freedom to select a brand of cake mix or to mix one up for ourselves from basic ingredients, the biggest consumer decisions are societal choices, not personal ones. Once our society has chosen what to produce, personal choices become extremely limited. Thus, to make basic consumption changes, we must start treating these choices as public matters. Transportation consumption is a good example.

It is no coincidence that Charles E. Wilson ("What's good for General Motors is good for the country"), former chairman of GM, was Secretary of Defense in 1956 when the decision was made to spend $33 billion of gasoline tax money on a nationwide freeway network. The result is the present freeway system, which Congress funded as a contribution to the national defense system. Meanwhile consumers have had to fight to maintain the existence of the nation's railways and other public transportation systems, despite the increasing cost of energy.

As the commitment to the freeway system increased air pollution, the federal government eventually imposed emission standards to control smog. The auto manufacturers chose to comply by use of the catalytic converter, despite a study by the National Academy of Sciences indicating that such a choice would be far less satisfactory than a complete change to stratified charge engines, such as those employed in Honda cars.[13] As an "add-on" the converter was much less expensive for the U.S. manufacturers because, among other reasons, the rights to the new engine design had already been sold to Honda by a U.S. firm and would have to have been bought back.

Catalytic converters use platinum (obtained by General Motors from South Africa) and palladium to reduce emission of carbon monoxide and hydrocarbons in engine exhaust. Unfortunately, these substances are replaced with sulphates and "sulphuric acid mist,"[14] which is injurious to human lungs, especially for people already suffering with breathing problems. The device also lowers gas mileage and has to be maintained every thirty to fifty thousand miles at a cost of $75 to $250. In sum, catalytic converters are expensive, replace one kind of pollution with another, and provide one of the many justifications for "necessary" U.S. cooperation with the apartheid South African government. And in 1983 Americans were treated to anti-Japanese propaganda by auto manufacturers to explain their closing of U.S. plants and increasing U.S. unemployment.

Official U.S. economic policy does not care about what consumption choices are available to us, only about the total level of consumption. Whatever we buy, the standard is "the more, the better." Auto accident costs, including hospital and funeral bills, raise the Gross National Product (GNP) and are considered signs of economic health. Jobs policy, instead of looking at what needs to get done, looks mainly at what level of consumption the wages paid will support, often without regard to the number of workers who obtain a basic livelihood from the employment. Food production, for example, generally has a lower profit margin than provision of luxury items. Therefore, fewer, higher-paid workers may actually provide more profits through their consumption than more workers paid the same total quantity of wages.

Personal consumption also becomes entwined with public policy when an individual cooperates with the production of unnecessary and harmful items because of the need for cash. Most of the time this cooperation is not illegal as defined by our country's laws, but the pressure to maintain our standard of living can provide "justification" even for illegal behavior.

In 1967, the B. F. Goodrich Company was asked to design a brake for the A7D jet fighter. For various reasons, the resulting brake failed most of its qualification tests. Kermit Vandiver, a technical writer for the company, was told to falsify the results in the test report. He writes:

Before coming to Goodrich in 1963, I had held a variety of jobs, each a little more pleasant, a little more rewarding than the last. At forty-two, with seven children, I had decided that the Goodrich Company would probably be my "home" for the rest of my working life. The job paid well, it was pleasant and challenging, and the future looked reasonably bright. My wife and I had bought a home and we were ready to settle down into a comfortable, middle-age, middle-class rut. If I refused to take part in the A7D fraud, I would have to either resign or be fired. The report would be written by someone anyway, but I would have the satisfaction of knowing I had had no part in the matter. But bills aren't paid with personal satisfaction, nor house payments with ethical principles. The next morning, I telephoned Lawson and told him I was ready to begin on the qualification report.[15]

The problems discussed in this section pervade our entire economic system, and years of effort by people working together in many ways will be required to make basic changes. It is important to carry on such work. But it is also necessary to recognize that there are ways open to most of us to begin to lead more satisfying lives in the here and now. If we do not find such ways, we cannot possibly maintain the strength and commitment necessary to make the biggest and most sweeping changes.

USING OUR GIFTS

One way we might start is by learning to recognize and use our personal gifts—the kind that are found in the human spirit rather than under Christmas trees:

All of us have a gift, a calling of our own whose exercise is high delight, even if we must sweat and suffer to meet its demands. That calling reaches out to find a real and useful place in the world, a task that is not waste or pretense.[16]

A few of us have the present good fortune to be able to exercise such gifts in our paid work and (if we also happen to be paid well) can even afford to give material support to others who are seeking this opportunity. Chapter VI discusses some ways more of us can begin to move closer to that ideal. But there are many other contexts in which we can express our gifts. The following exercises and activities are some ways to help you and others find and share your gifts.

1. *Evoking gifts.*

List all of the things you do, do well, and like to do. Get together with your family, community, and/or friends to exchange your insights about the list. Which are confirmed by your friends and family? How do you manifest them? What gets in the way? How does your job or your relationship to material things help you or hinder you in expressing your gifts in personally fulfilling ways and in sharing them with others? What does the expression of your particular gifts give back to the material world? How might you combine your gifts with the gifts of others to make needed changes? How could you develop your gifts over the next six months? One year? Five years? Ten years?

2. *Personal gift celebrations.*

Celebrations of personal gifts can be held at customary times of gift-giving, such as Christmas, birthdays, weddings, and anniversaries. Each celebration can include a time of reflection and sharing in which each person tells how the others have shared their gifts and special attributes with him or her and with the world. When one person, couple, or group is the focus, as on birthdays and anniversaries, participants can emphasize their particular gifts, affirming and supporting them. The central person or group may also take time to speak about what has helped enhance and nourish these gifts, and how obstacles to their growth and manifestation in the world have been overcome.

3. *Celebration of gifts.*

A church in Brattleboro, Vermont, recently gave each member who wanted to participate $50 to combine creatively with one of their gifts, the combined result to be returned in some manner to the church or wider community. The returns have come in many forms including artwork, crafts, storytelling, community projects, and, of course, increases in the original sums. While the church had expected monetary returns from the project, it got something deeper and more meaningful from many of its members—an expression of creativity, heart, and soul. Many participants have been empowered to go on giving to themselves and to the world in new ways as a result of this project.

4. *Creative giving.*

Try using gift-giving celebrations as times to give each other creations that express the qualities you see and/or share with the other. How can your gift bring out the master carver's "bell stand" hidden in the receiver or in the relationship you share?

5. *Sharing gifts with the planet and the material world.*

You can devise a session where each person in the group reflects on what she or he has received from the material world and is returning to it. This can also be a time for stating and recording intentions. What gifts do you have that can be shared with the earth to help it flourish and grow? How can they best be shared on the job or in your private, family, and community lives?

You can undoubtedly think of other exercises that will fit your own needs and those of your particular family, group, or community. The form of the exercise is relatively unimportant so long as it helps each person see her or his own gifts more clearly and to share them more fully with the world.

INCREASING COMMUNITY/REDUCING CONSUMPTION

Another way to change both the paid and unpaid work we do and the patterns of our material consumption is the restoration of networks of community. Much of the rest of this book is about people who are doing this. On a person-to-person basis, we can bring goods and services that have been turned into cash commodities back into the nonmoney economy: individual and community gardens, cooperative childcare and skill bartering are some means of doing this. We can also bring real control over the way we meet our food, housing, health, and energy needs back to our local communities by creating small-scale alternatives.

A third approach is to reduce actual and hoped-for personal material consumption. We can begin with the recognition that many "cheap" consumer goods are available only because of extremely low wages and deadening working conditions. Even if we ourselves are better paid than workers in other countries or in other occupations, reduction of material consumption can free us for other concerns. The more we *need* to buy, the more we need to work at cash jobs that just may not fulfill other needs.

How much of your time is thus traded for money? Taking an inventory of your time use and your priorities may help you see possibilities for change. The AFSC's Simple Living Program developed an exercise that may be useful:

Make a circle (balloon) in the center of a piece of paper and put your name in it. Around this balloon, make a balloon for each of the activities that occupies your time each day, such as work, family, sharing with others, spiritual life, and so on. The size of each balloon should represent the amount of time you give to that activity. Next draw a line from your balloon to each activity balloon, with the thickness of the line representing the strength of your commitment to that activity and the pleasure you receive from it. If you are doing this as a group, discuss with one another what your charts tell you about your own lives. For example, do you have a big balloon for work with only a thin line to it, and thick lines to family, sharing with friends, and spiritual life, but with small balloons for each of them? WHY? How does your balloon chart compare with what you would like it to look like? Do this exercise periodically if you decide to make significant changes.

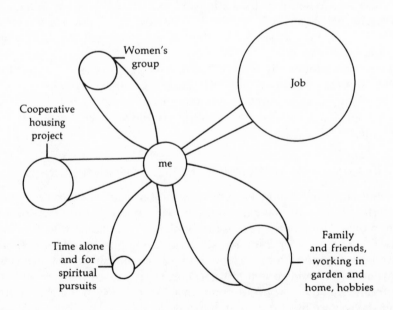

One important thing to recognize when looking at the time-money trade-off is that being unable to pay cash for a necessity may well mean more total hours of work for you in repairing the electrical wiring or in doing a childcare barter with a friend who has better electrical skills. In this context, though, we need to reexamine the division we are encouraged to make between "work" and "leisure," and look more toward an overall fulfilling life.

Changing long-established patterns of work and material consumption is a step-by-step process, even for someone like Gandhi. In recalling his decision to discard wealth and possessions in order to serve the people, Gandhi stated:

I cannot tell you with truth that, when this belief came to me, I discarded everything immediately. I must confess to you that progress at first was slow. And now, as I recall those days of struggle, I remember that it was also painful in the beginning. . . . But as days went by, I saw that I had to throw overboard many other things which I used to consider as mine, and a time came when it became a matter of positive joy to give up those things.[17]

You and I, if considering a commitment to simpler material living, may not wish to throw overboard as much as Gandhi did. The world's resources can probably support a higher standard of material comfort than Gandhi adopted for all of the world's people on a sustainable basis. Rather, we can adopt an attitude of stewardship and partnership with the natural world and with our sisters and brothers everywhere, by getting in the habit of asking questions about each choice instead of taking the status quo for granted. Is getting our clothes "white" more important than having unpolluted waters? Is the opportunity to purchase exotic foods more important than hungry families having control over enough land to grow basic foods? Is the use of aluminum in manufacturing soft drink cans more important than using that same aluminum for manufacture of light bicycle frames for basic transportation in hilly terrain? Each choice by each individual may seem small, but the combined effect creates the material, social, and spiritual climate that we live in.

POSSESSIONS AND PEACE

Our choices about work and possessions may ultimately affect our ability to participate in making world peace. Aside from the direct connection of wars fought for control of particular material resources (oil, for example), Adam Curle has found that people's attitude toward possession affects their openness and responsiveness to the needs and concerns of others in conflict situations. Curle, a Quaker social thinker, peace mediator, and psychologist, identifies two opposing systems of human awareness: "belonging-identity" and "awareness-identity." "Belonging-identity" is based on competitive and materialistic motives; it leads to personally unpeaceful, manipulative relationships, and socially and politically exploitative relationships. "Belonging-identity" people base their self-image on what belongs to them and what (club, regiment, etc.) they belong to. "Awareness-identity" is based on altruistic and empathetic motives; it leads to peaceful, loving, and supportive relationships. "Awareness-identity" people have a "self-image . . . based more upon what that awareness reveals of our nature (awareness-identity) than on what we amass in order to conceal further that nature from ourselves."[18]

Curle found, in his peace-mediating work with persons of primarily "belonging-identity," that "one can never reach the real person or the inner self, or even an honest fragment of the self. . . . I found that if one is talking to an image of this sort, very little real business gets transacted."

In dealing with those of "higher awareness," Curle found "a combination of wisdom, effectiveness, and humanity . . . and [there was] awareness of, sensitivity to and compassion for others."

If we are to contribute our wisdom to the search for world peace, a first step is reestablishing the balance point between consumption-centered and human-centered lives.

WHAT YOU CAN DO

1. List the goods and services on which your current way of living depends. Of these, which were not in general use seventy-five years ago? What advantages do they provide? What added costs?
2. Which of the goods and services on which you rely for comfort and survival depend on centralized sources of fuel, energy, water, transportation, or supply that are beyond your direct control? Could you in fact survive if these sources suddenly failed? What changes would you have to make? What alternatives are available? What alternatives ought to be available? Does our dependence on such sources help limit our freedom in relation to major political, social, and economic institutions?
3. Discuss with your friends and family ways you might lessen your cash needs. Which things can you do alone? In what areas might you trade skills with others?
4. For two weeks, pay close attention to the advertising to which you are exposed. What is it telling you about what you are as a human being? How does it seek to influence your goals and desires? Those of your children? What kinds of threats and promises does advertising use? Do these reflect reality or not? Record and discuss some ads that are especially striking for one reason or another. Analyze the influences and messages associated with our patterns of consumption and those of other segments of our society.
5. Find some popular magazines from Third World countries and discuss

the extent to which American consumption patterns are put forth as something to be aspired to in poor parts of the world.

6. List the possessions that you would need to live without great discomfort and inconvenience. What proportion are they of your total possessions? How do you define "great discomfort and inconvenience"? Try living without some of the nonessential for a period and sharing some of the others with neighbors and friends. Do your friends have something to share with you that makes new purchases unnecessary?

7. Which of the things that you work at *or* that you own:
   a. help you to be more active, self-reliant, creative, and convivial?
   b. promote passivity and dependence?
   c. enhance and enrich your spiritual life?
   d. help you to use your time in more effective and joyful ways?
   e. create a supportive and nurturing environment in which to live?
   f. help you to express your personality, individuality, and growth instead of pushing you into a standardized, mass-produced life?
   g. bring the families, groups, communities, and other networks that support and nourish you closer together?
   h. help you to be better stewards of energy, raw materials, and the natural environment?

8. Try saying no the next few times you are asked to solve any kind of a problem by making a purchase of goods that do not seem absolutely essential to you. What are the alternatives?

9. Divide into small groups of four or five. Each group is assigned a different annual income. If there are four groups, for instance, each member brings the following amount of money to the group: Group 1, $4,000 per year; Group 2, $8,000 per year; Group 3, $12,000 per year; and Group 4, $16,000 per year. Thus, if there are four players in each group, Group 1 will have $16,000, Group 2 $32,000 and so on. Each group then should take about one hour to figure out how they and their dependents would live on this income, to draw up a budget, and to discuss any other way their "way of life" would be affected by the income level. After an hour, bring the groups back together and exchange reports. Did the differences in income produce a difference in values? In actions? If you are in a continuing study group, try this exercise again when you finish this book, and see if your perception of the range of options has changed.

NOTES

1. Thomas Merton, *The Way of Chang Tzu*, (New York: New Directions, 1965).
2. Theodore Roszak, *Person/Planet* (Garden City, N.Y.: Doubleday, 1978), p. 216.
3. Harry Braverman, *Labor and Monopoly Capital* (New York: Monthly Review Press, 1976), p. 171.
4. Gandhi, *All Men Are Brothers*, p. 114, as quoted in *Young India*, November 5, 1925.

5. Braverman, *Labor and Monopoly Capital,* pp. 148–49.
6. Roszak, *Person/Planet,* pp. 214.
7. Braverman, *Labor and Monopoly Capital,* pp. 279–280.
8. Joan D. Gussow, Testimony before the Senate Commerce Committee, March 2, 1972, reprinted in *Journal of Nutrition Education,* Spring 1972, p. 48.
9. Ibid., p. 49.
10. John G. Neihardt, *When the Tree Flowered* (New York: Pocket Books, 1951, 1973), p. 33. Neihardt's fictionalized account, based on extensive interviews with Black Elk and other Oglala Sioux who remembered the prereservation period, is reinforced in Jeannette Mirsky, "The Dakota," in *Cooperation and Competition among Primitive Peoples,* ed. Margaret Mead (New York: McGraw-Hill, 1937), pp. 383–384.
11. Gary Sweatt in *Working Loose,* AFSC New Vocations Project (New York: Random House, 1971), p. 4.
12. *Alternative Celebrations Catalogue,* 4th ed. (Bloomington, Ind.: Alternatives, 1978), p. 160.
13. *New York Times,* October 15, 1973, p. 40.
14. Ibid.
15. Kermit Vandiver, "Why Should My Conscience Bother Me?" in *Sin in the Name of Profits,* ed. D. Obst (New York: Doubleday, 1972), p. 24.
16. Roszak, *Person/Planet,* p. 218.
17. Quoted in R. K. Prabhu and U. R. Rao, *The Mind of Mahatma Gandhi* (Ahmedabad, India: Navajivan, 1967), p. 187.
18. All quotations and concepts from Adam Curle, *Education for Liberation* (New York: Wiley, 1973), pp. 8–12.

SOURCES OF FURTHER INFORMATION

See Chapter VI for additional work-related resource groups and readings. See Chapter XI for additional "alternative way of life" related resource groups and readings.

Resource Groups

The Human Economy Center. Box 551, Amherst, Mass. 01004. Newsletter, speakers' bureau.

Bibliography

American Friends Service Committee. *South Africa: Challenge and Hope.* 1982. Available from: AFSC National Office, 1501 Cherry Street, Philadelphia, Pa. 19102. $5.95 ppd.; 10 or more copies, $2.50/copy + 20 percent postage.

Braverman, Harry. *Labor and Monopoly Capital: The Degradation of Work in the Twentieth Century.* New York: Monthly Review Press, 1976.

Corporate Examiner. Newsletter. Available from: Interfaith Center on Corporate Responsibility, 475 Riverside Drive, Room 566, New York, N.Y. 10115.

Domhoff, G. William. *The Higher Circles: The Governing Class in America.* New York: Random, 1971.

Goodman, Paul, and Percival Goodman. *Communitas: Means of Livelihood and Ways of Life.* New York: Vintage, 1974.

Illich, Ivan. *Toward a History of Needs.* New York: Pantheon, 1978.

Illich, Ivan. *Shadow Work.* Boston: Marion Boyers, 1981.

Jurgenson, Barbara. *How to Live Better on Less: A Guide for Waste Watchers.* Minneapolis: Augsburg, 1974.

Mander, Jerry. *Four Arguments for the Elimination of Television.* New York: Morrow Quill Paperbacks, 1978.

Mumford, Lewis. *The Myth of the Machine:* Vol. 1, *Technics and Human Development;* Vol. 2, *The Pentagon of Power.* New York: Harcourt, 1967, 1970.

Nash, Hugh, ed. *Progress as If Survival Mattered, 1981–1984.* San Francisco: Friends of the Earth, 1982.

Obst, David, ed. *Sin in the Name of Profit.* Garden City, New York: Doubleday, 1972.

Roszak, Theodore. *Person/Planet: The Creative Disintegration of Industrial Society.* Garden City, New York: Doubleday, 1978.

Schumacher, Ernest F. *Small Is Beautiful: Economics as If People Mattered.* New York: Harper & Row, 1973.

Shannon-Thornberry, Milo, ed. *The Alternate Celebrations Catalogue.* New York: Pilgrim Press, 1982. Available from Alternatives along with many excellent related publications. See next listing. $8.95/copy + 15 percent postage.

Smith-Durland, Eugenia. *Voluntary Simplicity Study Action Guide,* rev. ed. 1981. Small-group resource on the issue of alternative celebrations. Available from: Alternatives, Box 1707, Forest Park, Ga. 30051. $3/copy + 15 percent postage.

Zinn, Howard. *A People's History of the United States.* New York: Harper & Row, 1980.

CHAPTER II

Food

QUERIES

1. Do I take food for granted? What are my major considerations in choosing and buying my food?
2. Do I know what my food needs are? How do I feel about changing my diet to improve my health? To lessen hunger and starvation in the world? To lessen the exploitation of farmworkers? To preserve agricultural land and wilderness for future generations?
3. Could I use the land around my home to grow fruits and vegetables? Is there a community garden in my neighborhood, or could there be? Do I return my "waste" food garbage to the soil by composting?
4. Could I get along with fewer foods grown in other countries at the expense of that country's food supply—"cash crops," such as coffee, tea, and bananas?
5. Do I know what my protein requirements are? Am I consuming more protein than my body needs? Could I use my favorite cooking methods and flavors without using much meat?
6. Where do I buy my food? Is there an independent grocer, local farmers market, consumer co-op, or food-buying club that I could support instead of large supermarkets and agribusiness?
7. Can I get along with less packaged, canned, or convenience foods? Why do I buy these foods? Have I explored simple and quick methods of preparing and preserving basic food from scratch?
8. How are my eating habits and the cost of my food influenced by the media?
9. Can anything be done about the additives, preservatives, and pesticides in my food?
10. Are there conferences, workshops, or speakers in my community that could inform me and others about nutrition, unfamiliar foods, food co-ops, community gardens, domestic farm policies, and global food issues?
11. How could the business of food production and distribution be rightly operated to provide adequately for all the world's people? What is my role in making and implementing such food policy decisions?

Meals have been a basic way to gather with friends and relatives in all eras and in all cultures—both as part of the daily routine and on special occasions like birthdays and holidays. For every person in the world, the production, buying, preparation, or consumption of food is part of daily experience. Decisions about what we choose to eat, how it is prepared, and whether we eat at home or out have an impact on the entire food chain back to the farmer, the farm laborers, and the soil.

In order to take charge of this most basic aspect of human life, we need to be informed about how our food habits are literally a life-and-death matter for ourselves and others around the world. The control of our food system has become increasingly concentrated and profit-oriented, often at the expense of our nutrition, health, natural resources, and the farm families and workers who produce what we eat. The development of an integrated, worldwide food system has brought unintended side effects. As only one of many examples, six of the ten leading causes of death in the United States can be linked to unhealthful diet:[1] removal of vital nutrients and food fibers; the addition of excess salt and sugar in processing; harmful dietary fat; pesticide residues; chemical flavorings, colorings, and preservatives.

Nearly a fifth of humanity is chronically undernourished, and every minute, twenty-seven people—most of them, children—die from hunger or hunger-related diseases.[2] Nearly everywhere, soil and water resources are deteriorating. We are entering a period of unprecedented crisis regarding how we utilize the earth's carrying capacity for our species.

When we think of food crisis, we tend to think of famine. A "famine" may be defined as an episode in which a quarter of the population in an area starves to death. The first recorded population drop of this magnitude was in Bombay, India, in 1669–1670. In 1769–1770, a quarter of the Bengalese starved; in 1899–1900, famine devastated the populations of Baroda, Indore, and Rajputana; in 1943, two and one-half million starved in Bengal; in 1965–1966, U.S. grain shipments averted a similar famine in the same area.[3] Elsewhere there has been mass starvation in China in 1943, and in Biafra and the Sahel of Africa in the 1960s and 1970s.

These famines are tragic and dramatic, but we need to look beyond these isolated events to the more startling fact that *never, in all our thousands of years as a species, have we experienced the magnitude of chronic undernutrition that now exists.* There is no evidence to indicate that early man suffered the growth stunting and mental retardation from caloric and protein deficiency that is becoming common in many parts of the world today. Even contemporary "stone age" people in isolated parts of the world have better diets than those of many people in modern society. This malnourishment has many forms: heavily advertised infant formula, often overdiluted with contaminated water by parents who cannot afford to buy enough formula for their babies; junk food; or simply not enough food. It is no secret that in the United States some people eat pet food, scavenge garbage, and suffer malnutrition because they don't have the income to buy enough to eat and can't grow their own food.

The world is producing record-breaking crops—more than enough to feed everyone on earth as many calories as the average American eats (over 3,000 calories daily), including ample protein.[4] So why are people hungry?

The two separate food problems of famine and chronic malnutrition require different approaches. Famines resulting from war, drought, locusts, or floods are subject to emergency relief aid. But an end to chronic malnutrition demands fundamental changes in agricultural policy both here and abroad—from techniques that quickly destroy the land's usefulness to long-term, sustainable agriculture, from a plantation/peasant pattern of land tenure to genuine agrarian democracy, and from corporately controlled cash cropping to locally controlled food self-sufficiency. Interests that profit from the existing system tend to blame hunger on the lack of adequate technology in Third World countries or on "too many people," and seek simply to increase yields or to promote population control. If, however, hunger is seen as resulting from poverty and maldistribution of land and the resources to grow food, we must become involved with the sticky questions of equality and justice.

The overpopulation hypothesis can be tested by comparing China and India. China has half the cultivated acreage for each person that India has,[5] yet in twenty-five years, China has successfully eliminated malnutrition while many Indians still suffer from too little food. Similarly, in Mexico, most of the rural population suffers from malnourishment, whereas in Cuba, with less cultivated land per person, no one is underfed.[6] In other words, overpopulation does not seem to be the root cause of hunger; rather it is a symptom that tells us to look to other factors. High birth rates are often the result of poverty and maldistribution, not their cause. Many Third World parents will keep having large families as long as infant mortality is high, as long as children are their only social security, and as long as women do not have roles available to them that are as highly valued by their society as childrearing.

Although per capita food production is increasing in Asia and Latin America, in Africa it is decreasing and everywhere the number of undernourished is on the rise. Increasing malnutrition, accompanied by forecasts of higher food prices and lower per capita food production in the poorest countries by the year 2000, are ample indication that the current system is neither equitable nor practical. Though the global supermarket has been profitable, it is a disaster for millions of landless peasants and their compatriots in urban areas.

Forced colonial plantation agriculture, later replaced by multinational investment, shifted the agricultural production of Third World countries from self-sustaining food crops to cash or export crops. This has resulted in deteriorating soils, increased dependence on imported food, increased energy use, and malnutrition, as most of the cash generated goes outside the country or to a tiny percentage of local large landowners. A similar phenomenon can be found in many areas of the United States where soils and growing conditions are particularly suitable for profitable crops. Vacationers in Hawaii get a shock in the produce section of city supermarkets, finding that most fruits and vegetables sold in the "tropical paradise" are high-priced and shipped from the mainland, at least two thousand miles away. Hawaii's rich soil is controlled by multinationals that grow sugar cane and pineapples for export.

Many cash or export crops are luxury items of little nutritional value that require large amounts of low-paid labor. Multinational agribusiness, international lending agencies like the World Bank and the International Monetary Fund, and elite landholders are the ones who make the planting decisions, instead of the majority of the population who needs the food. Few Americans would willingly choose to have most of their basic food supply dependent on imports from other nations, and it is unlikely that the people of other countries feel differently.

Some examples of recent agricultural development in the Third World demonstrate how world food goals become distorted from feeding the hungry to maximizing profits for the privileged:

- In Senegal in Africa's Sahel region, multinational firms, assisted with public funds, grow eggplant, fruits, and vegetables to be air-freighted to Europe.[7]
- In Colombia, landowners have switched from wheat to carnations that are flown to the eastern seaboard of the United States and make eighty times the cash return of wheat per acre.[8]
- In Africa, during the last two decades, coffee production has increased fourfold, tea sixfold, sugar cane threefold, and cocoa and cotton have doubled.[9]
- In Nicaragua, between 1952 and 1967, cotton acreage quadrupled while the area planted with basic grains was cut in half.[10]

Another reason for this distortion is the attempt by many Third World countries to copy the Western, high technology development model. (See Chapter X for a full discussion of this.) Unfortunately, even governments that have the best of intentions for their people find themselves taking one step forward and two steps backward in their quest for cash to pay for imported machinery. According to Michael Manley, former prime minister of Jamaica, his country had to grow 20 tons of sugar cane in 1962 to pay for one Ford tractor. In 1980, the same Ford tractor cost Jamaica 41 tons.[11]

TEN FOOD-FIRST FUNDAMENTALS*

1. Every country in the world has the resources necessary for its people to free themselves from hunger.

2. To balance the planet's population and resources, we must now address the root cause of both hunger and high birth rates: the insecurity and poverty of the majority that results from the control over basic national resources by a few.

3. Hunger is only made worse when approached as a technical problem. Hunger can only be overcome by the transformation of social relationships in which the majority directly participates in building a democratic economic system.

4. Political and economic inequalities are the greatest stumbling block to development.

5. Safeguarding the world's agricultural environment and people freeing themselves from hunger are complementary goals.

6. Agriculture must become, first and foremost, a way for people to produce the food they need and, secondarily, a possible source of foreign exchange.

7. Our food security is not threatened by hungry people, but by a system that concentrates economic power into the hands of elites who profit by the generation of scarcity and the internationalization of food control.

8. Today, in every country in the world, people are working to democratize the control over food-producing resources.

9. Escape from hunger comes not through the redistribution of food, but only through the redistribution of control over food-producing resources.

10. For Americans distressed about the reality of hunger in a world of plenty, the tasks ahead are clear: work to remove those obstacles that prevent people from taking charge of their food-producing resources—obstacles that today are being built by our government, by U.S.-supported international agencies and U.S.-based corporations. Our work toward food self-reliance and democratization of our own economy allies us with the struggle of people in underdeveloped countries fighting for food self-determination.

*Taken from: FRANCES MOORE LAPPE and JOSEPH COLLINS, *Ten Food Myths.*

FOOD AID

Most Americans feel good about sending food to those who are starving around the world. The conventional objection often voiced to the Food for Peace Program (PL480) is that it just doesn't get food to those who really need it—it is believed there would be less hunger if only we could ensure that our food would go to those who need it most. When we look closely, however, we discover that the program was never designed to alleviate hunger. Congress stated the statute's purpose to be "to increase the consumption of U.S. agricultural commodities and to improve foreign relations of the United States."

Following World War II, there was so much food on the United States market that farmers couldn't sell it to paying customers. Prices dropped so low from this oversupply that farmers could not afford to produce it or even to store it. The Food for Peace program was created to help solve this problem of overproduction.

It would seem that sending food overseas would benefit both the American farmers and those who are hungry. In fact, its method of administration often means that those who are hungry become even hungrier.

Most Food for Peace aid is sent under Title I, which provides for the shipping of grain through commercial markets on a government-to-government basis. The United States finances contracts between private grain traders in this country and importers in the recipient nations. In the Third World country, the grain is then channeled to local commercial markets for sale to the people. Although the price is often lower than prevailing world prices, there is no assurance that the neediest can afford the American grain.

Though the price of Title I grain may be lower than world prices, it is still sold, and the loan taken out to buy it must be repaid in U.S. dollars. This obliges recipient countries to encourage the development of cash and export crops, such as cotton, coffee, or bananas, in order to generate foreign exchange to service an ever-increasing debt load. These export crops compete for land, water, labor, and fertilizer with the grain and the beans that originally sustained the local people, thus necessitating the import of more food. This self-perpetuating circle of debt ties recipient countries to the food aid "company store."

Donated foods have also been used as a vehicle to create a desire and commercial demand for unfamiliar foods that are not produced in the recipient nations, or even to put local producers out of business. The North American Congress on Latin America reports that massive Food for Peace dry milk donations to Costa Rica destroyed a thriving dairy industry. Now the grazing lands are used to raise beef, which is exported to U.S. hamburger chains. At the same time, the incidence of protein-calorie malnutrition is increasing.[12]

The Food for Peace program objectives state that it can "improve foreign relations of the United States," but the powerful rarely wish to aid the powerless by changing the balance of power. Leo Tolstoy explained this eloquently:

I sit on a man's back choking him and making him carry me, and yet assure myself and others that I am sorry for him and wish to lighten his load by all possible means—except by getting off his back.[13]

Sometimes our leaders are not even this subtle: at the 1974 world food conference, Secretary of Agriculture Earl Butz stated that "food is a weapon. It is a tool in our negotiating kit."

The best aid that we in the United States can give is to oppose corporate control and U.S. military and economic "aid" that distorts the growth and distribution of food, as well as to give emergency relief where necessary. And we can give unconditional aid to indigenous groups that are working to achieve self-determination and self-reliance. In Mali, in the Sahel region of West Africa, one American Friends Service Committee project helped two hundred traditional nomad families to reconstitute their herds after the six-year drought and to become self-sufficient in food by growing grain and vegetables to make food purchases unnecessary. Other examples of projects aiding self-determination are discussed in Chapter X.

PRESERVATION OF OUR AGRICULTURAL RESOURCES

Modern farming techniques create serious environmental hazards, ranging from simple soil destruction to full-scale desertification and deforestation (see Chapter X). High technology farming is extremely vulnerable to limitations of fossil fuel reserves. Such reliance on artificial fertilizers and chemical pest and weed control "mines" organic matter and reduces soil biomass, which in turn breaks down soil structure, increases water demand, wastes nutrients, and causes accelerated soil erosion. The short-term higher yields destroy a region's entire social structure by displacing small farmers, who sell out because they can't afford to buy the chemicals. Such a farming system can only exist on borrowed time as it is not self-regenerative.

As the use of the best arable land for export or cash crops continues, especially in the Third World, basic food crops are forced onto marginal lands such as steep hillsides, which are more ecologically vulnerable to damage. In cases where food aid has disrupted local food marketing, landowners have switched to livestock, often overgrazing marginal land that normally sustains a grain crop every several years in alternation with light grazing. These changes result in an eventual reduction in the sustainable carrying capacity of the land.

In conjunction with fair distribution of land and productive resources, long-term world food security depends upon the preservation of and return to traditional farming knowledge and practices, aided by "appropriate technology" (see p. 233) that assists in maintaining, rather than disrupts, the balance of nature. We often forget that, until very, very recently, these were the methods by which all the world's food was successfully produced. A system of sustainable agriculture depends upon many different factors: the way land is fertilized; the way pests are controlled; the way weeds are controlled; the methods of cultivation and the type of tools used; the patterns of planting; and the balance between the animal and vegetable foods raised.

The "Green Revolution," which promised high grain yields through scientifically developed seed varieties, has almost completely ignored principles of sustainable agriculture. In the Philippines, for example, in a twenty-year period, 75 percent of the country's ricelands were switched to high-yield seeds that require massive amounts of chemical fertilizers and pesticides. Native seed varieties of rice, corn, and vegetables, adapted to local conditions, are rapidly becoming extinct.[14] In the future it will be hard for farmers to return to cultivation technologies that are adapted to the land. Green Revolution plants also tend to be more vulnerable to pests and to use greater quantities of water than native plants. Higher densities of planting, made possible by use of herbicides instead of hand-weeding in large fields, also tend to decrease the protein content of grain.[15]

Chinese farming practices, a mixture of traditional knowledge and more recent discoveries, provide an illustration of "organic" methods of farming—an alternative often associated in the United States with holistic faddism, damaged, blemished fruits, and counterculturists ignorant of the realities of food production. The Chinese have increased their agricultural production by efficient use of labor without extensive use of machinery or artificial fertilizers. Weeding is done by hand instead of using herbicides. They have developed a system of "intercropping" where two or more crops grow simultaneously in one field, with staggered harvests allowing as much as a 50 percent increase in total annual yield.[16]

In addition to increased yield, intercropping illustrates other sustainable farming principles. Insect pest problems are greatly reduced: one variety of plants can be placed near another variety that repels the other plants' pests (many pests, for example, dislike onions and garlic and won't prey on plants nearby). Also, fields consisting of only one type of crop are much more vulnerable to pests, which like to travel directly from one plant to the next. Intercropping confuses them, since they usually will eat only one vegetable family. The intercropped plants can also nourish each other: corn, which uses a great deal of nitrogen from the soil, can be supplied with that nitrogen by beans, which take nitrogen from the air and "fix" it into the soil. In China other fertilizer consists of field stubble and compost made of human and animal waste (often in conjunction with biogas production), together with a limited amount of chemical fertilizer.[17]

The same sort of contrasts between sustainable and destructive approaches apply to the balance of production of vegetable versus meat foods. Some cultures, especially small populations of nomadic peoples and fishing peoples, have always relied heavily on nonvegetable sources of food. Most of the earth's population, however, has historically combined a mostly vegetable diet—including protein-rich grains and beans —with small quantities of meat, poultry, or fish, and indulged in a roasted pig or fried chicken for holidays and celebrations only. The American diet, however, has come to rely so heavily on animal foods that our land is being slowly destroyed, our water table is dropping, our remaining petroleum reserves are being squandered, and we are taking both grain and land to cultivate it out of the mouths of hungry people and our own children and grandchildren. A few statistics give the flavor of this situation:

- For every 16 pounds of grain and soy fed to beef cattle in the United States, we get back only one pound of meat on our plate.[18]
- To produce a one-pound steak requires 2,500 gallons of water, including that used in producing the feed.[19]
- We are losing two bushels of topsoil for every bushel of corn harvested on Iowa's sloping soils.[20] Most of that harvest is fed to livestock.
- To produce a pound of steak—500 calories of food energy—takes 10,000 calories of fossil fuel, expended mainly in producing the crops fed to livestock.[21]
- For every calorie of human energy the Chinese use growing rice, they harvest 53.5 calories of rice.[22]
- One-third of the value of *all* raw materials consumed for all purposes in the United States is consumed in livestock foods.[23]
- Livestock consume close to one-half the world's grain output, and by 1985, livestock are expected to eat even more grain than is eaten by people.[24]

A similar imbalance is found in our country's approach to vegetable, fruit, and grain farming. Three million acres of farmland are lost every year because of farming methods characterized by continuous planting of row crops and use of heavy equipment that compacts the soil, makes nutrient absorption by roots difficult, and encourages wind and water erosion. To maintain crop growth, more fertilizer is then needed, along with more energy to run bigger equipment to plow the hardened soil.

U.S. agriculture uses an annual average of 120 pounds of synthetic fertilizer per acre of cropland, which amounts to more than 200 pounds of fertilizer for every person in the country.[25] One effect of all this fertilizer use is nitrate contamination of groundwater, very harmful to human health. Another is phosphate contamination, which causes excessive algae growth that can consume all of the oxygen in a lake or stream, thus killing other plants and fish. Lake Erie's "death" (which was contributed to by a variety of polluting factors) is the most notorious example of this phenomenon. Many fertilizer and pesticide companies encourage application of their products on a fixed schedule, without regard for need at a particular moment or whether there is an effective, nonchemical alternative available in each instance.

There are other ways to farm, even in the Midwest Corn Belt. Since 1975, a team of researchers at Washington University's Center for the Biology of Natural Systems in St. Louis has investigated the economic viability of organic farms in that region. Here are some of their findings:[26]

- Soybean production per acre was 17 percent higher, and oat production 36 percent higher, on organic than conventional farms. Corn and wheat yields were 5 percent lower.
- A portion of an organic farmer's land is always planted with legumes or clover to replenish the soil, which is sometimes plowed under as "green manure" rather than harvested. The farmer may thus earn less total cash per acre. Operating costs, however, are 36 percent lower, so the net return per acre is often higher.
- Organic farmers use only 40 percent of the energy conventional farmers consume, including that used in petroleum-based fertilizers, insecticides, and herbicides.

Today there are perhaps eighty thousands farms in the United States trying some organic farming. Even more widely used is integrated pest management, which looks first at physical, biological, and farming technique controls, resorting to chemicals only when necessary. There are two hundred commercial organic farms in California, the leading state in the sales of organic food and one in which organic food criteria are codified in law.

One such operation is Star Route Farm in Bolinas, California. Warren and Marion Weber plant thirty acres with vegetables, fertilizing their soil with cow manure from a local dairy. The mild climate permits planting of nitrogen-fixing winter crop of vetch and Austrian peas, which are plowed under in the spring as green manure. No single crop is grown in the same place in succession, which further helps to maintain soil fertility. Most of Star Route Farm's produce is marketed through Veritable Vegetables, a collective produce warehouse described further in Chapter VI.

In this country, research on sustainable agriculture is generally not being done by agribusiness or publicly supported agencies. Rather, it is being done at places like the New Alchemy Institute in East Falmouth, Massachusetts, founded in 1969 and supported mainly by small private contributions. On its twelve-acre Cape Cod farm, which contains thirty separate research/exhibit areas open to the public, New Alchemy explores agriculture, aquaculture, wind systems, solar design, tree crops, and ecosystem modeling:

Our goal is to develop ecological approaches to food, energy, shelter and community design. The strategies we research emphasize a minimal reliance on fossil fuels and operate on a scale accessible to families and small enterprises. . . .

These projects share certain assumptions: that it is possible to live comfortably without jeopardizing future generations; that there can be a fruitful marriage of some modern technologies and some old ideals of stewardship; and that people can devise new syntheses of work, ethics and art.[27]

Some of New Alchemy's current projects include:

- A "six-pack bioshelter." This is a family-size, completely passive, solar-heated greenhouse (see p. 199), which is used to grow seedlings in the spring, and food, ornamental plants, and fish all year round. It can produce enough vegetables for a family of four throughout the year. A large, concrete fish pond absorbs heat on sunny days and releases the heat at night and on cloudy days. A small windmill on the roof operates a pond aerator, which gives oxygen to the fish and increases heat storage efficiency. A larger version of this greenhouse includes a mechanism for circulating fish-fertilized water to feed greenhouse plants.
- Hundreds of trees for fruit, nut forage (for pigs), and timber are being evaluated, selected, and developed for the Northeast climate.
- A solar food dryer, which easily preserves fruits, vegetables, and herbs, is constructable during a one-day workshop.
- In intensive, raised-bed gardens, high-yield, sustainable food production on small amounts of land is studied. Twenty raised beds cover less than one-tenth of an acre and produce enough vegetables during six months, without chemical fertilizers or pesticides, to feed ten adults three vegetable servings per day for a year. In the overall garden area, over one hundred different food crops have been tested using integrated biological pest controls and organically maintained soil fertility. One pest control method, a small light combined with a fan and catch-bag that attracts insects at night, provides some of the food for the fish raised in ponds and greenhouses.

In England, the late E. F. Schumacher and his Soil Association have used a reasonably successful tactic to promote organic farming research with larger growers. They have convinced those growers that they need a "lifeboat"—at least 5 percent of their land set aside to preserve and develop organic farming techniques—"just in case" their regular method of farming turns out not to be sustainable in the long run.[28] As Schumacher used to say, "Who could argue with that?"

ARE SMALL FARMS BEAUTIFUL?

In the United States, farms have become larger as farmers are forced out of production by the expense of capital, machinery, fuel, fertilizer, pesticides, and the increasing concentration of food processing and distribution, which means lower market prices for the farmer. Eight million farms operated in 1935. Two million, three hundred thousand remain, and of these just one percent produce over a third of all farm products on about a third of all farmland.[29] One effect of the drastic reduction in the number of farm families is a corresponding reduction of the family farmer's ability politically to influence policy decisions that affect the survival of the remaining smaller farms.

After commodities leave the farm gate, they are handled by twenty thousand companies, of which the top fifty take home 75 percent of the profits. A 1978 study shows that seventy-three companies account for nearly 75 percent of the food industry's $250 billion in revenues; fifteen companies supply 60 percent of all farm inputs (equipment, seed, fertilizer, pesticides); forty-nine companies receive 68 percent of all food processing revenues; and forty-four companies receive 77 percent of revenues from wholesale and retail distribution.[30] Consolidation limits competition, increases prices, and results in increased hunger.

Del Monte Corporation, now owned by Reynold's Tobacco, provides a good example of this consolidation of control over the growing, processing, and distribution of our food:

[It] is the world's largest canner of fruits and vegetables. But it does more than processing and canning. It manufactures its own cans and prints its own labels; it conducts its own agricultural research; it grows produce on its own land, as well as putting 10,000 farmers under production contracts; it distributes its produce through its own banana transports, tuna seiners, air-freight forwarding stations, ocean terminal and trucking operations; it operates its own warehouses; it maintains 58 sales offices throughout the world; and it caters 28 restaurants and provides food services to United Air Lines.[31]

Del Monte thus has the ability to compete better economically than the small farmer by obtaining more of the consumer's food dollar. As was discussed in Chapter I, the results of this superior "economic competitiveness" are increasing unemployment and employment at mindless and machine-minding jobs. It should be obvious even to city-readers that the knowledge, experience, and skill variety necessary to farm by sustainable agriculture principles is immensely greater than that necessary for most industrial society jobs.

Part of the strategy of agribusiness to compete economically is the exploitation of farmworkers. Campbell's controls nearly 90 percent of the soup market.[32] The people who harvest the tomatoes for that soup, the Ohio-based Farm Labor Organizing Committee (FLOC), have been on strike for years for fair wages and better working conditions. The majority of farmworkers have annual incomes below federal poverty guidelines and their children show signs of serious malnutrition, including growth retardation, rickets, and other vitamin deficiencies.

Instead of spreading the workload throughout the growing season by planting various crops needing maximum attention at different times, the agribusiness system of production depends on large quantities of cheap labor being available "on demand" for working and harvesting single-crop farms. Many farmworkers and their families are thus forced to lead a migratory life, often traveling considerable distances between brief jobs and living in improvised and unsanitary housing at each stop. Because each job is short and there are few alternatives, growers can play one group of workers against another if, for example, a crew asks for a raise or better working conditions. In past strikes, growers have brought in large numbers of undocumented workers, desperate for jobs, who had not been told a strike was in progress. Conversely, an undocumented worker knows that a protest of working conditions can quickly bring immigration authorities and deportation proceedings. It is illegal for an employer to call immigration authorities to break strikes, but this prohibition is difficult to enforce.

Concentration and integration of food production, processing, and distribution also results in environmental abuses, chemical residues and

Selma (small farms)								*Huron (corporate farms)*
11 .	.	.	.	Farm owners .	.	.	.	. 1
11 .	.	.	.	Resident owners	.	.	.	. 0
9 .	.	.	.	Farms	.	.	.	. 1
9 .	.	.	.	Resident farmers	.	.	.	. 0
7 .	.	.	. Resident owners/operators .	.	.	.	. 0
2 .	.	.	. Resident lessees/operators .	.	.	.	. 0
7 .	.	.	.	Full-time farmers	.	.	.	. 1
31 .	.	.	.	People on the land	.	.	.	. 0
$916,000 .	.	.	Gross value of production .	.	.	$590,000
$1,092,000	.	.	Property value	.	.	. $412,000
$25,394 .	.	.	Property taxes paid	.	.	. $8,627
9,036 .	.	.	Population .	.	.	. 2,539
287.	.	.	Number of businesses	.	.	. 55
22 .	.	.	. Manufacturers/processors .	.	.	. 11
0 .	.	.	. Corporate farm offices	.	.	. 18
$43,317,000	.	.	Retail taxable sales	.	.	$7,350,000
1 .	.	.	.	. Hospitals .	.	.	.	. 0
6 .	.	.	.	. Doctors	.	.	.	. 1
6 .	.	.	.	. Dentists	.	.	.	. 0
34 .	.	.	.	. Churches .	.	.	.	. 2

additives in our food, less nutritious foods, and adverse impacts on our farm communities. An example of the socioeconomic effects of large-scale farming is a study done by National Land for People, a nonprofit, small-farm advocacy organization in Fresno, California.[33] This organization compared two typical square miles (640 acres each) of close-by California farm land representing family-versus-corporate-style farming. The small farms around Selma grew the following crops in a square mile: 120 acres of yams; 10 acres of beans; 35 acres of peaches; 80 acres of cotton; 60 acres of alfalfa; 3.5 acres of berries; and 280 acres of raisins. Under large-sale farming around Huron, there were 320 acres of cotton and 320 acres of tomatoes. The chart offers a picture of the social fabric of these two towns.

Small farmers, then, can more than hold their own as efficient producers, but to offset the advantages enjoyed by big corporations they need more of the retail dollar. The Rural Economic Alternatives Project (REAP), an American Friends Service Committee effort, has been successful in developing alternative marketing outlets for family farmers in California's San Joaquin Valley. REAP's work began by organizing an association of growers now numbering about two hundred. Through this group it established several vigorous certified farmers' markets, launched a marketing cooperative with twenty-five of these same growers, helped refugee farmers from Laos get started in agricultural production, and co-sponsored workshops on alternative production techniques and integrated pest management.

In their first three years of marketing directly to consumers, members of the Stockton Farmers' Market Association sold over four million pounds of produce for a gross dollar volume of $1 million, and the consumers saved an estimated $500,000 on their produce purchases. The original market, located under the freeway in downtown Stockton, brings seventy-five or more farmers and five thousand customers together each Saturday at the peak of the growing season. Stockton area farmers are also servicing a number of additional markets that have sprung up in nearby counties, partly as a result of their successful example. One farmer jokingly reported that he's so busy going to farmers' markets now that he doesn't have time to get out in the fields and grow things! Actually, though it *is* a lot of work, the farmer can be assisted in the marketing by other family members and employees. In addition, one certified producer may voluntarily sell the products of up to two other such producers, relieving them of the burden of going each market day to sell directly to their customers.

As an additional outlet for their produce, fresh fruits and vegetables grown by members of the Stockton Farmers' Cooperative are pooled into larger lots and trucked into urban centers several times each week for distribution through wholesale markets and retail stores. Organized in the fall of 1980, the co-op has encountered the usual uphill struggle of any small, undercapitalized business facing competition from larger distributors who can supply an almost unlimited quantity and variety of products for their customers. Even so, the co-op has pulled through some difficult periods and now sells regularly to a chain of large, consumer co-op supermarkets in Berkeley, several other retail markets, community food stores, and small wholesale distributors including a San Francisco restaurant supplier and Veritable Vegetables (see Chapter VI).

Mack Warner, REAP organizer, observes:

We're facing some very large obstacles to our survival. No matter how successful we are at direct retail or co-op wholesale marketing, those larger economic forces can still knock you out if they are stacked against you as a small-scale operator. Tax shelters in agriculture that favor urban or corporate investors over the family farmer, credit policies that channel millions of dollars of Farmers Home Administration funds into the pockets of big-time operators rather than helping out the low-equity farmer as originally intended, and commodity price supports that do the same thing for the corporate growers, all these are ominous forces that make our future very insecure.

Even so, we have seen a noticeable renewal of interest in farming among some of our growers in this part of the Central Valley as a result of better marketing opportunities. More young farmers are remaining on the land and older farmers are once again experiencing a measure of hope that they can remain viable. We've learned that when you are small you have to work together to survive, not only with other farmers, but also in creative alliances with our urban brothers and sisters.

THE PERSONAL APPROACH

Typically, food habit changes have been viewed as the result of irresistable social forces produced by "women's desire for liberation from the kitchen" . . . [but] in a society truly dedicated to time savings, energy conservation, and women's liberation, the pressures that presumably have led to sugar-glazed frozen carrots could have led as well to eating vegetables raw—thus reducing preparation time to zero.

—JOAN GUSSOW[34]

Despite corporate dominance of our food system, food is an easier area than housing or energy in which to take charge of our lives. Many of us can grow some of our own food, and we can all make changes in what we eat, in where and how we shop, and in food preparation. By starting to change our own lives, our efforts will also reach the broader global family.

Change may not always come as easily as the decision to make the change. Most of our food habits are learned, and we need time both to do some "unlearning" of those habits and to gradually acquire new ones.

In many urban and rural areas there are alternatives to shopping at the chain grocery stores. One such alternative is the Boston Food Co-op, an unusually large co-op with an average membership of 2,000. Started as a student project in the early 1970s, it rapidly expanded its base, moved from its original university site, and became a leader in the community food co-op movement, giving direct aid and sponsorship to co-ops starting in other Boston neighborhoods. The Boston Food Co-op also founded the New England Food Cooperative Organization (NEFCO). NEFCO buys and stores produce, grains, and cheese for its members, which include most New England area food co-ops.

The Boston Food Co-op is unusual in that it is one of the few storefront co-ops to exclude nonmembers from shopping privileges. Members pay $5 per year and may participate in the co-op's decision-making boards and committees. Until recently, all members were also required to work two hours per month per adult in each household in order to shop at the co-op. Now, any members who are behind in their hours, or who choose not to work, pay a 15 percent surcharge on their grocery bill at the cash register. The curious can shop once as guests, but are expected to join if they wish to continue shopping. The co-op has engaged in various community outreach projects over the years, and currently operates an Elders' Co-op one day per week at a local community center.

Markup on wholesale price is low, averaging 16 percent and varying according to such factors as refrigeration costs and in-store labor required for preparation (cutting and wrapping cheeses, for example). Most items, such as spices, grains, beans, flours, and produce, are bagged by shoppers themselves in any quantity they choose. There are also canned goods, meat, and fish available. About seventy-five percent of the total hours worked at the co-op are by members, and the rest by a paid staff. Members' familiarity with the store's operation also cuts down on the total amount of paid or "official" labor required: if the mushroom box is empty, a shopper knows where to go in the cooler to bring out a new one.

Marilyn Bernstein, a laboratory technician, has balanced the co-op's checkbook monthly for eight years. With several people writing two to three hundred checks per month, she calls it "kind of a wild project." The balancing takes her three to six hours per month, so she's always ahead in her hours and has extra ones to "give away." Though she lives over a mile from the coop and usually must walk or take the bus carrying groceries, she shops there:

I like the atmosphere, and I like the feeling that the things the coop has to sell are selected thoughtfully. The food is good quality and tastes good. Some of the fruits and vegetables are chemical-free; nuts are available unsalted; there is a selection of rennetless cheeses for vegetarians. It's a nicer place to shop.

Many storefront food co-ops or "community food stores" don't require the level of member participation that the Boston Food Co-op does. Often, volunteer work is simply encouraged, in exchange for a discount on food purchases, with most of the work done by paid workers who own and run the store collectively. On the other hand, in food buying clubs, which tend to be quite small, members do all of the work. Typically, each household is responsible for a major task—such as shopping for produce at a wholesale market or sorting out and boxing members' pre-orders—once every month to six weeks. These clubs cannot always obtain wholesale prices as low as do larger co-ops, but there is no markup whatsoever.

Buying produce directly from a farmer or a farmers' market is yet another way to lessen your dependency on the corporate structure. Consumers get the benefit of fresh, seasonal produce at reduced costs. Bulk produce purchases for home canning, freezing, and drying are also much more easily and economically arranged when you deal directly with the farmer. Food waste is also reduced: often high-quality fresh produce cannot be sold through major marketing channels due to its "nonstandard" size or cosmetic blemishes or color variations. This is also true of canning-grade fruits and vegetables.

By working together with farmers, consumers can gain the benefits of direct marketing for their entire community. In 1977, the Massachusetts Federation of Farmers Markets was formed by local farmers market managers and representatives of consumer organizations. Today, the federation supports widespread development of farmers markets by providing training for market managers, technical assistance to consumer organizations, coordination of publicity campaigns, legal assistance, fund-raising assistance, and more. Other direct-marketing programs are also blossoming, such as the Wholesale Apple Marketing Project. Through coordinated efforts of the Massachusetts Department of Education, the USDA, and local farmers, small growers sell low-perishable produce, such as apples and carrots, direct to schools, hospitals, and other institutions. The recipients save 10 to 50 percent on the produce, while the farmers' revenue has increased by approximately 25 percent. Small farmers in Massachusetts also have formed producer cooperatives and, according to nutritionist Hugh Joseph, have moved into stable sales relationships with local supermarkets. With more farmers selling direct, Massachusetts can brag of both a healthy farm economy and a developing food self-reliance.

Gardening—in your backyard, on the roof, a terrace, a windowsill, or a solar greenhouse—can also provide a personal beginning for food self-reliance, as well as fresher, more delicious, and chemical-free produce. If you have no experience, there is much to learn. It can be especially frustrating the first couple of years as you find a different, unfamiliar bug on your plants each week and can't figure out if it's a friend or foe. Putting together your first garden plan using "intercropping" (or complementary) principles can also be mind-boggling: peas and onions like to be planted near each other, but tomatoes hate onions, but like carrots, but. . . .

If you don't have garden space available, or if you would just like some companionship and advice, community garden plots can also provide the opportunity to grow your own. In San Francisco, there are over fifty community gardens, each organized and worked collectively by its members, who share tools, knowledge, and labor. Most gardens have joined the San Francisco League of Urban Gardeners (SLUG), which promotes innovative use of land in urban areas and assists garden projects at schools, housing developments, and hospitals. At a recent meeting of SLUG, an elderly member spoke of the multifaceted value of gardening:

Community gardens projects accomplish more than just growing food for neighborhood families. They provide a focus for education. Our grandparents or great-grandparents did this for survival, whereas I think it is important for mental development as well . . . since we are all part of the earth.

Another member expressed appreciation for the variety of ethnic contacts her garden provided.

Community gardens are a nationwide movement. At a typical garden site in Oakland, California, twenty-five to thirty families each have a plot 10 feet by 15 feet, where they produce as much as $500 to $700 worth of produce in a single year. In Chicago, the community gardening program provides an important supplement to the diets of six thousand families. The Los Angeles Neighborhood Gardens and Farms program now includes more than two thousand families, who collectively produce more than $1 million worth of vegetables annually. In the Chapter IX, you will read about a Colorado community that uses solar greenhouses to increase their food supply throughout the year.

Poor communities in the inner city, where many chain stores have closed and food quality tends to be poor, can especially benefit from combining a number of alternative food strategies. Through the Detroit Anti-Hunger and Youth Advocacy Center, inner-city teenagers make a significant contribution to making high quality, affordable food available in their community. Started in 1975 by the American Friends Service Committee, the food section of the now-autonomous program sponsors teenage interns who comparison shop at local food stores, check food quality at local markets, and provide shopping services for the elderly and handicapped. Interns also teach nutrition to elementary school children, educate the community about domestic and international hunger, provide information about food cooperatives and food buying clubs to interested groups, and maintain a community garden whose products are shared with the community. The food programs are one approach to the project's focus on teaching young people leadership and organizing skills; exploring recognition of how racism functions and how Third World persons and white people can work together for racial justice; and providing practical experience and resources for meeting the basic human needs of their own communities.

WHAT'S FOR DINNER?

Shopping patterns aren't nearly as hard to change as eating patterns. In addition to our food selection and preparation reflecting our ethnic background, our food choices have been shaped by food companies' advertising and the processed foods they make available to us at the supermarket. There may be fifty varieties of cake mix on the supermarket shelf, but it is almost impossible to find whole rye (rye berries), which has a rich, nutty flavor and provides a wonderful substitute for rice at one-third to one-half the price. Cooking with whole, unprocessed foods is anything but dull: a typical reaction of a first-time shopper in a small, neighborhood food co-op is bewilderment at the variety of grains, beans, cheeses, dried fruits, soy products, seasonings, and sometimes even fresh produce that she or he has never seen before. Yet many Americans, if financially forced to lower their meat consumption, feel sentenced to macaroni and cheese or to cans of tasteless beans and low-priced soups.

What can you change to get a more nutritious, satisfying diet that sustains the body, the budget, and the land? How much of a role does meat play in your diet? With an understanding of plant protein values, anyone can get enough protein from plants alone without too many calories. Frances Moore Lappé, in her book *Diet for a Small Planet,* discusses in great detail how to utilize plant foods in proper proportion to get maximum protein value. She has also concluded that most people, especially if they eat some dairy products as part of a meatless diet, need not even worry about protein complementarity. (This generalization does not apply to pregnant or nursing women or to someone under a great deal of stress). *Diet for a Small Planet,* especially its tenth anniversary edition, is the best single introduction for someone making a transition to cooking with less meat, including among its recipes many main dishes that can be prepared in ten to thirty minutes.

The popularity of vegetarian cooking has put several excellent cookbooks on the market. A highlight of *Laurel's Kitchen* is a guide to cooking whole- or cracked-grain breakfast cereals, allowing you to experiment with the flavors and textures of different grains. *Tassajara Cooking* teaches you how to make a basic sauce or a vegetable pie, and then mentions ten to twenty variations of the ingredients or seasonings—feel free to spice the food as you always have! Molly Katzen's two cookbooks, *Moosewood* and *Enchanted Broccoli Forest,* are full of delicious vegetarian recipes, often of ethnic origin and easy to prepare. Friends, relatives, and immediate family may decide to overlook the missing meat or may not even notice!

If you and your kids are addicted to heavily processed, low-nutrition snacks, look for substitutes. Sugar drinks and pop are easy to replace with fruit juices: club soda or mineral water and juice combine well as a soda-replacement. Raisins, sunflower seeds, peanuts, and similar "crunchy" snack food are good substitutes for candy. Homemade cookies and quick breads are a good way to introduce whole wheat, rye, soy, and cornmeal flours. Make popcorn and sprinkle parmesan cheese over it.

If your lack of time tempts you to put a TV dinner in the oven or to stop at a fast-food outlet enroute home, you can start to change this by learning new cooking habits and by planning ahead. Try "Terry's Take-out Tofu" from *Diet for a Small Planet*—these tofu-cheeseburgers with onions and vegetables take about 15 minutes to fry up. Or invest in a wok or a large frying pan, start the spaghetti boiling, chop some vegetables and some meat, chicken, fish, or tofu, fry it all up together with spices, drain and add the spaghetti for a minute or two, and you have chow mein in about 20 minutes. Two students solved their time problem by cooking two or three main courses on the weekend, such as a pot of beans or a hearty vegetable soup, to last them all week. With the beans already prepared, it's easy to heat them up with a tortilla, cheese, and some fresh tomato. Or you can start with a basic dish and season it differently each night to give you a variety of flavors. (*Diet for a Small Planet* has a selection of one-pot stew meals that can sit in the fridge all week.) If you're preparing a tomato sauce for pasta tonight and planning pizza for later in the week, you can make enough sauce to use for both meals.

A time-consuming item such as beans doesn't necessarily mean you have to stay home all day and cook. If you're planning to have vegetarian chili, you can soak the beans the night before and save hours of cooking time. Or if you are adopting a mostly vegetarian diet, a pressure-cooker is a tool that can be worth the investment. (Shop around—the same brand, same size, varies in price from under $30 to $60.) In a pressure-cooker, lentils cook in 10 minutes, most beans in 20 minutes (instead of 2 to 3 hours), and even garbanzos (chick peas) cook in 45 minutes (instead of 4 hours). (Whole rye takes 35 minutes, but it's worth it!) *Recipes for a Small Planet*, by Ellen Buchman Ewald, contains a complete pressure-cooking chart.

If you have the storage space to purchase bulk amounts of the things you regularly consume, you will save on your overall shopping time. If you garden or have access to a farmer's market, the *Nutrition Survival Kit* gives good instructions to consumers on how to freeze, can, and store foods.

EDUCATION AND ACTION

Below we describe a few organizations that work toward ending hunger, preserving sustainable agriculture, and bringing about more public awareness of food, land, and nutrition issues. Many areas have projects you can join that focus on these issues—or if you have your own ideas, tell others and start your own!

Institute for Food and Development Policy (IFDP)

In 1972, Frances Moore Lappé published her first contribution to the area of food and nutrition in *Diet for a Small Planet*. Ten years later, in her tenth anniversary edition, she tells the story of her personal development from studying food issues alone in the library to becoming co-founder of the Institute for Food and Development Policy (IFDP). She talks about starting with a decision to learn about and understand world food problems, followed by making personal changes such as eating foods low on the food chain, and then spreading the word by typing and mimeographing a pamphlet to distribute to her friends. That pamphlet turned into *Diet for a Small Planet*.

The IFDP started with the idea to write *Food First—Beyond the Myths of Scarcity*. After writing that book, coauthors and founders Lappé and Joseph Collins developed a research and education center that focuses on food and agriculture. Through publications that include books, action guides, a slideshow, a comic book, a grade-school curriculum, and a quarterly newsletter, the institute constantly asks the question: why is there hunger in a world of plenty?

They started small, with three people, and have grown to include over ten staff people, plus volunteers, work-study students, interns, and a strong supporting membership. Lappé and Collins travel widely to talk with people about the roots of hunger and their personal experiences with economic injustice. They have met with farmers, peasants, consumers, students, planners, government officials, and church leaders all over the world. Their experiences and analyses offer the public invaluable insights to the real problems of, and possible solutions to, hunger. Most of the Institute's publications are listed in the Bibliography.

Center for Science in the Public Interest (CSPI)

The Center for Science in the Public Interest (CSPI) is a Washington-based organization that investigates and seeks solutions for consumer and environmental problems. Through its monthly publication, *Nutrition Action,* CSPI provides the public with reliable and current information about nutrition, the food industry, government regulation of foods, nutrition education, and food safety. It also includes book reviews, editorials, and resource lists. A few of their other publications include a "Sodium Scoreboard" poster; "Food: Where Nutrition, Politics, and Culture Meet," and "Chemical Additives in Booze."

Cornucopia Project

The Cornucopia Project has grown out of Rodale Press's forty years of concern about the problems with the food system in the United States. Its aim is to create an accessible body of information about the U.S. food system that can be used by all individuals and groups who are seeking to understand and improve it. Some Cornucopia Project studies are on a national scale, such as their book, *Empty Breadbasket? The Coming Challenge to America's Food Supply and What We Can Do About It.* Other studies examine the food system within individual states. Reports are now available on Pennsylvania, Maine, New York, New Jersey, Michigan, and California, while studies of most other states are currently underway. These studies document where each area is most vulnerable and what could be done to move in sustainable, affordable, and resource-efficient directions.

The Cornucopia Project reaches over twenty-five thousand people through its newsletter and publishes a variety of manuals to help people study where their food comes from and the costs of its production, processing, and transportation—including the hidden costs of ecological deterioration. They also provide ideas for community involvement in improving regional food problems. The manuals include: *Creating a Cornucopia in the City; The State of Your Food: A Manual for State Food Systems Analysis; Organizing a Local Cornucopia Project: A Manual for Changing Your Food System.* The project also distributes audiovisual aids.

COMMUNITY FOR CREATIVE NON-VIOLENCE (CCNV)

The Community for Creative Non-Violence is a Washington, D.C., group whose activities and organization are described more extensively in Chapter III and Chapter IV. One of its ongoing concerns has been food waste in the United States: on a daily basis they feed four to five hundred homeless people, with food mostly collected from the "waste piles" behind many of the local supermarkets and wholesale depots. In 1982, CCNV held a luncheon for thirty members of Congress and about one hundred reporters. The affair was organized to dramatize the House resolution that would make it easier for private groups and charitable organizations to distribute waste food to the needy. Keeping to the usual congressional dining style, CCNV members prepared a luncheon of fresh vegetables, fruits, and meats, including crab quiche. What was different about this meal was the origin of the food: all of it had been scavenged from their usual dumpster sources. More recently, on July 4, 1983, the CCNV sent some of its members to Kansas City where they joined over fifty people in a thirty-day fast that successfully pressured the United States Department of Agriculture into releasing millions of pounds of surplus food to America's hungry.

Father and Son in the Food Co-op Store

what does the food co-op mean to me?
working with my son jacob four and a half years old
wheeling out the produce
jacob sorting out the bruised or overripe peaches
        and tomatoes
snitching some fresh peas
putting out all the different breads

small hands dipping into the grain bins to check
        if they need refilling
cutting weighing wrapping and pricing all the
        fine cheeses
snitching a nibble of each as we work together
jake and i
four hours
                        go by
            one saturday morning each month
jacob's attention
out and eager and full of useful things to do
interested in his store
and how it works
and what he can do to help

as for me
that feeling at first
when i came to the cash register without pricing
        my own items
the slowness at first of my friends adding up
        my purchases on the cash register
oops, i forgot to bring a jar to put oil in
consciousness of what people do in stores
and how much sense and easy it is to recycle
unthinkable now to waste as much glass and paper and
        gas (we plan our shopping better now so that
            our once-a-week binge cuts down on driving)
a store of organics and
it's incredible that you get everything you need
        in such small space
without rows and rows of softdrinks and potato chips
        and cookies and cat foods and plastic stuff and
        muzak and everything wrapped
and nothing touchable or out of color
it's so refreshing to own your own store
it feels different
it feels fine
and you never do a quick shopping there
your friends and you stop to chat
you count up how much you save this time and decide
        to buy another share in the store
you don't feel so rushed
when the vibes are home grown and cooperatively
                        marketed

WHAT YOU CAN DO

1. List everything you eat in one day and analyze it for its nutritional
   value, social, political, and ecological considerations. *Laurel's Kitchen*

has the tables necessary to calculate individual needs and food compositions, along with excellent nutrition information. The USDA Food Composition Handbooks #8 and #456 also have complete food analysis information.

2. Make an inventory of your cupboards and refrigerator. What foods might you want to discontinue purchasing for nutritional, ecological, or social considerations? What foods might you want to add?

3. Go on your own supermarket awareness tour. Take some friends. Note the advertising, the packaging, the placement of items to get attention, the sales, the ingredients, and so forth. Are the ingredients included in the recipes in the cookbooks discussed in this chapter available? Can you do something to make them available?

Look for excessive use of plastic and paper bags. Do you see any smaller or irregular fruits and vegetables that are less expensive offered on sale? What happens to the produce that develops a bruise or bad spot, or the cheese with a mold spot? Check out the supermarket's dumpster, too.

4. Try meatless meals for a few days or a week. You may be in for a pleasant surprise. If decreasing meat consumption is difficult for you, try eating meat progressively fewer times a week or using only very small amounts for flavor. Have vegetarian potlucks that explore unfamiliar ingredients or focus on ethnic variety or protein complementarity. If your area has one, go out to dinner at a restaurant that features vegetarian specialties.

5. Join or start a neighborhood food co-op or buying club. The list of organizations and written materials in the Bibliography will help you get started.

6. Start a cooking co-op with several families, where each family cooks once or twice for others and delivers the meals or invites the others over. It won't work if you feel you have to clean your house or cook something fancy as if you're having guests for dinner.

7. Find out what your local schools serve for lunch. Do vending machines sell fruit or healthy snacks? Talk with other parents about what changes could be made to reflect more responsible food choices. Such choices as herb teas with honey, dried fruit and nut snacks, local produce, or baked goods could be offered with a note explaining why.

8. Try to get your local market to stock unprocessed foods in bulk. Ask if they would be willing to display nutrition information to promote use of whole foods. If they sell books, would they be willing to sell *Diet for a Small Planet, Laurel's Kitchen,* or *Food First?*

9. Learn about world economics, home economics, and hunger through a family project described in Chapter VII. Benefit UNICEF, too!

10. Hold a simulation meal, grouping people by continents for dinner. The number of people in each group might represent that continent's percentage of the world population. The number of plates and

utensils alloted each group might represent that continent's share of the world's GNP, and the amount of food served might represent that continent's daily, per-capita consumption of animal protein. (See chart for actual percentages.) Instruct people to deal with the situation realistically (i.e., the United States may sell food to allies, barter leftovers, etc.), but give away very little. Discuss feelings and reactions.

SHARE OF WORLD POPULATION (People)

Continent	Percent*
Africa	10
Asia	59
Europe	17
Latin America	8
North America	6

SHARE OF WORLD GNP (Plates and Utensils)

Continent	Percent
Africa	3
Asia	33
Europe	31
Latin America	5
North America	28

SHARE OF DAILY CONSUMPTION OF ANIMAL PROTEIN (Food)

Continent	Percent
Africa	8
Asia	23
Europe	26
Latin America	11
North America	22

*These figures are ten years old but work for the purposes of the game.

11. If you have a backyard, side lawns, or space for containers, try growing some of your own food. If you don't have the space, try your church, synagogue, public park, local schools, hospitals, vacant lots, and industrial lands for community garden sites.

12. Join or form a cooperative community cannery and process seasonal food to eat throughout the year. Look for other members of your community to pool resources, such as teachers, canning equipment, and jars. Churches and schools usually have institutional kitchens with enough space and equipment to get started.

13. Find out if there are any nearby farms that leave edibles in the fields. If there are, organize a gleaning program as a labor-intensive way for people on limited budgets to obtain fresh and nutritious fruits and vegetables (See Chapter V, for a description of one such project.) Food banks, soup kitchens, or other emergency food programs may be interested in the surplus.

NOTES

1. "Food Facts," published by Institute for Food and Development Policy, 1885 Mission Street, San Francisco, Calif. 94103 (April 1983).
2. Ibid.
3. Richard Strong, "World Hunger," *University Publishing* (Fall 1979), p. 6.
4. Frances Moore Lappé and Joseph Collins, *Food First: Beyond the Myth of Scarcity* (New York: Ballantine Books, 1978). p. 13.
5. Ibid., p. 18.
6. Ibid., p. 19.
7. Frances Moore Lappé and Joseph Collins, "World Hunger—Ten Myths," rev. ed., published by Institute for Food and Development Policy, 1885 Mission Street, San Francisco, Calif. 94103 (1978).
8. Ibid.
9. David Feldman and Peter Lawrence, "Global II Project on the Economic and Social Implications of Large-Scale Introduction of New Varieties of Foodgrains," *Africa Report* (Geneva: UNDP/UNRISD, 1975), p. 52.
10. Peter Dorner, "Export Agriculture and Economic Development," statement before Interfaith Center on Corporate Responsibility, New York, September 14, 1973 (Land Tenure Center, University of Wisconsin, Madison, Wis.), p. 6.
11. Michael Manley, speech at San Francisco State University, 1981.
12. "U.S. Government Aid," *Politics of Food Study Pamphlet III,* published by the Politics of Food Taskforce of the Ecumenical Peace Institute and the American Friends Service Committee, 2160 Lake Street, San Francisco, Calif. 94121.
13. Ibid.
14. Lappé and Collins, *Food First.*
15. Dana G. Dalrymple, "The Green Revolution and Protein Levels in Grain," Draft No. 2, published by U.S. Department of Agriculture, Economic Research Service, International Development Center (May 5, 1972).
16. Mary Harvey, "Agribusiness and the Food Crisis," *The Corporate Examiner,* published by Corporate Information Center, Room 846, 475 Riverside Drive, N.Y. 10027 (1974).
17. Ibid.
18. Frances Moore Lappé, *Diet for a Small Planet: Tenth Anniversary Edition* (New York: Ballantine Books, 1982), p. 69.
19. George Borgstrom (Michigan State University), presentation to the Annual Meeting of the American Association for the Advancement of Sciences, 1981.
20. William Brune (State Conservationist, Soil Conservation Service, Des Moines, Iowa), testimony before Senate Committee on Agriculture and Forestry, July 6, 1976.
21. Lappé, *Diet for a Small Planet,* p. 10.
22. Harvey, "Agribusiness and the Food Crisis."
23. Vivian E. Spencer, "Raw Materials in the U.S. Economy, 1900–1977," technical paper no. 47, prepared for the U.S. Department of Commerce and the U.S. Department of the Interior, Bureau of Mines, Table 2, p. 86.
24. David and Marcia Pimentel, *Food, Energy and Society* (New York: Halsted Press, 1979), p. 59; David Pimentel et al., "Energy and Land Constraints in Food Protein Production," *Science,* November 21, 1975.
25. "Organic Paths to Food Security," *Cornucopia Project Newsletter* (1982), available from the Cornucopia Project, 33 E. Minor Street, Emmaus, Pa. 18049.
26. Pete Engardio, "The Practice and Promise of Organic Farming," *Food Monitor,* January–February 1983, p. 21; available from World Hunger Year, 350 Broadway, Suite 209, New York, N.Y. 10013.
27. "Welcome to The New Alchemy Institute, 1982"; available from 237 Hatchville Road, East Falmouth, Mass. 02536.
28. E. F. Schumacher, *Good Work* (New York: Harper & Row, 1979), p. 106.
29. Don Reeves, "Tax Breaks: Writing Off the Family Farm," *Hunger,* no. 34 (September

1983); newsletter of the Interreligious Taskforce on U.S. Food Policy, 110 Maryland Ave. N.E., Washington, D.C. 20002.

30. Corporate Data Exchange, *Stock Ownership Directory No. 2—Agribusiness* (New York, 1978).

31. Jim Hightower, statement of the Food Action Campaign before the Monopoly Subcommittee of the Senate Select Committee on Small Business, December 10, 1973, p. 7.

32. Russell Parker, John Connor, and Willard Mueller, "Impact of Market Concentration on Rising Food Prices," testimony before the Subcommittee on Antitrust, Monopoly and Business Rights of the Committee on the Judiciary, U.S. Senate, 96th Congress, 1st Session on Rising Food Prices in the U.S., April 6, 1979 (U.S. Government Printing Office, 1979), p. 46.

33. *People, Land, Food Newsletter,* published by National Land for People (April 1979), pp. 72–73.

34. Joan Gussow, "Evaluation of the American Diet," *Journal of Home Economics,* November 1973.

SOURCES OF FURTHER INFORMAITON

Groups Mentioned in Chapter

Boston Food Coop. 449 Cambridge Street, Allston, Mass. 02134.

Center for Science in the Public Interest.* 1755 S Street, N.W., Washington, D.C. 20009.

Community for Creative Non-Violence. 1345 Euclid Street, N.W., Washington, D.C. 20009.

Cornucopia Project.* c/o Rodale Press, 33 East Minor Street, Emmaus, Pa. 18049.

Detroit Anti-Hunger/Youth Advocacy Center. 421 Drexel Street, Detroit, Mich. 48215

Institute for Food and Development Policy (Food First).* 1885 Mission Street, San Francisco, Calif. 94110.

Massachusetts Federation of Farmers'-Gardeners' Markets. C/o Department of Food and Agriculture, 100 Cambridge St., Boston, Mass. 02202

National Land for People. 2348 North Cornelia, Fresno, Calif. 93711.

New Alchemy Institute. 237 Hatchville Road, East Falmouth, Mass. 02536.

New England Food Cooperative Organization (NEFCO). 129 Franklin Street, Cambridge, Mass. 02139.

Rural Economic Alternatives Project (REAP). 405 East Lindsay, Stockton, Calif. 95202.

San Francisco League of Urban Gardeners (SLUG). C/o Producer/Consumer Project, AFSC, 2160 Lake Street, San Francisco, Calif. 94121.

Soil Association. Walnut Tree Manor, Haughley, Stowmarket IP14 3RS, England.

Stockton Farmers' Market Association. 405 East Lindsay, Stockton, Calif. 95202.

Additional Resource Groups

Farm, Food, and Regional Self-Reliance

Agricultural Marketing Project.* Center for Health Services, 2606 Westwood, Nashville, Tenn. 37204.

Center for Farm and Food Research, Inc. Box 88, Falls Village, Conn. 06031.

Hawaii Area Program. C/o American Friends Service Committee, Pacific South-

---

*Group offers extensive publications.

west Region. 980 North Fair Oaks Avenue, Pasadena, Calif. 91103.
Support for native Hawaiian land struggles.

Institute for Local Self-Reliance. 1717 18th Street, N.W., Washington, D.C.
20009.

The Integral Urban House. 1516 5th Street, Berkeley, Calif. Demonstration,
research, and consultation on ecologically integrated urban houses and
gardens.

Interreligious Task Force on U.S. Food Policy. 110 Maryland Avenue, N.W.,
Washington, D.C. 20002.

National Sharecroppers Fund and the Frank Porter Graham Center. Box 1029,
Pittsboro, N.C. 27312. Works to preserve the small family farm.

Producer/Consumer Project, American Friends Service Committee. 2160 Lake
Street, San Francisco, Calif. 94121.

Second Harvest, The National Foodbank Network. 1001 North Central, Suite
303, Phoenix, Ariz. 85004.

Food Cooperatives

Arizona/New Mexico Federation of Co-ops. 8812 4th Street, N.W., Alameda, N.
Mex. 87114. Produces a national directory.

Federation of Ohio River Co-ops. 320 Outebelt Street, Suite E, Columbus, Ohio
43213.

Federation of Southern Co-ops. 40 Marietta Street, Atlanta, Ga. 30303.

National Consumer Cooperative Bank. 2001 S Street, N.W., Washington, D.C.
20009.

North American Students of Cooperation (NASCO).* Box 7293, Ann Arbor,
Mich. 48107.

Nutrition Development Services. Archdiocese of Philadelphia, 222 North 17th
Street, Philadelphia, Pa. 19103.

U.S. Agricultural Policies/Farmworkers

American Agricultural Movement. 100 Maryland Avenue, N.E., Washington,
D.C. 20002.

American Agricultural Women. Route 1, Box 1748, Toppenish, Wash. 98948.

American Friends Service Committee, National Community Relations Division.
1501 Cherry Street, Philadelphia, Pa. 19102. Farmworker programs in
California, Florida, Arizona, Ohio, Texas, and New Jersey.

The Center for Rural Affairs. Box 405, Walthill, Nebr. 68067. Focus on Midwest
farming issues.

Emergency Land Fund. 564 Lee Street, S.W., Atlanta, Ga. 30310.

National Family Farm Coalition. 918 F Street, N.W., 2nd Floor, Washington, D.C.
20004.

National Farmers Union. Box 39251, Denver, Colo. 80239.

National Rural Center. 1828 L Street, N.W., Washington, D.C. 20036.

Rural America. 1346 Connecticut Avenue, N.W., Washington, D.C. 20036.

Exposing Roots of Hunger/Direct Assistance to Self-Help Efforts

American Friends Service Committee, International Division.* 1501 Cherry
Street, Philadelphia, Pa. 19102.

Bread for the World. 32 Union Square East, New York, N.Y. 10003. Christian
citizen movement with local chapters.

Community Nutrition Institute. 1146 19th Street, N.W., Washington, D.C. 20036. Monitors federal food programs and policy.

Food Research and Action. 2011 I Street, N.W., Washington, D.C. 20006. Seeks to improve nutrition of fixed-income people.

Food Research and Action Center. 1319 F Street, Washington, D.C. 20004. Offers organizing manuals and legislative updates.

OXFAM America.* 115 Broadway, Boston, Mass. 02116.

World Hunger/Global Development Program, American Friends Service Committee, New York Regional Office. 15 Rutherford Place, New York, N.Y. 10003.

World Hunger Year.* 350 Broadway, Room 209, New York, N.Y. 10018. Education policy advocacy.

Agricultural Marketing

Agricultural Marketing Project. Box 120495, Nashville, Tenn. 37211.

Bay Area Marketing Group. c/o American Friends Service Committee, 2160 Lake Street, San Francisco, Calif. 94121.

Earthwork/Center for Rural Studies. 3838 Blaisdell South, Minneapolis, Minn. 55409.

Pike Place Market Development Authority. 85 Pike Street, Room 500, Seattle, Wash. 98101.

Urban Agriculture

Agroecology Program. College Eight, University of California, Santa Cruz, Santa Cruz, Calif. 95064.

American Community Gardening Association. Box 8645, Ann Arbor, Mich. 48107.

Gardens for All.* 180 Flynn Avenue, Burlington, Vt. 05401.

Seattle Tilth Urban Agriculture Center. 4649 Sunnyside North, Seattle, Wash. 98103.

Bibliography

Farm, Food, and Regional Self-Reliance

Barnes, Peter, ed. *The People's Land: A Reader on Land Reform in the United States.* Emmaus, Pa.: Rodale Press, 1975.

Jackson, Was. *New Roots for Agriculture.* San Francisco: Friends of the Earth, 1980.

Merrill, Richard, ed. *Radical Agriculture.* New York: Harper Colophon Books, 1976.

Mooney, Pat Roy. *Seeds of the Earth: A Private or Public Resource?* 1980. Available from: Institute for Food and Development Policy, address above, $7.

Rain: Journal of Appropriate Technology. Available from: 2270 N.W. Irving, Portland, Oreg. 97210.

Vicente Guerrero: Building Community Self-Reliance. 1980. Slideshow on Mexican agricultural self-reliance. Available from: AFSC National Office, International Division, address above, $20.

Food Cooperatives

Co-op Handbook Collective. *The Food Co-op Handbook.* Boston: Houghton-Mifflin, 1975.

Food Co-ops, An Alternative to Shopping in Supermarkets. Boston: Beacon Press, 1974.
Nutrition Development Services. *Food Co-op and Buying Club Organization Kit.* Available from: Archdiocese of Philadelphia, 222 North 17th Street, Philadelphia, Pa. 19103.
Vellela, Tony. *Food Co-ops for Small Groups.* New York: Workman Publishing Company, 1975.

U.S. Agriculture Policies/Farmworkers

Berry, Wendell. *The Unsettling of America: Culture and Agriculture.* New York: Avon, 1978.
Fellmeth, Robert C. *Politics of Land.* New York: Grossman Publishers, 1973.
Goodwyn, Lawrence. *The Populist Moment: A Short History of Agrarian Revolt in America.* New York: Oxford University Press, 1978.
Hamburger, U.S.A. Slideshow/filmstrip on who controls our food system. Available from: AFSC regional offices. $75/$60; or rental.
McWilliams, Carey. *Factories in the Field.* Santa Barbara, Calif.: Peregrine Press, 1971.
The Small Farm Advocate. Newsletter. Available from: Center for Rural Affairs, Box 405, Walthill, Nebr. 68067. $7/year.
Weir, David, and Mark Shapiro. *Circle of Poison.* 1981. Report on the export of dangerous pesticides. Available from: Institute for Food and Development Policy, address above, $3.95.

Exposing Roots of Hunger / Direct Assistance to Self-Help Efforts

Agrarian Reform and Counter-Reform in Chile. Available from: Institute for Food and Development Policy, address above, $1.45.
Agribusiness Goes Bananas. Slideshow on multinationals in Philippines. Available from: Institute for Food and Development Policy, address above, $65.
Beckford, George L. *Persistent Poverty: Underdevelopment in Plantation Economies in the Third World.* New York: Oxford University Press, 1972.
Burbach, Roger, and Patricia Flynn. *Agribusiness in the Americas.* New York: Monthly Review Press, 1980.
Collins, Joseph, et al. *What Difference Could a Revolution Make? Food and Farming in the New Nicaragua.* 1982. Available from: Institute for Food and Development Policy, address above, $5.95.
Franke, Richard W., and Barbara Chasin. *Seeds of Famine: Ecological Destruction and the Development Dilemma in the West African Sahel.* Montclair, N.J.: Allanheld, Osmun and Company, 1980.
George, Susan. *How the Other Half Dies.* London: Penguin Books, 1976.
Gussow, Joan. *The Feeding Web: Issues in Nutritional Ecology.* Palo Alto, Calif.: Bull Publishing, 1978.
Hartmann, Betsy and James Boyce. *Needless Hunger: Voices from a Bangladesh Village.* 1979. Available from: Institute for Food and Development Policy, address above, $3.50.
Harty, Sheila. *Hucksters in the Classroom: A Review of Industry Propaganda in Schools.* Washington, D.C.: Center for the Study of Responsive Law, 1979.
Hightower, Jim. *Eat Your Heart Out.* New York: Vintage Books, 1975.
Lappé, Frances Moore, and Joseph Collins. *Food First: Beyond the Myth of Scarcity.* Boston: Houghton Mifflin, 1977. An excellent overview.

Lappé, Frances Moore, et al. *Aid as Obstacle: Twenty Questions About Our Foreign Aid and the Hungry.* 1980. Available from: Institute for Food and Development Policy, address above, $5.95.

Ledogar, Robert. *Hungry for Profits.* New York: IDOC, 1976.

Lerza, Catherine, and Michael Jacobson. *Food for People Not for Profit.* New York: Ballantine, 1975.

McGinnis, James. *Bread and Justice: Toward a New International Economic Order.* New York: Paulist Press, 1979.

Morgan, Dan. *Merchants of Grain.* New York: Viking, 1979.

Nelson, Jack A. *Hunger for Justice: The Politics of Food and Faith.* Maryknoll, N.Y.: Orbis Books, 1980.

Perelman, Michael. *Farming for Profit in a Hungry World: Capital and the Crisis in Agriculture.* Montclair, N.J.: Allanheld, Osmun and Company, 1977.

Trading the Future: How Booming Farm Exports Threaten Our Food Security. 1983. Available from: Institute for Food and Development Policy, address above, $8.95.

Tudge, Colin. *Future Food: Politics, Philosophy and Recipes for the 21st Century.* New York: Harmony Books, 1980.

Warnock, John. *Profit Hungry: The Food Industry in Canada.* Vancouver, B.C.: New Star Books, 1978.

World Hunger: Ten Myths. rev. ed. 1979. Available from: Institute for Food and Development Policy, address above, $2.95.

Urban Agriculture

Creasy, Rosaline. *The Complete Book of Edible Landscaping: Home Landscaping with Food-Bearing Plants and Resource-Saving Techniques.* San Francisco: Sierra Club, 1982.

Freeman, John A. *Survival Gardening.* Roch Hill, S.C.: John's Press, 1982.

Halpin, Ann, ed. *Organic Gardeners Complete Guide to Vegetables and Fruits.* Emmaus, Pa.: Rodale Press, 1982.

Leckie, Jim et al. *More Other Homes and Garbage: Designs for Self-Sufficient Living.* San Francisco: Sierra Club, 1981.

Naimark, Susan, ed. *A Handbook of Community Gardening.* New York: Charles Scribners Sons, 1982.

Newcomb, Duane G. *The Postage Stamp Garden Book: How to Grow All the Food You Can Eat in Very Little Space.* Los Angeles, Calif.: J. P. Tarcher, 1975.

Olkowski, Helga et al. *The Integral Urban House: Self-Reliant Living in the City.* San Francisco: Sierra Club, 1979.

Food and Nutrition

Brown, Edward. *Tassajara Cooking.* Berkeley, Calif.: Shambala Publications, 1973.

Ewald, Ellen B. *Recipes for a Small Planet.* New York: Ballantine, 1973.

Hertzberg, Ruth et al. *Putting Food By,* 3rd ed., Brattleboro, Ver.: Stephen Greene Press, 1982.

Katzen, Molly. *The Enchanted Broccoli Forest.* Berkeley, Calif.: Ten-Speed Press, 1982.

Katzen, Molly. *Moosewood Cookbook.* Berkeley, Calif.: Ten-Speed Press, 1977.

Lappé, Frances Moore. *Diet for a Small Planet,* Tenth Anniversary Edition. New York: Ballantine, 1982.

Longacre, Doris. *More With Less Cookbook.* Scottdale, Pa.: Herald Press, 1976.

Robertson, Laurel. *Laurel's Kitchen: A Handbook for Vegetarian Cookery and Nutrition.* Petaluma, Calif.: Nilgiri, 1976.

Winn, Grace, ed. *Simply Delicious, Quantity Cooking for Churches.* Available from: Alternatives, Box 1707, Forest Park, Ga.: 30051. $4.50/copy + 15 percent postage.

Nutrition Education Activities

Agricultural Marketing Project. *Eclipse of the Blue Moon Foods.* 1979. Available from: Alternatives, Box 1707, Forest Park, Ga. 30051. Includes: *Teachers Guide* (eighteen upper elementary lessons), $7.95; *Student Workbook,* $2.- 95; *Family Book,* $1; *A Handbook for Developing Community Food Education Programs,* $4.95; + 15 percent postage.

Brethren House Team. *Hunger Activities for Teens.* 1979. Available from: Alternatives, Box 1707, Forest Park, Ga. 30051. $2.25/copy + 15 percent postage.

Food for Everybody. Youth Magazine, special issue. August 1981. High school level. Available from: Alternatives, Box 1707, Forest Park, Ga. 30051. $1.95/copy + 15 percent postage.

Goodwin, Mary, and Gerry Pollen. *Creative Food Experiences for Children.* 1980. Available from: Center for Science in the Public Interest, 1755 S Street, Washington, D.C. 20009.

Katz, Deborah, and Mary Goodwin. *Food: Where Nutrition, Politics and Culture Meet.* Available from: Center for Science in the Public Interest, 1755 S Street, Washington, D.C. 20009.

Kishpaugh, Charles R., and E. Pauline. *Hungry Decisions: Making Life and Death Choices in Africa, Asia or Latin America.* Discipleship Resources, 1982. Reader works through to sixteen possible endings. Available from: Alternatives, Box 1707, Forest Park, Ga. 30051. $2.50/copy + 15 percent postage.

Rifas, Leonard. *Food First Comic.* 1982. Available from: Institute for Food and Development Policy, address above, $1.

Science for the People. *Feed, Need, Greed: A High School Food Education Curriculum.* 1980. Available from: Science for the People, 897 Main Street, Cambridge, Mass. 02138.

The Supermarket Tour: A Handbook for Education and Action. Available from: Ontario Public Interest Research Group, Provincial Office, Physics 226, University of Waterloo, Waterloo, Ontario, Canada.

CHAPTER III

Shelter

QUERIES

1. How are decisions made that affect shelter in my community? Who decides where and what kind of new housing gets built? Who decides where and what kind of old housing is torn down? What is the basis of these decisions?
2. What options are available for financing housing construction, purchase, and rehabilitation in my community?
3. Are "property values" rising in my neighborhood? If so, who is benefiting?
4. Have I considered a group household as a way to cut my financial burdens or to free me to explore life options that require less income? Would a group household be a way to find more community in my life?
5. Do all neighborhoods in my city or town receive equal amounts of "essential city services"? If not, why not?
6. Do I know how many people in my community are without shelter? Do I know who they are? Do I know what kind of shelter facilities my community provides? What are longer-range solutions?
7. Does my city or town have rent controls, controls on condominium conversions, or controls on housing demolitions? If yes, are they working well and how could they be made more effective? If no, who opposes these measures and how could effective measures be obtained?
8. How are building and housing codes enforced in my community? Is adequate assistance available for those too poor to maintain their homes? Are landlords required to maintain their buildings properly?
9. Does my community have an ordinance against housing discrimination? How well is it enforced?

Shelter is the physical basis around which our communities are built: it is where we live, where most of us work, where we often play. Our choices about shelter—and which choices are available for us to make—affect the entire spectrum of our lives, beyond the most basic needs to be kept warm, cool, dry, and safely enclosed against danger together with those with whom we have chosen to live. Some factors that limit our choices seem frustratingly to be under the control of others:

- New housing and commercial developments are often built on "cheap" land—covering the area's most fertile soil with buildings, roads, and lawns.
- Structurally sound, older buildings, which could shelter a large or medium-sized household (with a carpentry shop in the basement) are being demolished and replaced by three or four tiny, poor-quality living units, whose only benefit is higher profits for the landlord.
- You are forced to drive an hour to and from work because you can't afford closer housing.
- You are excluded from decent housing, either directly or through denial of financing, because of your race, national origin, or because you have children.
- When you are already sending the landlord one-third to one-half of your income every month, you find it difficult to care about learning to deal with simple plumbing problems or a broken latch yourself.
- The home your family always dreamed of owning has become an oppressive burden, because you alone don't have the skills, the time, or the money to do all the repairs it needs.
- You can't take significant, long-term steps to cut back your family's energy use—because you don't own your home.
- You don't want to put a lot of effort into developing the quality of the soil in the garden, when you may be evicted next month by higher rents or because the building gets sold.
- The nearest foodstore—or a building that could hold a community foodstore—is across the railroad tracks or two miles down the freeway, whether you live in a high-income housing development or a low-income housing project.
- You feel close to your community, have many friends and good community organizations, but feel trapped in your job because the rents and/or real estate prices are skyrocketing.

Sometimes even housing choices that seem to make good sense at the time cause unwelcome complications. An example is "gentrification," a phenomenon where young, usually white, professionals move into low-income and ethnic minority neighborhoods, fix up old houses, raise property values and rents, and force out the original residents. Jim Shoch, a long-time community organizer, observes that gentrification is usually begun by "pioneers," people who are committed to living simply and to a culturally and economically mixed neighborhood. The presence of these simple livers "creates a greater sense of comfort for those who come behind," who eventually displace most of the original residents.

This chapter will focus on housing affordability, community creation, and the interaction between them. When housing is affordable, people are free to choose their neighborhoods and to exert control over their communities. They are also freer to take closer looks at the kinds of shelter they want built and preserved.

BUILDING HOUSES

In simpler societies and simpler times, many people knew how to build their own shelters, and neighbors pitched in to "raise the roof" when necessary. Local materials were used—wood, animal skins, adobe bricks —and there was little to purchase or trade for. There was a lot less to know about: no plumbing, no electrical wiring, no sewer connections, no heat installations, no sprinkler systems for multiple dwellings and office buildings. In medieval and industrial cities, there were also a lot of fires, filth-spread disease, and dense air pollution due to wood and coal heating. Modern building codes have done much to ensure safe and sanitary dwellings, but many codes are so rigid that they prevent innovative and less expensive approaches, in areas such as energy efficiency and composting toilets.

OUTSIDE THE CITY

If you can obtain the land and the financing to do it yourself, owner-builder classes and guides have become popular in many areas (some resources are listed in the bibliography). The physical and psychological costs should not be minimized, however. In his review of *The Work Book*, Stewart Brand states that, "about 80 percent of the couples I know who have built a house or a boat, they build it, then they split up. Happened to me, too."[1]

Even in areas where poor people may own some land, they can't get the money to build a decent low-cost house on it. Kentucky Mountain Housing Development Corporation (KMHDC) works in Clay and Jackson Counties in Appalachia, building 20–25 new homes a year, doing major repairs on about 40 per year, and doing basic, inexpensive weatherization on about 400 per year. About thirty local people are employed on the regular construction, and seventeen more, mostly elderly, on the weatherization jobs.

The group, founded by a Church of the Brethren minister, has always had a strong base of financial support from a number of church bodies. This support, now over 50 percent of the budget since federal government cutbacks, funds materials and experienced workers; government funds are still used to pay the salaries of workers being trained. Frank Jones, KMHDC's Executive Director, explained that although they don't have as much money as they did in 1979, the same annual amount of work has been done because their labor force has become more experienced and efficient. At the same time, KMHDC has found itself serving "new low-income persons"—that is, those who have lost their jobs.

KMHDC encourages "all possible participation from the homeowner" in home construction and repair, even where heavy work is not possible. For example, a KMHDC worker may install a new door and buy the paint for an elderly homeowner to finish the job.

KMHDC has provided much decent housing, and Jones has noticed that the effects are felt in the community. New homeowners "really want to take care of their houses" and are more involved with their neighbors. One woman invited church members she had worked with for years to her home for the first time, since she was no longer ashamed for people to see where she lived!

CITY HOUSING

Before the Reagan Administration's extensive funding cutbacks, quite a bit of city housing in poor neighborhoods was built with subsidies or low-cost financing from various federal government programs. Some of these funds remain, but at a much lower level.

One group that was particularly successful in using these monies, as well as state funding and seed money from nonprofit organizations, is Inquilinos Boricuas en Accion (Puerto Rican Tenants in Action) of Boston's South End.[2] Formed in 1968 to fight neighborhood destruction by "redevelopment," by 1973 IBA had successfully fought for and supervised the rehabilitation of 207 apartments, mainly occupied by black and Puerto Rican families. It then moved on to the construction of a nineteen-story building with 201 apartments, serving the needs of mostly white, elderly residents of the neighborhood. Viviendas La Victoria I, completed in 1976, provided 73 apartments and 108 townhouses. Casa Borinquen, completed in 1977, rehabilitated 36 family apartments. Viviendas La Victoria II, completed in 1982, renovated 31 apartments and built 159 new townhouses. Though some of this housing is owned by the Boston Housing Authority, IBA's management firm oversees tenant selection, rent collection and maintenance. IBA, run by a board of directors of local residents elected at an annual community congress, also provides a variety of other programs, such as day care, residential security and crime prevention, and cultural and educational programs.

With cuts in government financing, IBA and other groups that build housing (such as Innovative Housing, Inc., discussed below) have been increasingly forced to use "tax-shelter financing." This has its good and bad points:

[W]ealthy private investors seek to shelter otherwise taxable income from taxation through rapid artificial "paper" depreciation the tax laws allow [for] housing and other capital goods. . . . The use of these tax shelters by and for community groups is a difficult, two-edged issue. Used creatively, they obviously provide substantial benefits to community groups, and in some cases represent the only way a housing venture can move ahead. On the other hand, they are a major loophole in the tax system, enabling doctors, dentists, lawyers, and others with overblown incomes to escape their rightful share of taxes, which, if paid, could provide the money communities need for housing and other programs. Something clearly is wrong with a system that permits communities to meet their needs only if they sell tax avoidance schemes to the rich.[3]

Money is also the major problem for moderate-income people who want to build or purchase a house in most parts of the United States. An innovative approach to this problem was announced in July 1983 by the San Francisco City and County Employees Pension Fund, when it made $25 million available for residential mortgages, restricted for the first ninety days of the program to union members and others with moderate incomes. The program also offered a more favorable interest arrangement than most currently available mortgages.

In spite of such scattered efforts, as long as high interest, high profits, and real estate speculation dominate the housing scene, affordability seems an illusive goal.

SHARING HOUSING AND SHARING CONTROL

GROUP HOUSEHOLDS

We are most familiar with group households as a living style of students and young singles who can't afford their "own" places. However, people who don't fit this description—couples, whole families, people of all ages —have turned to group living in recent years, both for financial reasons and for the community it can provide.

Group households can also be one key to living contentedly without great material consumption. Incomes can be reduced if washing machines, tools, automobiles, and houses are shared—and if less income is needed, we have more choices about what kind of work we do and how much time we have for things other than work. When we have people around to talk, sing, play, cook, and laugh with, we also have less need to go to a movie, watch television, or buy expensive gadgets that make a rote job a little shorter. More adults sharing a household can also help break down sex-segregated roles of child care, cooking, cleaning, and plumbing repair, and can relieve each one from having full responsibility for all these tasks.

Descriptions of life in two group households—one with a broad generational range and the other composed of single parents and their children —are included in Chapter VII. Another such household, Alpha Farm (see Chapter VI), includes income-sharing as part of its household economy. Some people are able to form households with people they already know, but many seek help from community bulletin boards, newspaper ads, and

an assortment of nonprofit and for-profit organizations that have sprung
up across the country to help people find housemates. Nationally, the
Shared Housing Resource Center promotes intergenerational shared
housing. As of May 1983, they reported more than seventy-five nonprofit
local groups helping older people, (70 percent of whom own their own
houses), to relieve loneliness, financial difficulties, and minor physical
difficulties with one or more housemates either of their own age or
another generation.

Certain kinds of issues, such as fair sharing of cleaning chores, seem
to arise in all households, and there are creative ways to deal with them.
A household that included two of the authors developed a chart to re-
mind the adults of their household chores: the outer paper circle with the
names rotates, and once a month jobs are changed.

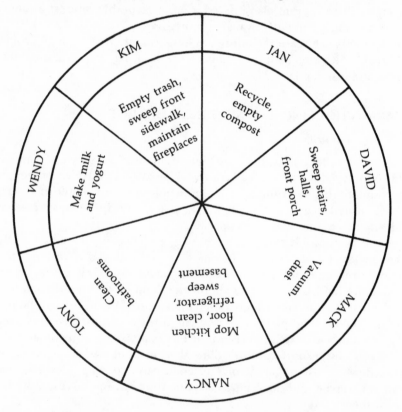

Other issues, such as attitudes toward child rearing, may not be so
easily dealt with. Even dish washing can be an important indicator of
one's ability to live responsibly with others. Lillian Willoughby, an older
member of a household in the Philadelphia Life Center, responded to a
question about mutual support in an intergenerational household by
talking about washing the dishes: "If you haven't learned to clean up after

yourself, you aren't likely to be washing anyone else's dishes. You haven't learned to give and take, only how to take. So then you're not likely to know how to be helpful in other, more difficult community situations."

Item 7 under "What You Can Do" at the end of this chapter suggests issues you may wish to examine if you are thinking about a group household. Some of the questions raised in items 1 through 3 at the end of Chapter IV may also be useful, particularly those that concern decision-making and conflict resolution.

CLUSTER HOUSING

With decreasing family size, most large houses that are suitable for group living are old and not being replaced. Even in large houses, few of our standard housing designs are ideal for long-term occupancy by singles or families who like some privacy but wish to share their common living areas, such as the kitchen and living room, with others.

In Holland and Denmark, both houses and apartment are being constructed with the assumption that they will be shared by several whole families or by singles who enjoy shared living. A common design is to place large, inviting common areas in the center, with two to four private sections around the outside of the circular design.

In the United States, Innovative Housing, a nonprofit organization, has decided to try a similar approach. Their initial construction project of low- and moderate-income housing, located in Fairfax, California, is primarily designed for singles and small, single-parent families. Each of their buildings will house one "cluster" of nine adults; each cluster will have a kitchen, a living room, and a dining room, linked by a common hallway. Bedrooms will be located on dead-end hallway branches, with one bathroom for every three individual units. The group hopes to follow this project with one that will house larger families, so that residents whose families grow will be able to move to other quarters that embody the same concepts.

The financing plan is to convert the housing into limited-equity housing cooperatives after five years, with Innovative Housing retaining ownership of some of the lower income units whose residents may be unable to afford the one-fourth to one-third monthly payment increase anticipated at the time of conversion due to the syndicated tax shelter financing method being used.

Innovative Housing feels that this long purchasing delay is necessary in order to nurture the shared living concept, which is totally unfamiliar to most Americans. Workshops introduce potential residents to group process and problem-solving techniques, and explore the hopes, fears, and expectations each person brings to the group. A low-cost counselor will be on call to assist clusters in working out serious problems that they are unable to deal with alone.

In forming the groups that will live in this and other shared housing projects, Innovative Housing is encouraging a number of ecologically sound, community-creating, and cost-cutting approaches: community gardens, bulk food-buying, workshop spaces, including space for some people to do their income-producing work at home, community-owned recreational equipment, and commonly owned vans, which could make a private car unnecessary. For the new construction (with off-street parking a zoning requirement), it costs one-third as much to "house" a car as a person, and the group is considering price reductions for residents without cars. Director Ann Howell describes most of those who have expressed interest in this way of life as "people committed to voluntary simplicity—people who are longing for saner ways of living for themselves, the community, and the planet."

LIMITED-EQUITY COOPERATIVES

Whether in new or existing buildings, limited-equity cooperatives are one way of combining housing affordability with control over one's shelter decisions.

"Limited equity" actually has a variety of definitions: the common denominator is that one does not expect to make a profit based on "value increase." When moving, residents may receive back only their original membership payment (down payment); or they may receive back the portion of their monthly payments that went to pay off the principal on a loan; or, to reflect inflation, they may receive back some increase over the amount they actually put in. This is quite a different view of "home ownership" than the one prevalent in our country:

The underlying principles of limited profit-taking are: (1) that the housing the cooperative owns is viewed as a resource for *use*, rather than for money-making; (2) that its housing is collective property rather than a collection of private investments; and (3) that the overall social benefit of keeping housing costs low outweighs any individual's need or desire to make a profit.[4]

The Aarti, a limited-equity housing cooperative located in San Francisco's low-income Tenderloin neighborhood, follows these principles quite strictly: members are committed to keeping a down payment unnecessary for cooperative membership, and have just begun to explore a method of paying long-term members back a portion of their "investment" when they move out.

Aarti began when Franciscan Charities, a Catholic organization committed to assisting the Tenderloin neighborhood, gave money to the Tenderloin Neighborhood Development Corporation (TNDC) for the purchase of a condemned, uninhabitable building that contained forty single-room units and had been empty for several years. In the summer of 1983, the tenants cooperative planned to sign a master lease with TNDC, the ultimate goal being full ownership by the cooperative.

After a period of renovation, financed by a loan from the City of San

Francisco, cooperative members moved in starting in June of 1982. The average age of residents is 30; both gay and straight; about half white, a quarter black, a quarter Latino; one-third women; half already residents of the neighborhood.

The building is run democratically by the whole cooperative membership; five hours minimum per week is required for housekeeping, maintenance, and committee work, though some members contribute more time. There are committees for screening new members, housekeeping, finance, maintenance, and overall administration. Those initially interested in moving in also made a five-hour minimum weekly "sweat equity" contribution during renovations. They did semiskilled work, such as stripping and staining hallway redwood paneling, building a roof garden, and exposing and cleaning attractive brick walls.

During the renovations, walls were removed on each of the three residential floors to create common living rooms, kitchens, and dining rooms. Food and meal sharing is optional. In the summer of 1983, a group of ten and a group of five each bought all their food together and cooked five to eight main meals each week, with the remainder of the residents buying and cooking on their own.

Wade Hudson, an Aarti resident, explained that a major reason for his membership was the financial freedom it gave him—now, and for the next ten to twenty years—to choose not to work a traditional, forty-hour-a-week job. He also explained his choice of such a large, semigroup-living situation: "For a long time, I've been interested in building a sense of family, a sense of community. I find Aarti rich and rewarding in terms of my involvement with such a number and diversity of people."

NEIGHBORHOOD PRESERVATION

Each year, two and one-half million Americans are displaced from their homes, and five hundred thousand lower-rent units are lost.[5] Displacement takes many forms: from the "simple" rent increase to the purposeful withdrawal of fire protection services from a whole section of a city; from the isolated act of an individual landlord to political and economic decisions by those who officially or unofficially control an area's housing supply. The authors of *Displacement: How to Fight It* observe:

In some senses, one can say that much of our country's history has been built on the principle of displacement: Native Americans starting in the seventeenth century, Mexicans from our Southwest during the nineteenth century, right through removal (and internment) of American citizens of Japanese ancestry from the West Coast during World War II and on into the urban renewal ("Negro removal" as it was then dubbed) program of the 1950s and 1960s.[6]

When fighting displacement, the first question that must be asked is: who is benefiting from the displacement? Real estate speculators? Owners of a factory who want to build on cheap land "cleared" by the city? Big housing developers? In all these cases, profit is the primary concern of the displacer who is seeking to control the housing decisions of the community. Solutions must be found that regain this control.

This section looks at five common ways people are displaced—through rent increases, condominium conversion, building demolition, city service cuts, and lack of essential maintenance—and ways some communities have fought back to ensure their survival.

RENT CONTROL AND CONDOMINIUM CONVERSION

As tenants well know, over the past decade rents have skyrocketed in most areas of the United States. The old guidepost that a family should be paying no more than one-quarter of its income for housing has become a bad joke as rent eats up one-third to one-half of many paychecks.

Rent control is the tenant's and community's most important defense against displacement and neighborhood destruction. It almost never prevents a landlord from making a fair return, but it does prevent unreasonable rent increases due to housing shortages and property speculation. Control on conversion of rental units to condominiums is another important factor in preserving a community's housing supply and keeping rents reasonable.

Many communities have tried rent control, with varying degrees of success. The most common reasons for ineffectiveness are wide loopholes, arising from political compromises that allow landlords to find ways to raise rents and to take rental units off the market.

One particularly successful example is found in Santa Monica, California, where a rent control ordinance was passed by ballot initiative in April 1979. Santa Monica is a moderate-income portion of Los Angeles County, about 75 percent white and 16 percent over age sixty-five. The older people, who are mostly renters with little interest in buying a home or apartment, have provided a strong base of support for rent control.

The initiative campaign was developed by Santa Monicans for Renters' Rights, a coalition of the local Democratic Club, the Campaign for Economic Democracy chapter, the Santa Monica Fair Housing Alliance, and the Ocean Park Electoral Network. The ordinance, defended by the same coalition, has survived two landlord-supported local ballot initiatives aimed at severely weakening rent control in 1979 and in 1983 as well as one initiative aimed at destroying effective rent control statewide. The coalition has also ensured the election of renter-advocates to the board that administers the ordinance (appointed boards have been a problem in some cities), as well as electing supportive members to the city council.

The rent board fixes rent increases annually, instead of by a pre-set percentage or formula. The typical annual increase has been 60 to 70 percent of the rise in the Consumer Price Index, which reflects the fact that a landlord's mortgage payments and certain other expenses do not rise with inflation. An extremely important feature of the law is that rent is not affected by a change of tenants; "vacancy decontrol" is the single largest loophole that guts the effectiveness of many statutes.

The board has quite wide powers to control attempted landlord abuses. A large percentage of the approximately one thousand petitions that have been received from tenants requesting a rent decrease due to building deterioration have been granted, as have a large percentage of the fifteen hundred petitions requesting refunds of illegally increased rents. If it can be shown that the landlord knew, or should have known, what the correct rent should be, triple damages are awarded. Illegal evictions have been controlled through an evolving variety of rules. For example, it was necessary to restrict the landlords' right to evict for the benefit of a relative to only one tenant per building, since some were evicting tenant after tenant supposedly for this purpose.

Tenants and landlords also ask the board for rulings on what renovations and improvements merit a rent increase: is this something that the normal rent should cover, or a substantial change in the property, entitling the landlord to a further fair return? Bill Allen, who finished his four-year term on the rent board in April of 1983, observed that as hard as the board worked to try to be fair, "it seems as if there is no carefully constructed balance acceptable to the landlord. The landlord usually not only wants to recover the money spent to put on a new roof, but wants to make a profit on it, too."

The rent control ordinance also strictly regulated the removal of rental units from the market, whether by demolition or by conversion to condominiums. Any demolition of a habitable or repairable building must be replaced by low- or moderate-income rental units. Condominium conversion is only permitted if the apartment is already inhabited by high-income persons, at a high-income rental, where the landlord cannot make a fair financial return and the supply of housing would not adversely be affected by the conversion. Since April of 1979, only fifty to sixty of Santa Monica's approximately thirty-six thousand rental units have been removed from the market.

Bill Allen feels that an important factor in Santa Monica's unusual success at passing and keeping its rent control ordinance is precisely because it is so strong: although landlord opposition is maximized, so is the active support from tenants who perceive that an effective ordinance is worth spending the time to fight for.

DEMOLITION

The Legal Services Anti-Displacement Project has set "two absolute goals": "the right to stay put," and "the absolute requirement that there be one-for-one (or more) replacement of lower-rent units withdrawn from the market." A Neighborhood Preservation Ordinance of the City of Berkeley, California, has successfully addressed these goals for over a decade by strictly regulating housing demolitions.

In order to receive a demolition permit for any housing, even single-family dwellings, an owner must show that the "demolition would not be materially detrimental to the housing needs and public interest of the affected neighborhood and the City of Berkeley," and that the developer has provided alternative housing for the residents at similar cost, quality, and within the same community, if desired. The developer must also show either that the house is "hazardous, unusable, or unrepairable" or that she or he will replace the housing with at least the same number of housing units, with the displaced residents having first choice in the new housing.

There have been very few housing demolitions in Berkeley during the past ten years: a few have occurred to permit replacement housing, a few for houses in extremely poor condition—usually gutted by fire—where repair is not feasible. One interesting adaptation, where zoning permits more than one housing unit per building, has been to raise a house and build another unit underneath, thus adding to the housing stock while maintaining the physical character of the neighborhood. Berkeley also has very strongly enforced restrictions on converting existing housing units to nonresidential use, further preserving the city's housing supply.

PEOPLE'S FIREHOUSE, INC.

People's Firehouse, Inc., is a community organization in the Northside section of Williamsburg, in Brooklyn, New York. Northside is home for twelve thousand people, three-fifths of them elderly, many speaking Polish, Italian, and Spanish. The organization is now involved in a number of housing preservation and other community services. But the struggle that People's Firehouse takes its name from is a stand against the destruction of the neighborhood by the withdrawal of fire protection: the most essential of city services for a densely populated, wood-frame house neighborhood sprinkled with paint factories, lumber yards, and liquified natural gas tanks.

By late 1975, Northside, which the city would have preferred "cleared" for industrial development, had already lost its police precinct, well-baby clinic, most hospital services, and half of its sanitation services. After the city announced the closing of the local fire station, two hundred residents decided to seize the men and equipment on November 21, 1975, the day before the scheduled closing. Legal proceedings delayed the closure for several days, but on Thanksgiving evening the word went out that the city was attempting to remove the fire engines. Hundreds of residents then surrounded the equipment, in an occupation that lasted for sixteen months. During that period, residents ran a People's Firehouse and responded to fires themselves (without fire equipment), documenting the delay and costs in lives and property.

After sixteen months, extremely limited and ineffective local service was restored. The community continued to gather documentation and to demonstrate at city hall, at the homes of the fire commissioner and mayor, as well as leafletting the Democratic National Convention.

Their most dramatic protest gesture came the day after a fire destroyed three buildings a block and a half from the firehouse when three broken hydrants prevented firefighters from extinguishing the blaze promptly. A contingent of neighborhood residents, mainly older people, blocked morning rush-hour traffic on the Brooklyn-Queens Expressway. . . . They caused a monster traffic jam extending some eighteen miles in both directions. The city finally gave in.[7]

The lack of adequate fire protection service left ten people dead during the two and a half years the station was closed. To prevent further deaths and injuries, People's Firehouse continues its monitoring of fire hydrants, installs free smoke detectors in homes where older people live, and collects regular data on "arson prone" buildings: those owing back taxes, in poor repair, and/or with a history of fires. Arson is the ultimate—and highly profitable—displacement weapon, and a low-income community of older housing that wishes to survive must unfortunately face the reality that a cleared, insurance-compensated lot can mean more to some people than a human life.

HOUSING MAINTENANCE

Housing maintenance can be expensive, and home ownership can mean little if one can't keep a roof over one's head. People can be forced to sell a house for lack of money to maintain it. Strict housing code enforcement, even when buildings are in quite liveable condition, can and has been used as a tactic to force poorer homeowners out of a neighborhood that has been targeted for "upgrading."

One approach to this problem is neighborhood skills-sharing. Very few of us have all the skills necessary for basic home maintenance—plumbing, electrical work, carpentry, painting, roofing—but we can exchange skills with our neighbors and learn about what we don't already know. Many communities have low-cost classes that can help. Tool-sharing can also make expensive purchases unnecessary. A community in Palo Alto, California, described in Chapter IV, is an example of such a long-term successful arrangement, though Palo Alto is not a community where people depend on skills-sharing for economic survival.

Older homeowners can have special problems with home repair, both in doing the work themselves and in finding the money to get help. One project that helps with basic maintenance—jobs with a limit of about $2,000—is Maintenance Central for Seniors, Inc., in Detroit, Michigan.

Maintenance Central workers do all kinds of home repairs for older persons otherwise unable to afford them—from furnace installations to roofs. They distribute a repair manual, which identifies tools and very simple repairs that can be done by householders. Executive Director Lawrence Humphrey explained that they are now trying to obtain funding for home appliance repair (refrigerators, radios, and televisions), which is especially essential for poor, single-person households whose residents find it hard to get around.

The project started through the efforts of one younger neighborhood resident and now employs one hundred people to do more than two hundred repair jobs per month. This is a cutback from pre-Reagan Administration levels. It received a one-year reprieve in 1983 under a special jobs bill, but with 60 percent of its regular funds cut, Maintenance Central faces an uncertain future.

HOMELESSNESS

In 1980, the Community for Creative Non-Violence (CCNV), in Washington, D.C., estimated in a report for Congress that 2.2 million Americans then lacked shelter. In 1982, they stated their belief that during 1983, "the number of homeless people in the United States could reach 3 million or more." About their own statistic, they say: "Not until [the homeless] come inside will we know for certain how many there are."[8]

Why are the homeless not inside? One of the myths about this subject was exploited by the mayor of Washington, D.C., during the winter of 1980, when

[h]e gathered two or three van-loads of reporters and camera crews and went on a tour of the downtown heat grates. . . . The mayor stopped at one grate after another and offered to drive the men to a city shelter. They respectfully declined.

No one asked why the men chose to remain where they were, for if they had inquired, they might have learned that there was—and is—good reason for the refusal: brutalization by armed guards; being put back on the streets at 5:30 A.M. in an unfamiliar area, with no place to go for at least two hours; theft of personal property; an abundance of lice and bedbugs. In spite of these problems, many of the men had tried the shelters, only to be turned away for lack of space. There would be no space left on the grates either, by the time they made the two- or three-mile trek back. Given the range of options open to them and previous experiences, the men on the grates had made a reasonable decision.[9]

CCNV has both tried to offer alternatives to these degrading conditions and to force Washington, D.C., and the nation, to acknowledge and house the homeless. Their own regular programs include a soup kitchen that daily serves three to five hundred people a morning meal; a free food store that distributes two to three hundred bags of groceries each day; a seven-days-a-week drop-in center (open from 7 A.M. to 6 P.M., when the shelters are closed) that provides shower, laundry, and bathroom facilities, hot and cold drinks, a place to relax, a mailing address, medical and legal services, and a hot evening meal; and a second drop-in center for people over age fifty, which includes an infirmary. Much of the food prepared is scavenged daily from supermarket dumpsters; the rest is donated or purchased with donated moneys.

These are some of the other things that CCNV has done:

- On New Year's Eve of 1976, they began to open their own home to the homeless. (The community itself is described in Chapter IV.) That winter they asked all eleven hundred churches, temples, and mosques in the area to follow their lead: only one said yes. The next winter, a second church offered help.
- In November 1978, CCNV informed the Secretary of the Interior that it would, together with Washington, D.C.'s homeless, move into the National Visitor Center on November 30. Hundreds of homeless came for shelter and food. When they were evicted after ten days, twenty-four people were arrested after spending the night in the middle of Massachusetts Avenue.
- In January of 1980, CCNV claimed the body of "John Doe," a homeless exposure victim; a public funeral procession, led by a horse-drawn cortege through downtown Washington, ended with public services in front of city hall.
- In March of 1980, community members poured blood on the altar at St. Matthew's Cathedral, after cathedral officials refused to keep the building open during a snowstorm and two people died nearby of exposure within the next three days.
- Starting in 1980, CCNV participated in a number of court cases that have succeeded in keeping shelters open and homelessness in the public eye.
- CCNV's census forms were publicly burned because census bureau procedures failed to count the homeless.
- CCNV members conducted a successful three-day public fast to secure additional shelter space for women.
- "Community members were twice arrested and removed from the Hilton Hotel for distributing copies of the Beatitudes to the U.S. Catholic Bishops at their yearly conference. The Church was being asked to be more sensitive and responsible to the needs of the poor."[10]
- On Thanksgiving day, 1981, seven hundred poor and homeless people were served dinner in Lafayette Park, across from the White House. That night, CCNV members and homeless people initiated "Reaganville," a tent encampment; they were arrested for sleeping in the park. The demonstration was continued twenty-four-hours-a-day for a month, using empty tents and awake volunteers. After a court battle, Reaganville was fully reinstituted a month later and the homeless slept in the tents until spring.
- On December 28, 1981, the Christian Feast of the Holy Innocents, a field of more than five hundred crosses was hammered into the

ground at Lafayette Park, each bearing the name or date of death of a homeless person who had died of exposure. They remained all winter, together with the tent encampment. On the last day of winter, another gathering planted new crosses representing victims of that winter, and the old crosses were each delivered to a member of Congress.

These are some of the results of CCNV's activities:

- Between December 1976 and the winter of 1981–82, the number of beds regularly available in Washington, D.C., for the homeless rose from 22 to 178 for women, and from 200 to 700 for men.
- As a result of the National Visitor Center action, CCNV was given the right to staff a new shelter for one month to create a model shelter program. This is what happened:

Within three days of the transition, Pierce [School] was at its capacity of 150 men, and within a week, numbers swelled as high as 216. Men slept on floors and tables while waiting for another building to open. . . .

It was obvious that a difference in atmosphere quickly attracted more people. They served one another meals, and helped maintain the building and staff the shelter. They began to assume the duties for which they had a responsibility and to which they had a right. . . . The system of participation by guests instilled in many a sense of possibility and the dignity that comes of being in control of one's environment and of service to others.[11]

- By 1980, an agreement had been negotiated with the city to contract the running of the city's shelters to the Washington Council of Churches, which has alleviated many of the degrading conditions.
- As a result of the participation of so many volunteers in CCNV's various actions, many of whom were college students and young working people who have since relocated, "a large pool of experienced shelter volunteers . . . spilled over into other cities to continue their efforts."[12] CCNV's example has also inspired groups in many other cities to confront the problem of homelessness in America.

For an example of a group addressing the problem of homeless families, see the description of Raphael House in Chapter IV.

HOMESTEADING IN THE 1980s

Detroit has many homeless people and many renters who can't afford both food and the living space they need. Detroit also has about ten thousand vacant houses: abandoned by owners who were unwilling or unable to pay back taxes, make needed repairs, or deal with estate proceedings. In 1980, the Detroit Chapter of ACORN (Association of Community Organizations for Reform Now) decided to do something about bringing these vacant houses and those who needed shelter together. This spurred an urban homesteading movement that has led to important protections for the squatter.

During the period of the campaign, a program instituted by Detroit's mayor has distributed by lottery 149 homes, with 76 people actually living in the homes by August 1983. But ACORN organizer Jeryl Davis calls the mayor's program a "poor excuse" for a solution to Detroit's housing problem. Most of Detroit's structurally sound abandoned houses are torn down by the city at a cost of $3,000 to $5,000—or left empty waiting for arson to do the job.

So ACORN "squatted" sixty families in abandoned houses. In one confrontation, eight ACORN members were arrested. The organization also backed squatters in court battles, repeatedly requested assistance from the city council, and worked at keeping the issue in the public eye.

In the meantime, squatters used "sweat equity" to make their new houses safe and comfortable. With only the money they would have otherwise paid for rent, they and their friends did the needed repairs. ACORN nationally is supporting a bill that has already passed the House of Representatives and would make grants and loans available for housing rehabilitation in such circumstances.

On July 27, 1983, the three-year campaign resulted in the passage by the Detroit City Council, on a 9 to 0 vote, of a comprehensive ordinance protecting squatters. The ordinance recognizes squatter's rights to use an abandoned house for shelter, while giving the owner a chance to redeem the house over a period of three years. An urban homesteader files a notice of intent to "abate a nuisance" with the City Building Safety Department, which inspects the house, informs the homesteader of the measures necessary to make it safe, and informs the owner of the homesteader's intent to do so. At any point during the next three years, the owner may pay any back taxes and utility bills, *plus* the value of the homesteader's labor and materials used in improving the owner's property. If the owner does not do so, the homesteader is not responsible for back taxes or utilities and will receive title to the house from the city at a price still to be worked out. ACORN's position is that the price should be $1.

As of August 1983, Detroit's mayor was refusing to implement the ordinance, though it had officially become law—and ACORN was gearing up to continue the fight for as long as necessary to preserve Detroit's housing for the use of its citizens.

WHAT YOU CAN DO

1. Volunteer—alone or in a group—at an emergency shelter in your community. Discuss what you learn about who is using the shelter and why they are homeless.

2. Distribute a questionnaire among your friends, neighbors, or community organization to determine what home maintenance skills each of you has. Talk about how you can help each other or make maintenance tasks lighter by doing them in the company of others.

3. List the ways that your choices—or lack of choices—about shelter affect your own life. Are you satisfied with your situation? If not, what options are open to you—as an individual or in working with others?

4. If the streets in your neighborhood aren't being cleaned, check those in the neighborhood of the street cleaning department supervisor. If they're clean, picket her or his house. (This effective tactic was used by residents of the San Francisco neighborhood of Bernal Heights.)

5. Find out what your area's property tax assessment is—and the assessed value of the building you live in. Figure out what proportion of your rent covers property taxes. Add a generous estimate of your landlord's maintenance costs and utilities, if she or he pays them. How much are you paying to buy your landlord a building? Are there other alternatives?

6. Learn about what administrative boards and agencies make decisions about shelter in your community. Some possibilities are zoning boards, planning commissions, antidiscrimination or human rights commissions, and building inspection departments. What are the avenues for citizen input? If there is a shelter decision coming up that adversely affects your community, such as a house demolition, learn more about these processes by organizing a group to protest it before the appropriate board. Was the protest effective? If not, what changes would make it more effective?

7. If you are interested in starting or joining a shared household, here are some issues you can begin to explore—both with yourself and with others:

   • Would the members of your household share a common life-style or standard of living? Some possibilities are vegetarianism, recycling, simple living, gardening, and abstinence from smoking, alcohol, or drugs.
   • Do you like the other people?
   • Do you want your living companions to share your principles, values, or spiritual beliefs? Do you want them to share your recreational interests?
   • Would household members share any possessions? Which ones? Any special rules concerning possessions?
   • Would household members share chores? How would you allocate these chores?
   • Would household members share similar sexual attitudes?
   • Would household members share child rearing? Do you have common attitudes about it? What are they? How would you structure shared child rearing?

- Would you seek diversity or similarity of age, ethnic background, work, or interests?
- Would you buy food together? Would you prepare food together?
- Are you looking for a long-term or short-term living situation? Do you view shared living as a long-term or short-term part of your life?
- Does the physical layout of a house or apartment allow adequate privacy? Will each person have her or his own room? If not, are there other options for providing sharers privacy when necessary? Is there room for guests?
- Does the physical layout of a house or apartment encourage interaction among household members?
- If you are "moving into someone else's home," how can you become a full and comfortable member of the household?
- Who will handle household money? Who will pay household bills?
- Will all members contribute money to the household equally? Will contributions be set by the quality of the space available to each person (including common areas)? By income? By income, taking into consideration a household's commitment to a member's nonincome-producing activity?
- Will household members have similar schedules? If not, will you ever see each other? Do you care?
- How will you select new housemates? Should everyone agree?
- How large a household do you want? How might the number of people affect the answers to some of the other questions?

NOTES

1. Stewart Brand, ed., *The Next Whole Earth Catalog* (Sausalito, Calif: Point, 1980), p. 223.
2. Chester Hartman, Dennis Keating, and Richard LeGates, *Displacement: How to Fight It,* published by Legal Services Anti-Displacement Project of the National Housing Law Project, 2150 Shattuck Avenue, #300, Berkeley, Calif. 94704 (1982), pp. 195–198.
3. Ibid., p. 198.
4. Ibid., p. 177.
5. Ibid., p. 3.
6. Ibid., p. 4.
7. Ibid., p. 76.
8. Mary Ellen Hombs and Mitch Snyder, *Homelessness: A Forced March to Nowhere* (Washington, D.C.: Community for Creative Non-Violence, 1982), p. xvi.
9. Ibid., p. 57.
10. Ibid., p. 100.
11. Ibid., p. 97.
12. Ibid.

SOURCES OF FURTHER INFORMATION

Groups Mentioned in Chapter

Community for Creative Non-Violence. 1345 Euclid Street, N.W., Washington, D.C. 20009.

Detroit ACORN. 2230 Witherell, Detroit, Mich. 48201.

Innovative Housing. Box 1174, Mill Valley, Calif. 94941.

Inquilinos Boricuas en Accion. 405 Shawmut Avenue, Boston, Mass. 02118.

Kentucky Mountain Housing Development Corporation. Box 431, Manchester, Ky. 40962.

Maintenance Central for Seniors, Inc. 3750 Woodward Avenue, Detroit, Mich. 48202.

People's Firehouse, Inc. 113 Berry Street, Brooklyn, N.Y. 11211.

San Francisco City and County Employees Pension Fund. 770 Golden Gate Avenue, San Francisco, Calif. 94102.

Santa Monica Rent Control Board. 1685 Main Street, Santa Monica, Calif. 90401.

Shared Housing Resource Center, Inc. 6344 Greene Street, Philadelphia, Pa. 19144.

Tenderloin Neighborhood Development Corporation. 474 Eddy Street, San Francisco, Calif. 94109.

Additional Resource Groups

California Housing Action and Information Network (CHAIN). 1107 9th Street, Suite 1017, Sacramento, Calif. 95814. Rent control campaign experience.

Center for Community Change. 1000 Wisconsin Avenue, N.W., Washington, D.C. 20007.

Center for Metropolitan Action. Queens College, Flushing, N.Y. 11367. Low-income housing.

Citizen Action. 1501 Euclid Avenue, #500, Cleveland, Ohio 44115. Many issues, including redlining and arson. National organization.

Conference on Alternative State and Local Policies. 2000 Florida Avenue, N.W., Washington, D.C. 20009.

Fair Housing for Children Coalition. Box 5877, Santa Monica, Calif. 90405.

Housing Assistance Council. 1025 Vermont Avenue, N.W., #606, Washington, D.C. 20005. Rural housing.

Housing Rights for Children Project. 6501 Telegraph Avenue, Oakland, Calif. 94609.

Institute for Community Economics. 151 Montague City Road, Greenfield, Mass. 01301. Urban and rural land trusts.

Low Income Housing Information Service and Coalition. 323 8th Street, N.E., Washington, D.C. 20002.

National Association of Housing Cooperatives. 1012 14th Street, N.W., Suite 805, Washington, D.C. 20005.

National Association of Neighborhoods. 1651 Fuller Street, N.W., Washington, D.C. 20009.

National Coalition for the Homeless. 105 East 22 Street, New York, N.Y. 10010.

National Committee Against Discrimination in Housing. 1425 H Street, N.W., #410, Washington, D.C. 20005.

National Consumer Cooperative Bank. 2001 S Street, N.W., Washington, D.C. 20009.

National People's Action/National Training and Information Center. 954 West Washington Blvd., Chicago, Ill. 60607.

National Rural Housing Coalition. 1016 16 Street, N.W., #8G, Washington, D.C. 20036.

National Tenant Organization. Box 208, Parksville, N.Y. 12768. Public housing
and subsidized private housing tenants.

National Tenants Union. 380 East Main Street, East Orange, N.J. 07018.

New Jersey Tenants' Organization. Box 1142, Fort Lee, N.J. 07024. Rent control
campaign experience.

Owner-Builder Center. 1516 5th Street, Berkeley, Calif. 94710.

Planners Network. 1901 Q Street N.W., Washington, D.C. 20009.

Rural America. 1900 M Street N.W., #320, Washington, D.C. 20036.

Bibliography

Construction, Design, Legal Guidance

Alexander, C., et al. *A Pattern Language: Towns, Building, Construction.* Oxford:
Oxford University Press, 1977.

Brann, Donald R. *How to Remodel Buildings.* 1978. Available from: Easi-Bild, Box
315, Briarcliff Manor, N.Y. 10510.

Institute for Community Economics. *The Community Land Trust: A Guide for a New
Model for Land Tenure in America.* 1972. Available from: Institute for Community Economics, 120 Boylston Street, Boston, Mass. 02116. $7.50.

Jackson, Albert, and David Day. *Tools and How to Use Them.* New York: Alfred A.
Knopf, 1978.

Kaswan, Jaques. *Converting Multi-Unit Housing into Affordable Cooperatives.* 1983.
Available from: Jaques Kaswan, Community Development Associatives,
1740 Walnut Street, Berkeley, Calif. 94709.

Kern, Ken. *The Owner-Built Home.* Totowa, N.J.: Charles Scribner's Sons, 1975.

Kern, Ken. *The Owner-Built Homestead.* Totowa, N.J.: Charles Scribner's Sons,
1974.

Kern, Ken, and Evelyn Turner. *The Work Book: Personal Politics of Building Your Own
Home.* 1979. Available from: Owner-Builder Publications, Box 817,
North Fork, Calif. 93643.

Papanek, Victor. *Design for the Real World.* New York: Bantam Books, 1982.

Reader's Digest, Eds. *Complete Do-It-Yourself Manual.* New York: Random House,
1973.

Reader's Digest, Eds. *Fix-It-Yourself Manual.* New York: Random House, 1977.

Turner, John. *Housing by People: Towards Autonomy in Building Environments.* New
York: Pantheon, 1977.

Vital, Edmund. *Building Regulations: A Self-Help Guide for the Owner-Builder.* Totowa,
N.J.: Charles Scribner's Sons, 1979.

Organizing

Blumberg, Richard, and James Grow. *The Rights of Tenants.. The Basic ACLU Guide
to a Tenant's Rights.* New York: Avon Books, 1979.

Cassidy, Robert. *Livable Cities: A Grass-Roots Guide to Rebuilding Urban America.* New
York: Holt, Rinehart and Winston, 1980.

Gilderbloom, John, et al., eds. *Rent Control: A Source Book.* 1981. Available from:
Housing Information Center, Foundation for National Progress, Box
3396, Santa Barbara, Calif. 93105. $7.95.

Hartman, Chester, et al. *Displacement: How to Fight It.* 1982. Available from: Legal
Services Anti-Displacement Project of the National Housing Law Pro-

ject, 2150 Shattuck Avenue, #300, Berkeley, Calif. 94704. $7.95. The best book available on many aspects of housing organizing.

Hombs, Mary Ellen, and Mitch Snyder. *Homelessness: A Forced March to Nowhere.* Washington, D.C.: Community for Creative Non-Violence, 1982.

People's Firehouse #1. A twenty-five minute, color film documentary. Available from: Third World Newsreel, 160 Fifth Avenue, Suite 911, New York, N.Y. 10010. $50 rental.

Shelterforce. Quarterly journal. Available from: National Tenants Union, address above.

Stone, Michael. *People Before Property: A Real Estate Primer and Research Guide.* Available from: Urban Planning Aid, 120 Boylston Street, Boston, Mass. 02006.

Trust for Public Land. *Citizens Action Manual: A Guide to Recycling Vacant Property in Your Neighborhood.* 1979. Available from: 82 2nd Street, San Francisco, Calif. 94105. Free. (This group has six regional offices around the United States.)

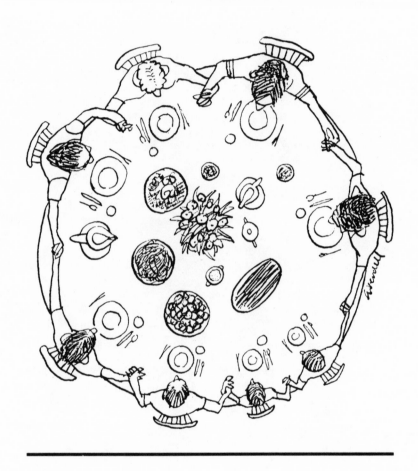

CHAPTER IV

Community

QUERIES

1. What does the word *community* mean to me?
2. Am I fearful of commitments involved with community? What commitments *are* required of me? What commitments do I expect from others?
3. What kinds of support groups might aid my personal growth?
4. Are there ways that working with others could give me the power I need to make changes in my neighborhood, state, nation, and world?
5. What problems of others do I see that might be helped by stronger community?
6. What communities am I already part of? How could more "community" be created within them?
7. How might community make living with fewer possessions more possible and/or more desirable?
8. Could a consensus decision-making process (instead of majority rule) contribute to the strength and vision of a community I am part of?

Most people are, or have been, part of some kind of community—but most of us would like more. People can work together or interact without any real sense of community or meaningful sharing as, for example, when people work in the same office or factory, but hardly know one another.

A community of sharing, action, concern, or spirit must be consciously begun, developed, and nurtured. This is not always an easy task. But most people discover that a sense of having something in common brings much more joy and fulfillment to their lives than the "easy" road of staying apart.

What is community? It can be as small as an individual household (see Chapter III) and as large as the entire ecological system. The Ozark Area Community Congress, located in the Ozark watershed areas of Missouri, Oklahoma, and Arkansas, takes this broadest view: "Ozark Area Community Congress is a representational body. It represents many things, including human agencies, organizations, philosophies, beliefs. . . . It

represents watersheds, rivers, forests, animals, the whole bioregion.
. . . We do not represent only human populations, and we take our
mandate from the ecology and not simply from human concerns."[1]

This chapter will discuss types of communities within this range: neighborhoods, religious-centered communities, social and political goal-ori-
ented communities. It will also look at ideas, methods, and techniques
that can be useful for any kind of community, new or existing, in exploring its goals, making decisions, and learning how to be together.

YOUR NEIGHBORHOOD AS COMMUNITY

In the other types of communities we'll look at, participants are partly
or entirely self-selected: they worship at the same church; they oppose
nuclear weapons; they live and work together for the purpose of feeding
and sheltering the hungry and homeless of a major city.

A neighborhood is different. Residents may worship in a variety of
places or no place; they may hold a wide variety of political views; they
may be of a number of different ethnic cultures and primary language
groups; they may work mostly in other neighborhoods and other cities
and towns. Projects that create community within a neighborhood need
to find ways to reach across these social barriers to the human concerns
all the residents share.

The Richmond District is a mostly middle-class neighborhood of about
sixty-three thousand in the northwest corner of San Francisco that has
been home to a changing variety of ethnic groups since the 1880s. Among
the earlier residents were Irish, French, Eastern European and Sephardic
Jews, and Russians fleeing World War I and the 1917 revolution. On a
Sunday morning, one can still buy a kosher chicken or enter a bakery and
be surrounded by six or seven Russian conversations. More recently, the
neighborhood has become a preferred residence of Chinese, Japanese,
Korean, and Vietnamese families who are able to escape the crowded,
substandard housing of lower-income ghettos; they comprise about 50
percent of the district's population, and there are many Asian-language
churches and Asian grocery stores.

Since 1970, a number of people and organizations have attempted to
create community in the neighborhood as a whole. Their history illustrates both the rewards and difficulties of this sort of effort.

After Earth Day in 1970, the local YMCA drew two hundred people to
talks on environmental issues. After one of these talks, twelve people
decided to form Richmond Environmental Action (REA), the first and
longest-lasting neighborhood recycling group in San Francisco. At the
height of its organizing activities, REA was collecting cans, bottles, and
newspapers at twelve garages plus at a central lot each Saturday morning,
utilizing a total of one hundred volunteers. It currently operates only at
a centralized location, but six days a week, utilizing a combination of paid

and much less volunteer labor. It does a large volume of recycling, but no longer is the "community-creating" activity it once was.

Richmond Involved in Safe Energy (RISE) is the sole survivor of several neighborhood organizations formed in the late 1970s affiliated with San Francisco's People Against Nuclear Power. In addition to participating in city- and region-wide events, over the years RISE has sponsored numerous street-corner tables and educational programs at the local public library on nuclear power, safe energy, and, most recently, nuclear weapons. The active group has remained small; however, in June of 1983, one RISE member collected over seven hundred signatures in one week from Richmond residents of every age and ethnic background supporting those (including several neighborhood women) who had been arrested while blockading the Livermore Laboratory, the United States' main nuclear weapons design facility.

The Neighborhood Women's Network was started in 1979 by an unemployed social worker and single mother, Renee Renaud, then an eleven-year neighborhood resident. She stapled on telephone poles throughout the Richmond District invitations to "women of all ages, races and religions" to attend four weekly potluck meetings in her tiny living room. After a month, the crowd of women, ranging in age from teens to those in their sixties, moved to a local church's basement, where monthly potluck dinners are still held. At some potlucks, all attending introduce themselves and share whatever needs, concerns, useful information, or funny stories they wish. At others, programs have ranged from sing-alongs to slides of a member's trip to refugee camps in Cambodia, to Buddhist Art, to an acupressure demonstration. Members write up their skills, needs, and what they like to do for fun for a directory, which is distributed only to those who participate. Recent additional activities were a Richmond District history walk, a tour of Chinatown herbal shops, a camping group, a vegetarian potluck-recipe exchange, and a child-care exchange network. A past activity was a discussion group based on an earlier version of this book, which started the editor of this edition writing on the subject!

Despite the success of these groups, many community people were frustrated by the limited multiethnic participation. In June of 1983, their efforts culminated in the opening of the Richmond District Neighborhood Center, three years after a multiethnic board of directors came together to stop the San Francisco School Board from bulldozing three old school buildings and leasing the land to condominium developers. The center houses a number of groups: Self Help for the Elderly, which provides meals and programs six days a week for Chinese-language elders; the Community Music Center, which offers low-cost music lessons and neighborhood performance groups; the San Francisco Special Olympics, which sponsors sports activities for the mentally disabled; a cross-cultural preschool/child-care center, including staff who speak Chinese,

Japanese, and Vietnamese; a Richmond YMCA after-school youth program; evening dance/exercise classes and a Saturday morning T'ai Chi class. Evening and weekend space is available at low cost to all community organizations for meetings, and educational and cultural activities. Renee, who helped with the center's organizing, describes its opening as "the first time in the almost one hundred years since we became the Richmond District that there is a single connecting place for all the diverse people who live here."

STARTING A SMALLER COMMUNITY

Many different groupings of people can form the basis for building community. In November 1974, Dorothy Fadiman, a housewife and mother of two, shared her vision of community with parents and teachers at the elementary school her children attended. The first meeting drew more than fifty people, who filled out this Community Interest Sheet:

Your Name _____
Address _____
Phone Number_____

Please indicate your level of interest in any of the following projects by noting one of the below:

    A. *Participant*—Interested in the idea, would use it if it developed.
    B. *Worker*—Would be willing to work on it as it develops.
    C. *Organizer*—Willing to help organize the original plans.

1. Sunday meeting   once a week_____   once a month_____
    Participant_____   Worker_____   Organizer_____
2. Food co-op
    Participant_____   Worker_____   Organizer_____
3. Services exchange
    Participant_____   Worker_____   Organizer_____
4. Goods exchange
    Participant_____   Worker_____   Organizer_____
5. Job referrals within the community
    Participant_____   Worker_____   Organizer_____
6. Community-oriented childcare
    Participant_____   Worker_____   Organizer_____
7. More shared parenting
    Full days_____   Weekends_____   Longer_____
    Participant_____   Worker_____   Organizer_____
8. Community garden
    Participant_____   Worker_____   Organizer_____
9. Political action/Discussion group
    Participant_____   Worker_____   Organizer_____
10. Cooking cooperatives
    Participant_____   Worker_____   Organizer_____
11. Drama group
    Participant_____   Worker_____   Organizer_____

12. Single parents discussion
     Participant_____   Worker_____   Organizer_____
13. Yoga
     Participant_____   Worker_____   Organizer_____
14. Medical
     Participant_____   Worker_____   Organizer_____

Each person who expressed interest in being an organizer met with those who had checked either the "participant" or "worker" category in a specific area. From this original survey, several three-family cooking co-ops developed. Each family took turns cooking one major meal a week and delivering it to the other two homes. These groupings lasted up to five years; the families then found that this arrangement did not suit their needs as children grew older. The concept is carried on, however, by other families who now have small children. The same has been true of children's play groups.

A ten-person drama group continued for about a year and a half, as did a monthly "Sunday Meeting"—for people of all religious backgrounds. In June of 1983, a number of people from the 1974 community regathered to form a periodic "silent prayer meeting for the planet."

The most basic need expressed by many members of the group was to "get their houses in order." Growing out of the services exchange, about a dozen adults still gather monthly at a member's house to do "whatever needs to be done": wiring, painting, cleaning closets, washing windows, insulating attics, planting gardens. Necessary tools are contributed by anyone who has them. A big midday potluck gives these long-time friends time to catch up on the events of the month; in December, the work session is skipped and the families go Christmas caroling together.

Over the years each family has saved much in time and money, but Dorothy Fadiman feels there has been a more important benefit: "I have a deep sense that if I need anything, I can ask these people, and they know they can call on me."

The Philadelphia Life Center

The Philadelphia Life Center began in 1970–71 as part of the Movement for a New Society (MNS)—a national communication network of nonviolent training and action groups. There were many influences that created MNS and the Life Center, but Quakers who were radical social activists probably had the strongest influence. As of mid-1983, the Life Center consisted of eighteen group households that have chosen to locate in the same small section of West Philadelphia. The MNS office and other facilities associated with the Life Center are also in the neighborhood.

For the initial years, all Life Center residents were also members of

MNS, and all MNS members were expected to live in Life Center houses. Now there is more flexibility in both directions, with MNS members living elsewhere and with many household members active in other organizations, such as the Jobs with Peace Coalition, Central Philadelphia Friends Meeting, and reevaluation counseling. This change reflects in part a conscious attempt to avoid isolation of the community from the rest of society. Member Lynne Shivers comments on this common problem facing communities: "We have created our own values, jargon, and forms of recreation, and they are proof that we have created a real alternative community. Yet, the differences sometimes put newcomers off."

Although many of the households have social contacts, the core of the community aspect of the Life Center is the forty-five members of MNS who work closely together politically as well as in a variety of neighborhood activities. For many years, the dominant activity of MNS members was a program that taught the skills needed to build nonviolent social change movements. Both nine-month and two-week training programs were offered, with about 25 percent of the participants from other countries. In the fall of 1982, these programs were discontinued for an extended evaluation by the community; as of the fall of 1983, they were slowly being restarted in somewhat different form. Three MNS members live in and staff The Crossing, a hospitality and conference center that can house fourteen people overnight and meetings of up to fifty, where the trainings take place.

MNS members staff New Society Publishers, which publishes and distributes books on nonviolent social change and on methods for working together collectively. Community member Lillian Willoughby explained that "New Society Publishers is now making a real push to put books concerning nonviolence everywhere—in libraries, in schools, and around the world." The Transnational Collective, another MNS group, facilitates the international distribution and the community's other international contacts.

The Life Center has established a Land Trust, which has gradually acquired five of the eighteen group households and the MNS office. Since the time and method of acquisition—and therefore the prices—varied widely, the Land Trust pools the total amount of mortgage payments, taxes, insurance, and most of the maintenance for the five group households, and residents make equal monthly payments no matter which house they live in. Community members are very active in the running of a neighborhood food cooperative and in support of a neighborhood credit union sponsored by the activist Calvary Church, which is providing a method for neighborhood residents to invest their money in their own community. One member runs a neighborhood car repair shop; another teaches at a neighborhood school and leads the local girl scout troop.

Community members provide support for each other in a variety of ways. A basic one is an application of the early Quaker practice of the "clearness meeting." A clearness meeting is called to help a person make a decision (membership, entering or leaving a group or house, choosing personal priorities). The person making the decision invites others to provide support and challenge. Another support mechanism has been small groups that have varied over the years: women, men, Jews, Catholics, working class individuals, the Racism Task Force, and Wonderful Older Women.

Has the Life Center succeeded as a community? Member Lynne Shivers thinks so:

Reflecting on our twelve-year history, we see that the community has released a great deal of energy and imagination among its members. We have supported and challenged each other to be whole people, responsible to ourselves and others and to society as a whole. We have learned that living in a community takes discipline, commitment, energy, and a willingness to solve problems. Yet, we are pleased and proud that we have created a lively political community that continues to develop initiatives and be part of the nonviolent U.S. social change movement.

COMMUNITIES OF RELIGIOUS CONCERN

YOUR OWN PLACE OF WORSHIP

University Christian Church (Disciples of Christ) of Hyattsville, Maryland, is a church that pays a lot of attention to the creation of community —both within the 110 family, integrated membership and in their surrounding area.

Within the church, half of those who attend services also attend adult Sunday School, with class topics ranging from traditional Bible study to self-improvement to Jesus Christ Superstar to a ten-week series on simple living. There are three different monthly sets of social events: a dinner potluck, an "after-dinner potluck," and season-oriented events, such as square dances and Thanksgiving dinners. There is a Mother's Club with monthly programs, such as on speech development and on when to call the doctor, and a Father's Club was recently formed.

When the federal government cut back basic health services for women, infants, and children, the church opened its doors to an evening clinic, aimed at filling the gap. Church members volunteer their help at the clinic, along with other members of an interdenominational service group.

Church members also continue their fifteen-year outside involvement in a recreational program at a "reform school" for boys from nearby Washington, D.C., and visit two local nursing homes once each week, bringing refreshments and various recreational programs.

Judy Torgerson, mother of three young children and a church elder, is proud of her church's service commitment as well as its internal strength. "We put our focus on making visitors welcome," she says—a deceptively simple statement that provides an important key to the nurturing of community.

COMMUNITY AND CREATIVE NONVIOLENCE

Some of the work of Washington, D.C.,'s Community for Creative Non-Violence has already been described in Chapter III. But what is the meaning of "community" in their name? Why are they a community, and how do they live together, work together, make decisions together?

Mary Ellen Hombs came to the community twelve years ago with a feeling that participation in mass demonstrations did not give expression to the deep religious basis of her opposition to the Vietnam War. She found that "people working and living together was the answer," an uncommon interpretation of the Christian Gospel's mandate that two or more people must come together to feel the presence of the Holy Spirit. This principle forms the core of the community, which now includes people of many (and no) religious backgrounds, black and white, people who were successful businessmen and suburban housewives as well as convicts and people who have been poor all their lives. A basic belief in nonviolence is the only membership requirement.

The community numbers thirty to forty-five, half of which have been members at least two years, a quarter at least five years. Many first come for food or shelter; many come to give a summer, a semester, a year of their lives; some arrive and leave the same day; some come for a week and are still there two years later.

Mary Ellen observes that "it is not easy, physically or mentally, to stay in the community a long time." Besides running their seven-day-a-week kitchen, drop-in centers and infirmary, the community undertakes intense campaigns for months at a time involving vigils, fasting, and civil disobedience. Nobody has outside employment; long-term members receive room, board, clothing, and minimal personal expenses entirely from donations. All live in three households, with twenty-four in the largest house, which has nine bedrooms.

Short-term members who have some money can at first have difficulty understanding a long and emotional discussion about finding a way for a West Coast member to visit her family or why some community members cannot join them for an "inexpensive" social event. The community tries hard to involve all who offer their work in the entire spectrum of their activities as well as fully involving them in the consensus decision-making process. This can bring a rapid understanding of the community's work and basis, as well as offering an opportunity for each new member to express his or her gifts and to contribute new insights. All major and minor decisions are made by consensus of all community members, with the exception of any who may withdraw from considering a particular question because they feel they are not sufficiently knowledgeable or will not be there to experience the consequences.

How could a group who is inspired by CCNV begin to explore its own possibilities? Mary Ellen stresses that the "most central thing is working together in some way, having a commitment to work that allows you to begin to transcend the personal differences in the group and to begin to get an overriding sense of thinking in community terms." For her, that initial sense has remained: "Why I'm here now is why I was here the first day. The kinds of things I can do in community that are impossible to do individually are what keeps me here. I found a place I could put all the parts of me together and have them mean something."

RAPHAEL HOUSE—MORE THAN SHELTER

From 1971 to 1976, the sisters and brothers of the Holy Order of MANS ran Raphael House, then San Francisco's only shelter for women and children, as most shelters are run: dinner, breakfast, out in the streets for the daytime, with a limit of three nights. When they lost their building (which was razed for a parking lot), they had an opportunity to evaluate whether their work was truly providing the service needed by homeless families. They decided the new Raphael House would have to be a place where entire families could stay long enough to make a difference, until they had a decent place to live, a source of income, or both. They have also created a community that provides for needs other than simple shelter and food.

In 1977, the new Raphael House opened in a renovated hospital. Forty-six brothers and sisters of the ecumenical Christian order live in the house, along with up to fifty people who need shelter—pregnant women, women with children, men with children, and whole families. Over half are there due to marital difficulties, including domestic violence; the rest have a variety of financial problems. Although Raphael House shelters around five hundred people per year, 74 percent of families who apply are turned away due to lack of space. A typical stay is at least one month and often as much as two months, as a family saves enough money for a rent deposit. Assistance with basic furniture, blankets, and kitchen utensils is provided to help the family get a reasonable start.

The brothers and sisters accept new Raphael House residents as part of their community. Everyone eats the same food together in cheerful dining rooms, where both permanent and temporary residents share the chores. Children are cared for while a parent is looking for work or housing; counseling and other referrals are provided by professional brothers and sisters, as well as outside psychologists and lawyers. Residents are welcome to attend religious services, but are not expected to do so.

Raphael House is financially possible only through vows of commitment to voluntary poverty, which the order also calls voluntary simplicity and holy simplicity. The members live very simply and do all the work required for the maintenance of the house themselves. Eight sisters and brothers work at outside jobs and turn their salaries over to support the rest of the brothers and sisters, with an annual surplus being donated to the house. All salaries and profits from Brother Juniper's Breadbox, a small restaurant on the premises, are similarly used. Residents pay a fee covering about one-fourth to one-third of the actual cost of shelter, food, and other services; the remainder is made up through individual contributions and foundation grants for special projects, such as building renovations.

Many former Raphael House residents remain in contact through participation in one or more activities: sewing groups for basic clothing and children's gifts; a pottery workshop; weekly parenting groups, which deal with subjects ranging from budgeting to nonviolent discipline of children; seasonal picnics and holiday celebrations.

With three hundred elderly tenants living in the same block, Raphael House organized a Neighborhood Senior Association, which aims at bringing "the missing part of the family" into the community. There are chamber music concerts, a sewing group, a community college creative writing class, and Sunday afternoon teas. Some of the older people enjoy giving potluck lunches on the roof garden for the children; others sew items that are sold at an annual fund-raising bazaar they organize and sponsor for the house. Another service that especially benefits the elderly is Brother Juniper's Breadbox, an inexpensive public restaurant that serves homemade soups and enormous half-sandwiches, providing a place to socialize, meet neighbors, and find help in crisis situations.

One mother who has been sheltered described her feelings about the community this way:

At first, I was scared but they really made me feel at ease and helped me out a lot. I've made a lot of friends—we're like one big family. I think that's what helped me the most. I've learned a lot about myself and others staying here. I've got more self confidence and don't put myself down like I used to.[2]

POLITICAL AND SOCIAL CHANGE COMMUNITIES

DEATH AND TAXES

The "affinity group" developed as a basic unit of the 1970s movement against nuclear power; it has spread as a form of organization to numerous movements of the 1980s. Affinity groups most often form to support persons who engage in civil disobedience: blockading the gate of a military base, occupying a nuclear power plant site, blocking traffic to protest evictions. Most affinity groups contain ten to twenty people and are generally affiliated with one or more umbrella organizations. In California, for example, such organizations (and their issues) are the Abalone

Alliance (nuclear power and safe energy), the Livermore Action Group (nuclear weapons), the Vandenberg Action Coalition (MX missiles), and the Port Chicago Campaign (American military involvement in Central America).

Those being arrested make tactical decisions together and support each other in and out of jail. Other affinity group members observe police actions during the arrests, do follow-up legal and political work, and help the families of those in jail deal with the situation. Many affinity groups continue to do political work together after the particular action for which they were formed is over; some go even further and become ongoing, close-knit communities.

Death and Taxes is an affinity group community whose activities span all four of the above organizations—and more. It is hardly a typical affinity group; rather their first six months together shows the range of possibilities open to twenty women and men, age twenty-three to thirty-eight, who are passionately concerned with this wide variety of issues.

Death and Taxes formed in January 1983, after the Vandenberg Action Coalition had called for a blockade of the roads leading to Vandenberg Air Force Base, where the MX nuclear missile was to be tested. Members were concerned about panic reactions within the coalition about the possibility of being shot at the base and wanted to act to quiet the fears as well as to call attention to the quality of base security. After camping for two days in thirteen inches of rainfall, they (together with members from two other affinity groups) scaled the base fence. They then put a special personal item each had brought symbolic of peace and transformation from war into the center of a circle and joined hands in a spiritual ceremony. Following the ceremony, they hiked cross-country toward a group of Minuteman missile silos, which were being retrofitted to contain first-strike-capability nuclear weapons. Amazingly, they reached their goal despite a line of military personnel blocking their way; members walked between the soldiers, walked up to the missile silos, and wrote peace messages on them. They were arrested only after leaving a second set of silos and were released the same night after being "banned" from the base.

In February, Death and Taxes acted on its own. In order to protest the maneuvers of American troops on the Honduras/Nicaragua border, nine members chained themselves to all the front doors of the San Francisco Federal Building one early Thursday morning. They spent five days in jail and were released with "time served" on Monday in the face of a packed courtroom.

In March, two affinity group members joined fifteen to twenty other people—including former electroshock patients—in blockading the entrance of Herrick Hospital in Berkeley, which continues to administer electroshock as a psychiatric treatment; about eight to ten other members attended to support the action. Those arrested were released within several hours.

In June, most of Death and Taxes returned to Vandenberg Air Force Base. Their object: to prevent the first test firing of the MX by being a continuous presence within the launch danger zone. Along with members of other affinity groups, never numbering more than fifty, they took turns observing the launch site for unusual activity from a hill just outside the base. They also went onto the base itself for one- to three-day periods, trying to get as close as possible to the launch pad while not being arrested.

Joe Johnston, who explained that their presence delayed the launch ten to fourteen days, observed that it is "very empowering to feel that such a small number of people can exert such a powerful influence." Only two Death and Taxes members were actually arrested; one received thirty days in jail and the other received five days.

Upon returning home, one member participated in a blockade of the Livermore Nuclear Weapons Laboratory and subsequently facilitated numerous jail meetings during a two-week sentence. Other members held several bake sales to raise funds for legal expenses.

In July, after President Reagan suddenly ordered all Nicaraguan consulates to close, Death and Taxes opened a symbolic Nicaraguan consulate in front of the vacated offices and passed out literature on Central American issues. Also in July, several members joined a blockade at Concord Naval Weapons Station, where weapons are shipped out of Port Chicago to Central America, and they spent several days in jail there.

Only one affinity group member is a student; most are craftspeople or hold "alternative" or political jobs that give them the flexibility to risk frequent arrest. Two members staff the statewide Abalone Alliance office, and other members have covered the office while they were participating in an action. All decision-making is by consensus. Member Cissy Wallace, who has done consulting work with governments and international agencies, states that her participation in Death and Taxes has "taught me something about building a different kind of society—one where everyone is equal." She feels she has "learned the meaning of personal empowerment." Equally notable, every person interviewed seven months after the group's formation used the words "friends," "love, "support," and "family" when speaking of the group. It was clear that these concepts are the basis of their strength and creativity.

A STRIKE COMMUNITY

What happens when you take a stand you feel you must take—and you find that traditional support communities, such as your neighbors and your church, have turned away from you? This is part of the story of the Willmar 8, eight bank tellers and bookkeepers who walked a picket line through two Minnesota winters because of their outrage at being asked to train a young inexperienced male to be their supervisor. The eight women of this small Minnesota city were churchgoers; none had previously been trade union members; one stated that she "had to look up the meaning of *feminism* in the dictionary."

An unusual film documentary on the Willmar 8, directed by Lee Grant, offers an opportunity to watch and discuss the reaction of these women's neighbors and church members, and the development among themselves of a strong and beautiful sense of community that allowed them to stand together for so long. The documentary is available from California Newsreel with a resource and discussion manual, including a special supplement for church groups. The sex discrimination issues the women struck about are discussed in the Chapter VI.

A LEARNING COMMUNITY

Highlander Center, located in New Market, Tennessee, is an extraordinary example of a learning community—a label often applied to "university communities" where caring and sharing is hard to find in giant lecture halls and set curricula. Highlander's history and methods are described in this excerpt from a letter (October 14, 1982) by Ronald Dellums and Andrew Young nominating the Highlander Center to receive the Nobel Peace Prize:

Founded in 1932 by Myles Horton, Highlander Center has realized for half a century the commonly unfulfilled responsibility of education for developing the dignity and equality of all people. It has played a central role in virtually every significant movement for social justice in the South—the worker-initiated labor union organizing in the 30's and 40's, the Civil Rights Movement in the 50's and 60's, and the struggle to overcome endemic poverty in Appalachia in the 70's and 80's. . . . For decades it was the only place in the South where Blacks and Whites could gather to learn, eat and live together as equals. . . .

The story of a song provides an example of how Highlander's influence spreads. In the 1940s two Black tobacco workers on strike in North Carolina brought to Highlander a spiritual they had been singing on the picket line. Zilphia Horton, Highlander's music director, recognized the power of that spiritual. With the help of folk singer Pete Seeger . . . she re-arranged the words and music to create "We Shall Overcome" as we know it today. . . . It has since spread around the world, inspiring people everywhere who are struggling for peace and social justice.

Humankind's quest for lasting justice and peace has proven to advance with agonizing gradualness. Mindful of this, Highlander, when it chooses a principal focus, commits its modest resources for a decade or more and develops strategies designed to move progressively towards its larger goals. It patiently lays the groundwork over many years, strengthening and spawning many organizations, developing networks among individuals and organizations working toward the same ends, and always relating the possibilities of a given moment to long-range objectives.

. . . In the 1960s, when Highlander turned its primary attention away from civil rights and toward Appalachian poverty, only a small handful of groups in the area were working on the issue. Today over fifty community organizations are banded together into a strong coalition—the Appalachian Alliance. . . .

How much progress toward social justice and peace in the South and across the United States would never have occurred, were it not for Highlander? We can never know, and that is how this modest little-known democratic institution in the mountains of Tennessee prefers it.

Highlander is not shy, however, about explaining its methods—methods that are heavily committed to creating community. The Highlander staff is itself a community; they share child care, eat together about half the time, and make policy decisions together—everyone from the research director to the cook.

Education at Highlander takes place mostly in weekend and week-long workshops. Several group representatives from a number of communities that have the same problem—toxic waste dumps, for example—are invited to come together with staff members, who are initially viewed by many as "the experts." They are surprised to find that most workshops begin by setting up decision-making groups and by turning over control of scheduling, content, and format to the participants. Myles Horton explains why:

How do you help people grow? We don't think you help that person grow by giving them information, facts, teaching them techniques, training them to do something that *we* know is good for them. . . . What I try to do is give that person learning experiences that involve doing something with and for his fellow men, which he can analyze and learn from. . . .

People are socialized to think very little of themselves . . . so the first thing we have to do is show respect to those people, and show that we think they are people of worth. . . . They had always been told their experiences were not important. . . . We have to get them to talk about those experiences and analyze them. . . . Then it becomes a group experience, and they start learning from each other, the learning of the group of course is the old business of being more than the sum of the individuals—something happens when they start criticizing, analyzing, trying to understand each other, and trying to learn from each other.

Our experience is that we want a group of people who will go back and work together—people are struggling against odds that are insurmountable for one person, that's why they came together as a group. When they go back and start struggling, and the opposition comes in, most people aren't strong enough as individuals to withstand that opposition. It's a terrific sort of opposition—they threaten to fire them, threaten to run them out of the community, threaten to isolate them, so you've got to be strong to stand up to that. We deal with real tough problems, not just little petty reforms with nothing that anyone objects to.[3]

After workshop participants have shared and discussed their experiences, and perhaps been taught some basic research methods to find out additional information they may need, a Highlander staff member generally points out the need for them to take the rest of the members of their groups through a similar process when they return home, thus learning to work together as a community. Highlander's success shows that this lesson has been well learned.

MAKING DECISIONS BY CONSENSUS

In community, the means we use are an integral part of the ends we are seeking. How do we relate to one another and how do we make decisions in our communities?

In a consensus decision-making process, participants try to explore together and reach a common decision, rather than taking a majority vote. This can take time, especially when people are used to taking the approach of "winning" enough votes for one or another position. Particularly when concern is high and principled differences exist, consensus decision-making is something that has to be learned and practiced in order to be done well.

Members need to get to know and trust each other. How to use the skills each member brings and how to deal with high emotions and personality clashes is also important knowledge. In working toward successful consensus decision-making processes, a number of groups have found the following ideas helpful. These are discussed in more depth in *The Resource Manual for a Living Revolution:*

1. Start meetings with brief periods of "excitement sharing" in which members tell the group about something new or interesting that has occurred in their lives recently. People thus have the chance to get to know one another and to start on a positive note.

2. Decide the agenda and how time is to be used at the beginning of the meeting. This avoids the classic situation in which the first item on the agenda—no matter how unimportant—takes up 40 to 70 percent of the meeting time.

3. Take care of each other. Set aside regular times when group members can deal with their feelings toward one another and toward the group itself. We think better together if our heads are not all clogged up with old resentments, bad feelings, and uncertainties unrelated to the issue at hand.

4. Emotions are not always unrelated to the issue at hand—but it may be helpful to "allow" people to express them and to find out how they are affecting assessment of what should "rationally" be done. Try going around the circle twice: the first time, each person expresses only their emotions about the difficult choice; the second time, each person says what they think should be done. You may be surprised at the content of the eventual consensus.

5. When things start to drag or get bogged down, a short but active game or jumping up and down can get people's energy flowing and raise the level of interest. If a discussion gets very heavy and discor-

dant, don't be afraid to call a break. People can often work things out informally in ways that can't be handled while a meeting is under way.

6. The facilitator/chairperson should see to it that everyone gets to participate in discussion—even those who initially feel they have little or nothing to contribute. Shy people often need to be encouraged and talky ones helped to listen. Particularly if a group is large, it is often helpful to break into smaller groups to discuss an issue. This gives more opportunity for input from everyone.

7. Switch roles from meeting to meeting. All members should get a chance to facilitate or take notes. This approach encourages everyone to learn these skills and can help deal with any sexism or racism that might otherwise creep into choice of roles.

8. Have meeting evaluations. It is important for people to tell each other that they have done well; we give far too few compliments in this society. We also need to know where and how we can do better in the future.

9. Have fun together. People who do nothing but work together can easily get tired of each other's company.

10. Find ways of supporting one another outside of the area where you are working together. Taking time to listen to and enjoy each other is a good way to help build group solidarity and trust.

This is a very incomplete list, and none of these suggestions is a magic formula. They are simply a few ideas for working more effectively together in ways that emphasize our care for one another.

WHAT YOU CAN DO

1. If you are interested in figuring out what kinds of community are possible, the following questions may be useful:
   a. How do we practice community right now?
   b. What kinds of community exist around us?
   c. How would community help us be the people we want to be and live the kinds of lives we want to live?
   d. How can we begin to build community where we now live?
   e. Are we close to people we would like to build community with? What prevents us from moving ahead? Who are the people we trust? With whom do we have things in common? Does this help us define our community?

2. If you are interested in building community with particular people, the following questions might help you find out if there is a common understanding of the commitments involved:
   a. Would the members of your community share common principles, values, or spiritual beliefs (and practices)? What are they?
   b. Would members share a common life-style or standard of living?

   c. How would you make decisions? How would leadership roles be distributed? How would tasks be distributed?

   d. How much diversity of age, ethnic or socioeconomic background, and other characteristics would you seek or accept?

   e. What commitments would the community ask of people who seek to join? What is your minimal expectation for the community (without which you leave, or it dissolves, or it is something different)? What is the community's expectation of you?

   f. What are the most important things for community members to agree on? Would you join the community as you have described it? If not, what else would you need?

3. If you are interested in evaluating the feelings and process within an existing community, the following questions may be useful. These questions do not assess the more concrete accomplishments and programs of a community:

   a. How are people *feeling* about the community and group interaction?

   b. Is personal competitiveness among group members a problem? Is cooperation a reality?

   c. Do you have a few "leaders" or does everyone pull his or her weight?

   d. Do you often have meetings that are all talk and no action?

   e. Have you tried consensus decision-making? If so, how is it working? Do a few people always get their way?

   f. How are differences of opinion and personal conflicts handled within the group?

   g. How open can group members be about doubts, differences, personal feelings of weakness, etc.?

   h. How much time do you spend on personal caring and sharing with one another in addition to project or work activity?

NOTES

1. "Interview with David Haenke," *Planet Drum*, no. 4 (Winter 1982), p. 3.
2. *Tenderloin Times* 7, no. 8 (August 1983), p. 7.
3. From a transcript of a living-room conversation (November 5, 1981) with Myles Horton, attended by several of the authors and the editor.

SOURCES OF FURTHER INFORMATION

Groups Mentioned in Chapter

Abalone Alliance. 2940 16th Street, San Francisco, Calif. 94103.

Community for Creative Non-Violence. 1345 Euclid Street, N.W., Washington, D.C. 20009.

Highlander Center. New Market, Tenn. 37820.

Livermore Action Group. 3126 Shattuck Avenue, Berkeley, Calif. 94703.
Philadelphia Life Center/Movement for a New Society. 4722 Baltimore, Philadelphia, Pa. 19143.
Port Chicago Campaign. c/o AFSC, 2160 Lake Street, San Francisco, Calif. 94118.
Raphael House. 1065 Sutter Street, San Francisco, Calif. 94109.
Vandenberg Action Coalition. c/o Livermore Action Group, 3126 Shattuck Avenue, Berkeley, Calif. 94703.
Willmar 8. Film available from: California Newsreel, 630 Natoma Street, San Francisco, Calif. 94103.

Additional Resource Groups

The Barter Project. 1214 16th Street, N.W., Washington, D.C. 20036. Technical assistance to groups.
Community Alternatives Society. 1937 West 2nd Avenue, Vancouver, B.C. V6J 1J2. Canadian co-op housing and co-op development.
Institute for Local Self-Reliance. 1717 18th Street, N.W., Washington, D.C. 20009. Newsletter. Promotes urban neighborhood self-reliance and self-determination.
Neighborhood Services Project, American Friends Service Committee, Middle Atlantic Region. 317 East 25th Street, Baltimore, Md. 21218. Seeks to strengthen neighborhoods that are experiencing racial or ethnic conflict.

Bibliography

On Communities

Adams, Frank, with Myles Horton. *Unearthing Seeds of Fire: The Idea of Highlander.* Winston Salem, N.C.: John F. Blair, 1975.
Chapman, Paul. *Clusters: Life Style Alternatives for Families and Single People.* Stoughton, Mass.: Packard Manse. Available from: Alternatives, Box 1707, Forest Park, Ga. 30051. $3 + 15 percent postage.
Communities: A Journal of Cooperative Living. Monthly. Available from: c/o Twin Oaks, Box 426, Louisa, Va. 23093.
Community Publications Cooperative. *A Guide to Cooperative Alternatives.* 1979. Available from: Box 426, Louisa, Va. 23093. $5.95.
Goodman, Paul, and Percival Goodman. *Communitas: Means of Livelihood and Ways of Life.* New York: Vintage, 1960.
Journal of Community Communications. Box 996, Berkeley, Calif. 94701. $9/yr. individuals, $15 institutions.
Kriyananda, Swami. *Cooperative Communities: How to Start Them and Why.* Berkeley, Calif.: Ananda Publications, 1972.
Morris, David, and Karl Hess. *Neighborhood Power: The New Localism.* Boston: Beacon Press, 1975.
Raimy, Eric. *Shared Houses, Shared Lives.* Boston: Houghton Mifflin, 1979.
Whitney, Norman J. *Experiments in Community: Ephrata, Amish, Doukhobors, Shakers, Bruderhof, and Monteverde.* Wallingford, Pa.: Pendle Hill Publications, 1983.
Zablocki, Benjamin. *The Joyful Community: An Account of the Bruderhof, A Communal*

Movement Now in Its Third Generation. Chicago: University of Chicago Press, 1980.

On Group Process/Organizing†

Biagi, Bob. *Working Together: A Manual for Helping Groups Work More Effectively.* 1978. Available from: Citizen Involvement Training Project, c/o Univ. of Mass., Amherst, Mass. 01003. $6.

Center for Conflict Resolution. *Building United Judgement: A Handbook for Consensus Decision-making.* Philadelphia: New Society. $5.95.

Center for Conflict Resolution. *A Manual for Group Facilitators,* 2nd ed. Philadelphia: New Society, $5.

Coover, Virginia, et al. *Resource Manual for a Living Revolution,* rev. ed. Philadelphia: New Society, 1981. $7.95.

Doyle, Michael, and David Straus. *How to Make Meetings Work.* New York: Jove Pubns.: 1977.

Fisher, Roger, and William Ury. *Getting to Yes: Negotiating Agreement Without Giving In.* Boston: Houghton Mifflin, 1981.

Lakey, Berit. *Meeting Facilitation: The No Magic Method.* Philadelphia: New Society, 1975. 50¢

Rosenberg, Marshall. *A Model for Nonviolent Communication.* Philadelphia: New Society, 1983. $3.95.

Taylor, Richard K. *Blockade! Guide to Nonviolent Intervention.* Maryknoll, N.Y.: Orbis Books, 1977.

Training/Action Affinity Group. *Building Social Change Communities.* Philadelphia: New Society, 1979. $3.95.

Woodrow, Peter. *Clearness: Processes for Supporting Individuals and Groups in Decision-Making.* Philadelphia: New Society, 1976. $1.75.

---

†Many of the books in this section are published and/or distributed by New Society Publishers, a collective discussed in the chapter text. Books are available from 4722 Baltimore Ave., Philadelphia, Penn. 19143, at indicated price plus postage: $1, first book; 40¢ /additional book.

CHAPTER V

Aging and Elders

QUERIES

1. Are there programs in my community that allow elders to remain independent? If I could instantly initiate one, what would it be?
2. Is there a specific age at which I think other people (or myself) are no longer able to work? Learn new things? Have fun? Enjoy sexual relationships? What is that age and why do I feel this way?
3. Do I think people much younger than I are too inexperienced or immature to make good judgments? On what do I base this opinion?
4. Do I have friendships with people more than five to ten years younger than I? More than five to ten years older than I? If not, why not?
5. Whatever my age, have I written an autobiography that looks at my life's experiences and accomplishments at various life stages? Have I shared this information with my family and friends?
6. Do the media tell us there is a "best" age to be? Do I spend money or hours of my life simply trying to look older or younger than I am?
7. Am I retired with inadequate income? Will I be retired with inadequate income? Does "living simply" speak to these questions? Do federal and state government programs speak to these questions? Does building strong "alternative communities" speak to these questions?
8. Can older people make a special contribution to transforming our communities and the world?
9. How can younger people assist older people who are facing some special problems of aging, such as chronic illness, isolation, and vulnerability to crime?
10. How can older people assist younger people with family problems, problems of self-identity, or problems of "learning the ropes" in work or in political activities?
11. How can elders build support groups to help handle their special problems?

"THE BEST AGE IS THE AGE YOU ARE"

What is aging? The Gray Panthers, an intergenerational organization whose motto is "Age and Youth in Action," think of aging as "growth during the total life span from birth to death in personal development, social involvement, and self-fulfillment."

This is a very different view from the dominant one in our society, which equates a worthwhile life with being young and acting young. This view is very useful for the promotion of a variety of commercial products and for justifying the discarding of older workers to live out the remainder of their "worthless" lives at poverty-level incomes. It is a view that is extremely damaging to the older person, who, in addition to experiencing more obvious forms of discrimination, comes to feel increasingly worthless and superfluous to the workings of society. It is also a view that is extremely damaging to people of all ages: it stifles honest and open communication between generations, and it can keep people from making important changes in their lives because they feel they are "too old" —even if they have just celebrated their thirtieth birthday. It can also keep older people from asking for or getting the help they need: if one has to ask for help in lifting a heavy box, one is no longer an "independent person"; if one is a "sensitive" younger person, help will not be offered for fear of suggesting that the older person is "over the hill." Our society's whole view of aging sets up a dynamic of pretense, falsity, and dishonesty that can be hard to break through.

One reason this breakthrough is difficult is our extreme age stratification. Children in school are discouraged from playing with or learning from children even one grade older or younger; housing is stratified into singles' neighborhoods, family neighborhoods, old people's housing; social groupings often limit themselves to a span of a decade at most, even when the possibility exists in the neighborhood or the workplace for interaction across generations. This isolation hurts people of all ages by limiting the variety of views and experiences available to them. It especially hurts older people who become increasingly isolated as their peers begin to die and who may end up "without a friend in the world."

The stereotypes connected with aging are also damaging. Dr. Alex Comfort observes that

if we insist that there is a group of people which, on a fixed calendar basis, becomes unintelligent, asexual, unemployable, and crazy, the people so designated will be under pressure to be unintelligent, asexual, unemployable, and crazy.[1]

Despite the pressure to conform to these stereotypes, most older people resist. It comes as a surprise to many younger *and* older people that 89 percent of people over age sixty-five live totally self-sufficiently in the community. Seven percent are confined to their beds or homes, and only

4 percent are institutionalized.[2] So *the* problem of aging is not nursing homes (although nursing home conditions certainly present many problems).

Many older people continue to work for pay full- or part-time. Many others, as they have more time, increase their activity in the community's political affairs or pursue classes, such as writing, astronomy, or European history. A large number do hours of essential volunteer work per week in programs at hospitals, food distribution centers, emergency shelters, or telephone crisis lines, serving people of all ages. But not all the statistics are positive, especially for elderly minorities and women.

For example, a comprehensive poll conducted by Louis Harris & Associates found that

in every problem area except one (not enough education), the elderly black feel far more burdened by very serious problems than do the elderly white. They report more fear of crime (twice as much as the white group); more poor health; more than three times as many say not having enough money to live on is a serious problem. The same proportions are shown in respect to not having enough medical care when compared to the white group.[3]

Over half of the women over sixty-five are widowed, and one-third live alone, as compared to one in seven men over age sixty-five. In addition to isolation, these women face a heavy financial burden: 80 percent of retirement age women have no access to pensions; one-third of all widows have incomes below official poverty levels, and less than 10 percent of widows receive pension survivor benefits.[4] The quality of survivors' benefits is a point that does not occur to many younger people when they negotiate union contracts, evaluate an employer's pension plan, or make decisions about putting money into the bank for use after retirement. But it may become a matter of economic survival for one's much-loved spouse and can seriously diminish the quality of his or her remaining lifetime.

The quality of "life after retirement" is also very much determined by one's view of it. Wonderful Older Women, a support collective of the Philadelphia Life Center, points out that "elders are taken seriously and respected for their role if they believe they have a role. One must continue to believe one has a continuing role as a person." But age is not the only factor that affects the feeling of whether one is being taken seriously. The same Harris poll cited above observed that

One in ten of those 65 and over feel they have specific skills which no one gives them a chance to use. This feeling exists not only among the retired; a like number of those still employed feel they have unused skills. However, this is not a problem exclusive to older Americans; many others in our society feel they have no chance to use present skills or would like the chance to learn new ones.[5]

The rest of this chapter will deal with this essential question of usefulness, control, and dignity, as well as with the economics of aging and the

ways in which people of all ages can support each other and learn from
each other. Our philosophy behind the question of how to "take charge"
of our aging is well-expressed by Kathleen Lammers, San Francisco Gray
Panthers' staff person: "People have the right to a life of dignity from the
moment they enter this planet to the moment they leave this planet."

ECONOMICS AND AGING WITH DIGNITY

As of 1983, Social Security, Medicare, and Medicaid, all basic programs
that provide economic sustenance to older people, were under massive
attack from both governmental and private sources. Since most of the
national and regional organizations that represent elders were already
working actively on these issues, we choose to deal in this section with
smaller-scale actions being taken in various communities by elders who
are taking charge of their economic predicaments. In doing this, we have
no intention of minimizing the crucial importance of the Social Security,
Medicare, and Medicaid fight, but rather wish to share with people additional approaches that may be available in the areas of work, food, medicine, and housing.

WORK

Many people look forward to retirement with eagerness and with plans
for new projects and pursuits. A thirty-six-year-old relative of the editor
can tell you at any moment how many years, months, weeks, and days are
left until her retirement at age sixty-five. On the other hand, many older
people enjoy their work and would like to continue a full- or part-time
schedule past an arbitrary retirement date, either at the same job or in
a different line of work. Many others, despite very simple living styles, are
unable to cover their basic financial needs from Social Security payments
that reflect a lifetime of low-paying jobs.

Age-discrimination in employment has a number of reasons and
manifestations. Some employers prefer to fire (illegally) or retire an older
worker early (at a lower pension) whose pay has increased with seniority
and hire a younger worker at a lower salary. Some assembly lines are
timed so only the youngest and most physically fit workers can handle the
speed; the General Motors assembly plant at Lordstown is famous for
having workers whose average age is in their twenties. Workers who can't
make the pace quit from exhaustion or are fired. More subtle discrimination results from the stereotypes discussed earlier in this chapter, where
older people themselves, as well as their employers, may assume they can
no longer do a good job simply because of their age.

There are agencies in a number of communities that place older people
who have lost their jobs, wish to change jobs, or have been forced to retire
in both full- and part-time positions—but that task will never be easy until
employers are both convinced and required to disregard age in making

hiring choices. One employer whose special efforts may help others to make this transition voluntarily is Texas Refinery Corporation, a manufacturer of heavy-duty lubricants and protective coatings. Over 20 percent of the company's nationwide sales force are sixty-five or older, and nearly 20 percent of the company's newly hired salespersons are over sixty. Many work full-time, but they also have the option of part-time schedules.

Texas Refinery's sixty-five-year-old president, Wesley Sears, explained the policy as "just good business. Over the years our older salespeople have provided us with many millions of dollars of profitable sales. In a way, you might say that we have helped them. But we don't look at it this way. We work with many older individuals because we have found they help us."

The age of these salespeople is especially surprising to many, including customers, because the job often involves climbing on roofs in order to assess the particular materials necessary for each building. One seventy-year-old salesman commented, "It scares the heck out of me when they grab ahold of me and hang on . . . helping me over ladders because they think I need the assistance!"

Hopefully, more employers will become convinced to hire older workers by examples such as Texas Refinery, but it hasn't happened yet. A salesperson in his eighties commented, "The good thing about Texas Refinery is that they give the older workers like me a chance to prove they have these qualities [of self-confidence and ability]. Most companies wouldn't even talk to me."

FOOD

Many people, particularly elders, have diets that are inadequate in calories or essential vitamins or food types—while much edible food goes to waste. The Grey Bears of Santa Cruz, California, an organization of people over age sixty, is determined to put an end to wasted food while helping its members to obtain a decent diet.

The project started when some young college students discovered their garden had produced more than they could use and decided to donate the surplus to older people who needed the food. From this beginning, the Grey Bears now collect, pack, and distribute 4,000 bags of food per week to their 4,000 members; 700 more are on the waiting list until capacity can be expanded. Only four paid staff members, plus numerous volunteers, do all the necessary work to distribute 2.5 million pounds of food annually at 37 distribution sites, as well as to make 400 home deliveries to shut-ins.

A major source of food is gleaning from the fields of commercial growers. Each day that the weather is suitable, twenty to thirty members pick produce for about an hour and a half that otherwise would have been plowed under or discarded. An example is lettuce that does not fit to a

standard size of twenty-four per box. Growers were reluctant to cooperate, until one major grower tried the program and recommended it to the
others.

Some of the produce picked is distributed in Santa Cruz County, but
quite a bit is traded with food banks in surrounding communities: lettuce
for melons, broccoli for outdated muffins. In this way, all the counties
achieve a variety in their grocery bags. Outdated food is also collected
from supermarkets, and many area residents donate the crop from their
gardens' fruit trees to Grey Bears pickers.

Joan Roberts, associate director of the Grey Bears, explained that they
have "a strong commitment to recycling and to not waste anything." This
commitment has become a major source of the group's fund-raising.
Members do extensive recycling of newspapers, glass, aluminum, and
cardboard, and collect usable items for rummage sales—in addition to
raising funds from private contributions and state, county, and city agencies. Roberts also feels that the work fills needs other than nutrition and
conservation: "Members enjoy the physical activity in a noncompetitive
atmosphere, and also are able to be with a community of people who
share the same needs and concerns."

DRUG AND MEDICAL COSTS

The National Gray Panthers have a goal "to build . . . a new and just
economic system which will transcend the profit motive, eliminate the
concentration of corporate power, and serve human needs through democratic means." The North Coast Gray Panthers's comprehensive health
care campaign seems a good example of an approach that may help
achieve this goal.

In 1981, the North Coast Gray Panthers (of mostly rural Humboldt and
Del Norte Counties, California) decided to take on what Convener Bill
Landis calls "the Four Horsemen of Economic Ruin: doctor's fees, hospi-
tal costs, drug costs, and Medi-gap costs."

They began with a survey of pharmacy prices and discovered wide
discrepancies for the same drug, as well as pharmacies that were not
complying with the state law that requires telephone quotation of prescription prices. Pharmacies were also found that were not helpful with
substitution of less expensive "generic" drugs (see Chapter VIII) con-
taining the same formula as "brand-name" prescriptions.

Two years later, prescription prices have become much more equalized
in the counties, and a follow-up survey continues to keep residents on top
of the situation. In the meantime, the Gray Panthers moved on to the full
range of related problems, with surveys comparing charges by medical
laboratories, by local hospitals, and, more recently, by funeral directors.
They were joined in this last survey by the local Senior Resource Center
and the Retired Senior Volunteer Program. The local Panther chapter is
also active in the national organization's campaign to preserve and im-

prove Medicare and Medicaid coverage, and has distributed information comparing the costs of "Medi-gap insurance," insurance to cover the costs Medicare increasingly doesn't.

The Gray Panthers' activities have had a strong impact, which was recently underlined when the county's medical society formed a committee to meet with them about finding solutions to the county's medical problems. Since the Panthers are a multigenerational organization, one of the major issues they are discussing is how to get medical assistance for the "new poor" of all ages, the numerous unemployed of the area. As a result, some doctors have offered to provide low-cost and free services as necessary.

HOUSING

The financial, social, and emotional aspects of housing for elders are deeply intertwined. Seventy percent of older people own their homes, and most of the rest have also lived in the same place for many years. When incomes shrink at retirement, half-empty houses or apartments can be difficult to maintain and pay for; this issue becomes particularly difficult after the death of a spouse. Despite social attitudes that often pressure them to "move to a smaller place" or move in with relatives, most people wish to remain in their own homes, or at least in their own communities. It is especially important to consider these issues carefully when one has lots of time, rather than feeling pressured to act quickly after a death or a severe change in financial circumstances.

Several approaches to these issues are discussed in Chapter III. One example is subsidized housing specially built by a community organization. Another approach for elderly poor homeowners is Maintenance Central in Detroit, a service that can do basic home maintenance.

A third approach, which goes beyond commonly accepted ideas, is shared housing, either by age peers or intergenerational. Although the potential for house-sharing is enormous, it is taking time for it to gain acceptance in a society where both privacy lines and age lines have been strongly drawn. There are cultural differences in the present degree of openness toward house-sharing: a study in the Los Angeles area found minority elders, and especially blacks, more favorable toward house-sharing than "Anglos."[6]

If we are able to involve people of all ages actively in our long-term work to create strong communities with institutions that make human sense, the "special problem" of housing our elders may no longer seem different from that of creating housing that meets the needs of everyone.

INDEPENDENCE, CONTROL, AND DIGNITY

In addition to being able to afford food, medicine, and housing, we need to be able to understand and control our relationship with them.

Being in good physical and mental health is one of the most important requirements for independent living. When we have some difficulties with health or stamina, a bit of the right kind of physical help, access to good transportation, or use of medications in the right manner and quantity can restore the ability to live independently.

The Health Support Council for Capitol Hill Seniors, of Denver, Colorado, sponsors a variety of programs that deal with these issues. A primary focus is information: since 1975, over sixty forums have been held on subjects such as Nutrition, Hearing Aids, How to Stay Well with Daily Exercise, and Health Insurance: How much do you Need? The group's definition of health subjects is broad: a 1982 forum, Our Health and the Air We Breathe, featured a doctor from the University of Colorado Department of Preventive Medicine and the chairman of the Colorado Air Quality Control Commission. A large variety of class series have been offered, including a "worry clinic," yoga, CPR training, "coping support groups," a psychology class on "living, values, and remembering," and a writing class on "reminiscing for the past and present." Capitol Hill neighborhood residents keep informed of these programs and a variety of useful health information through the *Sta-Well News*, the group's regular publication.

One particularly interesting approach to independent living sponsored by the Health Support Council was a pilot program that demonstrated the effectiveness of an occupational therapist. Ethlyn Christensen, who was the organization's president for six years, explained that the need and potential became clear to her when she broke her kneecap. The doctor sent her home, stating he was sure she "could manage," but without any assistance or advice about how to make needed adjustments. She set to work with the hope of helping others fare better than she did, and in 1978 and 1979, the Health Support Council received funding from state agencies for an occupational therapist to teach injured elders how to maintain themselves at home. The therapist also pinpointed difficulties in the home that are particularly dangerous for older people and helped make changes that would prevent future accidents. Though this program was extremely successful, and some similar services are now offered by another community agency, the Health Support Council has been unable to obtain further funding for this service due to federal and state budget cutbacks.

STAYING IN THE HOME

A variety of other programs have been tried in many communities to help older people stay out of institutions. A very simple one is "telephone reassurance," a regular phone call at the same time each day to make sure the recipient is okay. Another is the "home helper"—paid for by the individual, a community organization, or a government agency—who helps with housework or shopping. Some communities have groups of "shoppers," volunteers who either take older people shopping or shop for them as necessary. (See Chapter II for an example accomplished by inner-city teenagers.) "Meals on Wheels," funded by both private and government sources, has provided nutritious meals to shut-ins for a number of years, generally delivered by volunteers. An interesting variation of this arose in the neighborhood of the Philadelphia Life Center, when the program lost its government funding recently. A local church organized a number of groups of neighbors, each group responsible for cooking one meal per day for one person. An aluminum dish is provided so the recipient can either eat the meal when it is delivered by that day's cook or reheat it if she or he prefers to eat it at another time.

Even people who need quite a bit of assistance need not move to a nursing home. Group households of elders who together can hire a live-in helper (sometimes with outside financial assistance) are being tried, including quite a few in Florida. For shut-ins who either live alone or with a relative, adult day-care programs, long common in Scandinavia, have begun to develop in this country during the past few years. A person is transported to the day location several days per week, where he or she has an opportunity to make new friends, eat a good meal, do exercises, play cards, watch movies, and generally socialize with others. Such programs also restore independence and control to the person who has been providing care in the home.

Even when people can no longer stay in their homes, control over their environment need not be completely lost. A small percentage of nursing homes across the nation now have nursing home resident councils, where those who are able can either make suggestions about or actually control issues of food, scheduling, program, mistreatment by aides, outside trips, and staffing levels. Two organizations—the Association of Nursing Home Resident Councils and the National Citizens Coalition on Nursing Home Reform—provide support for and information about these efforts.

TRANSPORTATION

Lack of decent public transportation limits the lives of people of all ages. Even communities that have comprehensive service but high fares put similar limits on poorer people. This problem is especially difficult for elders who may be living on low Social Security payments and are no longer easily able to walk medium distances, especially if they are carrying groceries or library books.

In San Francisco, during a period when the basic bus fare has risen from 25 cents to 60 cents, a strong alliance of older people has kept fare for those over age sixty-five at 5 cents a ride. A monthly pass costs $2.50, and a yearly pass $25.00. BART, the interurban train linking a number of San Francisco Bay Area communities, also has a low, over-sixty-five fare of 10 percent of the normal ticket price. The success of these fares is particularly obvious at midday, when younger people find themselves in a minority on many transit lines.

Accessibility also becomes a problem in communities with poor public transit, in high crime areas, and where ailments make it hard to get on and off a bus. A variety of approaches have been tried: "kneeling" buses, dial-a-van, lower-cost taxi vouchers, volunteer ride givers. With the exception of modifications to buses themselves, a common problem with many of these approaches is that they are available only for food shopping or for doctor's appointments and not for "nonessential" trips, such as visiting a friend, attending religious services or a concert, or going to look at the ocean because it's a nice day. Unless our communities become more neighborhood-oriented, requiring less travel to enjoy the whole variety of life, equal access to transportation must be seen as a crucial issue for guaranteeing decent living for older people.

DRUG ABUSE

Drug abuse is a term usually reserved by older people for teenagers and "junkies"—but many are themselves unwitting victims of drug abuse.

This may happen in many ways: shyness about causing the doctor "too much trouble"; lack of understanding of how different medications may interact with each other and of the specific directions for their use; feeling unqualified to make a judgment as to one's need for a particular medication—feeling that one cannot question a doctor's opinion; receiving prescriptions from a number of different specialists who don't know what other medications one is already taking.

A doctor or a pharmacist often has an opportunity to catch any problems that result from prescription medications, but over-the-counter medications present particular drug abuse problems. Instead of "staying well with daily exercise" and eating decent meals, television and radio ads overencourage the use of laxatives for "irregularity" and the use of antacids and other medications for upset stomachs—not to mention one hundred different headache medications instead of increased friendships, a "worry clinic," or a "coping support group."

SRx, the San Francisco Department of Public Health's Senior Medication Education Program, is trying to make a dent in abuse of both prescription and nonprescription drugs. Founded in 1977, the program initially hoped to rely heavily on pharmacists for drug education. Although partially successful, especially when pharmacy student interns were available on-site, the program found that the business aspect of running a pharmacy tended to interfere both with the pharmacist's time and interest in patient education.

The program now works primarily in two areas: education of health-care providers to sensitize them to the most important problems, and direct education of older people. Program staff and pharmacy students might give a "mini-course" on a common problem, such as sleeping medications, or a more general talk on wise use of medications. The program has been fortunate to have instructors available who speak the many languages of local elders, including a number of Chinese dialects. The program has also relied on peer education: eight older volunteers formed the STEP Troupe (Senior Theatre Education Project), which presents one-act musical performances, such as "How to Stay Alive While Living," emphasizing the importance of patients taking responsibility for their own bodies.

Kathryn Eng, Program Director, estimates that 3,500 to 4,000 older San Franciscans have been directly reached by SRx's program, and 35,-000 through its broadly distributed educational materials. In addition to the problems mentioned above, two others she feels are often overlooked are "skimping" because of medication costs and nonrecognition of aspirin, alcohol, and cigarettes as drugs. Many health-care providers and many older people do not mention these at all when surveyed about drug use—until they are more carefully questioned.

As of September 1983, funding had just been received from a consortium of eight foundations to expand San Francisco's model program to six Bay Area counties. For other communities, the program has prepared a manual on how to develop a medication misuse program, including a history of what did and didn't work, sample questionnaires, and sample class outlines for both elders and health care providers (see Bibliography for ordering details).

SUPPORTING EACH OTHER/LEARNING FROM EACH OTHER

Many elders become increasingly isolated, both from their own peer groups and from other generations. Participation with groups and programs that offer companionship, understanding, intellectual stimulation, or the opportunity to help others can make the difference between a frightening feeling of helplessness and uselessness and a full, dignified continuation of one's life.

In July 1982, Gay and Lesbian Outreach to Elders (GLOE) began to address the special problems of the estimated twenty thousand gays and lesbians over the age of sixty who live in San Francisco. (There are similar programs in a number of cities, including Philadelphia and New York.) Stafford Buckley, one of two half-time GLOE staff persons, explained why the project started:

Those now over 60 grew up and had careers when being gay or lesbian was even less socially sanctioned than it is now. They were told they were bad people, and they felt they were bad people, and out of necessity most kept their sexual identity hidden. Now, living in a society that segregates both older people *and* gay people, as well as a society that denies that older people have any sexual orientation, they are at a great risk of isolation. They are not welcomed by their heterosexual age peers, and they are not welcomed by younger gays and lesbians.

Older gays and lesbians also run into special legal and medical problems. A long-time partner can be denied access to a hospital room or nursing home, or be denied the right to make important medical decisions or funeral arrangements permitted to "next-of-kin." Similarly, many older gays and lesbians have been rejected by most or all of their close relatives, and friendship networks that have taken the place of family may be denied visiting access by "family only" restrictions common for the seriously ill. Unless careful legal arrangements are made, a bank account that was intended to supplement a surviving partner's retirement income may go by inheritance laws to the same, estranged relatives.

The staff and a sizeable group of mostly younger volunteers offer counseling and work with other social service providers to make them sensitive to these issues. But most of GLOE's work is directed at breaking through the isolation surrounding gay and lesbian elders. Its main method of doing this is through an extensive program of group events: writing groups, drop-in rap groups, cooking groups, neighborhood rap groups, women's groups, as well as lunches and other social events. Despite an extensive gay and lesbian cultural network in San Francisco, these programs are publicized mostly through the mainstream press because older gays and lesbians are generally not part of that alternative network. Buckley observes, "For many, coming to something we sponsor is the first time they've ever been to a gay event."

After a year of operation, GLOE programs have over two hundred older participants. For those who are not able to get around easily, volunteers have started a "Friendly Visiting" program, using regular visits to go on an outing, run small errands, or to just sit and talk. (The Friendly Visitor program is an example of many programs that have followed the model of the New York International Ladies Garment Workers Union [ILGWU], which employs ninety Friendly Visitors, mostly retired, to visit almost thirty thousand retirees to offer companionship and assistance with Medicaid, Medicare, housing, health and social service information.)

One seventy-year-old lesbian woman made clear that GLOE's approach is working well: "I feel very close to many of the people, and I know that whatever happens, I won't be all alone. It's like having an extended family. That means a great deal to me, and I'm speaking from my heart."

EDUCATION

Older people, with more time to explore their interests, enthusiastically support a wide variety of educational programs. In many communities, these are on a small scale, such as the Health Support Council's classes, but they also range to the massive scale of New York City Community College's special offerings at sixty locations, which started when foreign-born Brooklyn elders asked for an English class "so we can talk to our grandchildren."

Many elders prefer to attend regular college classes, which, in the case of community colleges, are open on the same basis to people of all ages. The editor's father received an A.A. degree from a community college after retirement. The University of San Francisco (USF), a private institution, encourages elders to attend up to four classes per quarter taught by emeritus professors, at a charge of $150 for three quarters—or to audit regular classes. USF also has a unique library that collects the work of writers over age fifty, presently containing seven thousand manuscripts from over three thousand contributors around the world: mostly fiction, poetry, and autobiography. Besides being used by students, the library is made available to historians who may wish accounts of certain periods, such as World War I, and has become a resource for sociologists and anthropologists as well.

INTERGENERATIONAL STUDY

If older and younger people wish to get to know each other better, one way is to study together. In Sarasota, Florida, Gray Panthers have, for the past several years, conducted a study program with a local high school that recently won the Florida Educational Foundation's award for "Most Outstanding Program Between Youth and Aged."

The award-winning 1982–83 program covered three subject areas of mutual interest: Environmental Problems, Alcohol and Drug Abuse, and Growing Up in a Nuclear World. During the school year, the Gray Panther Interage Task Force and the Riverview High School Student Council met jointly once each month. In between meetings, fifteen to twenty Gray Panthers and fifteen to twenty students worked together on a continuing basis, gathering information on these subject areas and meeting with local people who had relevant expertise. The year culminated with an all-day Saturday workshop that involved about sixty Gray Panthers and one hundred and twenty students. Each workshop was given three times, so participants could attend all three if they wished.

More informal activities grew out of this association. The older and younger people have parties together, and the Panthers invite the high school students to accompany them on lobbying trips to their congressman. They also have invited students to attend local meetings on the city's health problems, pointing out that they and their parents also need health care. Growing out of this year's focus, students also began accompanying Gray Panthers to meetings of the local Coalition for a Nuclear Freeze.

Convener Clifford Carstedt is enthusiastic about plans to expand the program to additional high schools, although this will put a strain on Panther resources:

You can almost choose any problem you want, and find a joint interest. We find that the thinking of younger and older people is quite similar, which is sometimes startling to both parties. The older people start out thinking the kids are too immature, and the kids start out thinking the older people are too senile. When they find that both are bright and anxious to learn, this tends to tear down old barriers that we have built up in our culture. Expanding the program will be spreading the Gray Panthers a little thin, but we will just have to do it—it's extremely worthwhile.

Foster Grandparents

The Foster Grandparents is another intergenerational program with quite a different focus. It is a federally funded program of ACTION (which administers the Peace Corps) and has operated in many local communities since 1965. Other funding sources augment many of the local programs.

Poverty-level persons aged sixty and older are trained and employed four hours a day, five days per week to work with "high-risk" children: children who are ill, neglected, battered, emotionally disturbed, or mentally retarded. A Foster Grandparent typically gives two hours of individual attention to two children per day, usually at an institution, school, or day-care center. That individual attention may consist of "comfort and hugs; help with academic skills and/or school projects; a 'confidant' role for the child; time—to play games, read a story, admire a new achievement, or simply sit by while the child plays; a conversation with the past."[7]

In addition to emotional rewards, the program pays Grandparents $2.00 per hour, plus carfare and lunch. This stipend does not count as income for any purpose, so does not preclude eligibility for low-income programs.

OTHER APPROACHES

In addition to the Gray Panthers, there are a number of other national organizations with local affiliates that are active around issues affecting older people, mostly in the area of legislative lobbying. The largest is the American Association of Retired Persons (AARP). Also very large is the National Council of Senior Citizens (NCSC), an organization with numerous local affiliates throughout the United States, including retired members of particular union locals and "legislative councils" in various cities and states. The Older Women's League (OWL) lobbies in the areas of pension rights, employment discrimination, Social Security reform, access to health-care insurance, and respite care for women giving care to the chronically ill.

An older person need not be politically active as an "older person" or only on "older person" issues, as a number of the projects described elsewhere in this book make clear. The organizer of Domestic Workers Rights (see Chapter VI) is over sixty-five, and the Kansas Electric Shock Coalition (see Chapter IX) was spearheaded by both younger and older members of the Wichita Gray Panthers. Raphael House, now directed by a younger woman (see Chapter IV) was begun and shepherded for five years to its present status by an eighty-five-year-old woman. Different life stages may legitimately be marked by important differences—but age alone should never limit one's assessment of abilities, interests, and concerns.

WHAT YOU CAN DO

1. There are a number of different ways to approach a life review. These are some suggestions from the Reminiscing class given at the Health Support Council for Capitol Hill Seniors:
   a. Pick five events that shaped your life.
   b. Write about five "firsts" in your life (first kiss? first job?)
   c. Pick one or more of the following topics and trace its effects throughout your lifetime, from childhood to your present age: teachers, guests, cars, mountains, cooking, values, marriage, divorce, love, holidays, vacations, inventions, romance, solitude, fun, fear, friends, surprises, phone calls, food, work, play, bosses, illness, candy, dresses, suits, disillusionment, hobbies, encouragement, coats, hair, recipes, grandparents, secrets, sunrises, farms, cities, pets, houses, tears, triumphs, accomplishments, meals, lovers, spouses, airplanes, war(s), hugs, holding hands, schools, shopping, budgets, birthdays, life ambitions, money, religion, equality for women, laughter, health, physical fitness, children.
   d. Keep a journal. "As you begin to get into closer touch with who you *were,* your insights about who you are right now will need recording, will even demand jotting down!"
2. Take some time to examine choices you have made about contact with people of other generations. If you feel that your age contacts are too narrow, first consider individual choices that could make a difference: choice of housing or neighborhood; participation in volunteer work at a local school or at a program for elders; inviting your older or younger co-worker along on a picnic. Also consider what kinds of changes could be made by a few people: an intergenerational program at a local school; inviting a local organization of older people to participate in planning meetings for a neighborhood food co-op.
3. Examine the factors that determine whether you are or will be secure around retirement age: Social Security, pensions, savings; medical coverage; availability of help with physical disabilities; availability of human beings that care. What personal and political actions can you

make now to improve the picture? What trade-offs do particular choices imply? (Example: voluntarily choosing to earn less income now can mean lower Social Security payments, pensions, and savings; becoming part of a supportive, long-term community that is conscious of this problem could balance the loss of cash income.)

NOTES

1. Ronald Gross, Beatrice Gross, and Sylvia Seidman, eds., *The New Old: Struggling for Decent Aging* (Garden City, N.Y.: Anchor Press/Doubleday, 1978), p. 79.
2. Ibid., p. 9.
3. Ibid., p. 100.
4. Ibid., p. 51 (also, Older Women's League, membership pamphlet).
5. Ibid., p. 118.
6. Stephen R. McConnell and Carolyn E. Usher, *Intergenerational House-Sharing: Summary Report and Resource Manual,* Andrus Gerontology Center, University of Southern California, Los Angeles, Calif. 90007, October 1979, p. 4.
7. Brochure, Foster Grandparents program.

SOURCES OF FURTHER INFORMATION

Groups Mentioned in Chapter

American Association of Retired Persons. 215 Long Beach Boulevard, Long Beach, Calif. 90801.

Association of Nursing Home Resident Councils. C/o National Citizens Coalition on Nursing Home Reform, listed below.

Foster Grandparents. 806 Connecticut Avenue, N.W., Room M-1006, Washington, D.C. 20525.

Gay and Lesbian Outreach to Elders. 1853 Market Street, San Francisco, Calif. 94103.

Gray Panthers, National Office. 3635 Chestnut Street, Philadelphia, Pa. 19104.

Gray Panthers, North Coast (California) Chapter. 1910 California Street, Eureka, Calif. 95501.

Gray Panthers, Sarasota Chapter. C/o Clifford Carstedt, 6515 Waterford Circle, Sarasota, Fla. 33583.

Grey Bears. 1298 Fair Avenue, Santa Cruz, Calif. 95060.

Health Support Council for Capitol Hill Seniors. 1420 Ogden, Denver, Colo. 80218.

National Citizens Coalition on Nursing Home Reform. 1424 16th Street, N.W., Room 204, Washington, D.C. 20036.

National Council of Senior Citizens. 925 15th Street, N.W., Washington, D.C. 20005.

Older Women's League (OWL). 1325 G Street, N.W., Lower Level-B, Washington, D.C. 20005.

SRx. 101 Grove Street, Room 204, San Francisco, Calif. 94102.

University of San Francisco, Fromm Institute, Koret Living Library. 538 University Center, 2130 Fulton Street, San Francisco, Calif. 94117.

Additional Resource Groups

Americans for Better Care. Box 18820, Cleveland, Ohio 44118. Nursing home reform.

Economic Rights Project: Feminization of Poverty Conference, American Friends Service Committee, New York Regional Office. 15 Rutherford Place, New York, N.Y. 10003.

National Association of Meal Programs. Box 6959, Pittsburgh, Pa. 15212.

National Senior Citizens Law Center. 1424 16th Street, N.W., Suite 300, Washington, D.C. 20036.

Senior Action in a Gay Environment (SAGE). 208 West 13th Street, New York, N.Y. 10011.

Bibliography

Blau, Zena Smith. *Old Age in a Changing Society,* 2nd ed. New York: Franklin Watts, 1981.

Bolles, Richard N. *The Three Boxes of Life (And How to Get Out of Them).* Berkeley, Calif.: Ten-Speed Press, 1981.

Butler, Robert. *Why Survive? Being Old in America.* New York: Harper & Row, 1977.

Christensen, Alice, and David Rankin. *Easy Does It Yoga for Older People,* rev. ed. San Francisco: Harper & Row, 1979.

Comfort, Alex. *A Good Age.* New York: Simon & Schuster, 1978.

Cross, K. Patricia. *Adults as Learners: Increasing Participation and Facilitating Learning.* San Francisco: Jossey-Bass, 1981.

Curtin, Sharon. *Nobody Ever Died of Old Age: In Praise of Old People.* Boston: Little, Brown & Co, 1973.

DeBeauvoir, Simone. *The Coming of Age.* New York: Putnam, 1972.

Directory of Cooperative Living for Older Persons. Available from: c/o National Ministries, American Baptist Churches, Valley Forge, Pa. 19481.

Eng, Kathryn. *Preventing Geriatric Medication Misuse: A Manual for Developing a Model Program.* Available from: Department of Public Health, 101 Grove Street, Room 204, San Francisco, Calif. 94102. $10.35 ppd.

Gray Panthers. *Blueprint for a New Age: A Gray Panther History.* Available from: 3635 Chestnut Street, Philadelphia, Pa. 19104. $3. Also: *Gray Panther Manual I for Organizing* (comp. Harriet Perretz), $6.50; *Gray Panther Manual II for Training* (comp. Frances Klefter), $6.50; both manuals, $11.

Gross, Ronald. *The Lifelong Learner.* New York: Simon and Schuster, 1977.

Gross, Ronald, et al., eds. *The New Old: Struggling for Decent Aging.* Garden City, N.Y.: Anchor/Doubleday, 1978.

Horn, Linda, and Elma Griesel. *Nursing Homes: A Citizens' Action Guide.* Boston: Beacon Press, 1977.

Jackson, Jacquelyne J. *Minorities and Aging.* Belmont, Calif.: Wadsworth Pub., 1979.

Jorgenson, James. *The Graying of America: Retirement and Why You Can't Afford It.* Garden City, N.Y.: Doubleday, 1980.

Koch, Kenneth. *I Never Told Anyone: Teaching Poetry Writing in a Nursing Home.* New York: Random House, 1978.

McDowell, Donna. *The New Older Citizen's Guide: Advocacy and Action.* 1977. Available from: Office for the Aging, Pennsylvania Dept. of Public Works, Bureau of Public Education, Box 2675, Harrisburg, Pa. 17120.

OWL (Older Women's League), address above, has the following *Gray Papers* available, $2.50 each ppd: #3, *Older Women and Health Care: Strategy for Survival;* #4, *Older Women and Pensions: Catch 22;* #5, *Welfare: The End of the Line for Women;* #6, *The Disillusionment of Divorce for Older Women;* #7, *Till Death Do Us Part: Caregivers of Severely Disabled Husbands;* #8, *Not Even for Dogcatcher: Employment Discrimination and Older Women.*

Paull, Irene, and Bulbul. *Everybody's Studying Us: The Ironies of Aging in the Pepsi Generation.* 1976. Available from: Valcono Press, c/o California Association of Older Americans, 330 Ellis Street, San Francisco, Calif. 94102. $3.95.

Pelletier, Kenneth R. *Longevity: Fulfilling Our Biological Potential.* New York: Delta, 1981.

Rubin, Lillian B. *Women of a Certain Age: The Midlife Search for Self.* New York: Harper & Row, 1979.

Schulz, James H. *The Economics of Aging,* 2nd ed. Belmont, Calif.: Wadsworth Pub., 1979.

Shanks, Ann Zane. *Old Is What You Get: Dialogues on Aging by the Old and the Young.* New York: Viking, 1976.

Shields, Laurie. *Displaced Homemakers: Organizing for a New Life.* New York: McGraw-Hill, 1980.

Sigelman, Daniel W. *Your Money or Your Health, A Senior Citizens Guide to Avoiding High Charging Medicare Doctors.* 1980. Available from: Public Citizen, Box 19404, Washington, D.C. 20036.

Silverstone, Barbara, and Helen Kandel Hyman. *You and Your Aging Parent: The Modern Family's Guide to Emotional, Physical and Financial Problems.* New York: Pantheon, 1982.

Zimmerman, William. *How to Tape Instant Oral Biographies,* 3rd rev. ed. 1982. Available from: Guarionex Press, 201 W. 77 Street, New York, N.Y. 10024. $5.95 ppd.

CHAPTER VI

Work

QUERIES

1. At work, am I able to participate in decisions regarding myself and my co-workers? Do I know my rights under my union contract and/or under state and federal labor laws?
2. If I could be doing any kind of work I wanted to, would I continue in my present job? What kind of work would I prefer? Why?
3. Do I feel trapped in my job by a mortgage, high unemployment, kids, medical bills, etc.? Could I make a five-year plan for changing the situation?
4. Are certain kinds of jobs in my community done by people of one race or ethnic background?
5. Is there a way that more of us can begin to work with the day-to-day necessities, instead of with weapons, luxuries, or elaborate paper shuffling?
6. Does the company I work for pollute the air? Pollute the water? Use chemicals and additives for cosmetic reasons? Use a cheaper, more dangerous ingredient or process when a safer one is available? Do I know how to find out?
7. Is the work that is done in my home divided by sex or by available time and abilities?
8. Is my work physically dangerous to me? To my unborn children? To my mental stability? To my having any intelligence left to use for the rest of my waking hours?
9. What sort of unpaid work do I already do at home or in my community that fulfills basic human needs? Would it be possible to expand this to paid work, or could I expand my unpaid work to replace some of my need for cash income?
10. Why is there so much unemployment? What could be done about it?

: : : : :

Of course it scares me that I don't know where I will be working in September. There was a lot of security in my last job.

—Single mother of two children

You can democratize a workplace all you want, but no one's ever going to go to work in a steel furnace if it's not to feed his babies.

—*United Steelworkers presidential candidate,*
speaking with student supporters

About half of the carpenters I know don't have a full set of ten fingers.

—*Carpenter*[1]

If we could get this thing going right, we could all finish fast and knock off by noon or two. We could hire someone to come in and play the guitar or the flute or something while we work. I bet I could play a harmonica while I stitched. You know, strap it around my head like Dylan.

Yeah sure. They'd let you play the harmonica just like they'd let you go to the bathroom.

—*Two assemblyline workers at a Ping-Pong factory*[2]

She'd be making $30,000 if she were a man.

—*Supervisor's compliment on a job performance evaluation*

What do you mean, do I like my work? It's work—everybody has to work. You gotta make money somehow.

—*Baker, Whole Earth Bread Store, Palo Alto, California*

I think that it's impossible to get enough support at home to make up for what has happened in the course of working, but that's what we all want.

—*Construction worker*[3]

At first I gave in, then I felt used, now I'm always saying no. But it doesn't seem to sink in that when I say no, I mean no. I also gained eighty pounds in hopes that my employer would find me unattractive.

—*Domestic worker*

The difference is the conditions we work under. We want to be treated like people, not animals.

—*Farm workers, Salinas, California*

There are no mentally qualified minorities for supervisory positions.

—*High-level supervisor in large Northern California public agency,*
upon being accused of discrimination in promotions

What can a steward say for someone who just wants to take Fridays off? If those kids would come up with a demand like 'four-day weeks in the summer,' maybe the union would push for it. . . . But they don't make a demand. All they want to do is say 'Fuck it.' So how can the union fight for them?

—*Older union member, Helena Rubenstein factory*[4]

No, I don't like my job, but it's hard to change jobs. I'm fifty now. There are certain things that my wife is used to and doesn't want to give up. If we were to make some changes together, then maybe it would be possible.

—Engineer

I was always crabby when I went home and I couldn't understand it until I learned that the stresses and strains of noise apparently have their effects on people's emotional health.

—Printer[5]

And the breaks are very good for your circulation. You have to run all the way there and all the way back.

—Assemblyline worker, Bumblebee tunafish factory[6]

I'm twenty-three years old and if I go into the bathroom and a forty-year-old supervisor follows me in there and looks under the stall to see if I'm in there, I think that's pretty crazy. But that's not an uncommon practice. I feel like I'm an adult and should have the right not to be treated like a child who can't be trusted.

—Telephone company operator[7]

We came to San Antonio to work, not to die. But Reagan economics has nothing trickling down to us. I have gone as far as I can go with our lives. My wife, Kay, and I are hard-working people that have been reduced to beggars almost.

—Suicide note, unemployed Ohio couple found dead in their car in Texas[8]

:   :   :   :   :

Boredom, insecurity, race discrimination, sex discrimination, physical danger, stress, dissatisfaction, lack of activism, disrespect, inhuman conditions, despair. There's a lot about our work that needs changing. And work changes are some of the hardest ones to make. While some of us who are young, childless, or starting from a strong financial base may be able to make dramatic, rapid changes, most of us face difficult obstacles to transforming our work lives. Many of these obstacles are built into the nation's economic system. It's not as easy as trying tofu burgers instead of hamburgers for dinner.

Chapter I discussed the kind of opportunity most people would like to have in their work: responsibility *to* our work that it should be well done; and responsibility *for* our work that it should be well used. Few of our jobs fulfill this ideal. Many of us feel trapped in our present job situation— if we have one—by already incurred financial obligations, lack of alternative skills, lack of support from co-workers or family, or lack of apparent choice in the community. There are, however, ways in which most of us can begin to make our day-to-day work lives more equitable and more bearable in traditional work situations. Many people are also exploring alternative work situations, as well as strategies for fulfilling their material needs that make less cash earnings necessary.

Many of these actions involve risks and sacrifices—retaliatory firing for reporting health and safety hazards, long strikes, experimenting with collective process and collective responsibility instead of taking orders and automatically receiving a paycheck, dependence on the weather for agricultural survival. There are also powerful forces who do not see workers' taking charge of their lives as being in their interest. These corporations assert their right to locate jobs where they will, hire whom they will, pay what they will, and run the workplace as they will without interference from workers, unions, local communities, state, national, or international governments.

For most of us, the short-term strategy must be to challenge this absolute control. In the long-term, we need constantly to be looking for ways to put all of the control where it belongs: in the hands of a workplace's workers and local community.

CHANGES IN TRADITIONAL WORK SITUATIONS

ORGANIZING TOGETHER AND UNIONS

While everyone is aware of a union's function in achieving higher wages and benefits, many nonunion people are unaware that the most important protection achieved in many union contracts is the grievance procedure and the right not to be fired except for "good cause." The importance of various other contract provisions varies from industry to industry: health and safety protections, seniority rights, or the right to refuse overtime can be crucial factors in determining a worker's quality of life.

Labor laws give some protection to people who are organizing a union or enforcing union rights, but the degree of that protection has lagged far behind the need—especially in the length of time it takes to get reinstated when illegally fired, for example, or in the miniscule penalty given an employer who repeatedly violates the labor laws. It is usually cheaper to fire organizers—and to take the subsequent penalties—than to pay union wages. Of course, such tactics are not ultimately effective if the rest of the workers stand solid and refuse to be intimidated.

For those who want maximum participation in the unionizing process, it is possible to organize an independent union, but this is often very difficult to sustain financially when matched against an employer with far greater resources. When looking for an existing union to bring in or affiliate with, it is important to remember that not all unions are alike, and within your industry there may be a choice of two or three different unions that could represent you. A crucial issue is union democracy: does the membership control the decision-making process of the local and of the bargaining unit (the individual workplace or group of workplaces)? Or are there a few officers who seem to run everything? Is the union leadership and membership sensitive to important issues, such as sex and

race discrimination? Does the union publish contracts and union literature in languages other than English where necessary? What sort of
contract protections have been won by this union elsewhere? There are
many resources that can give you suggestions about choosing, winning,
and keeping an effective union; some are listed in the Bibliography.

Household Workers Rights—a workers' organization that is not yet a
"union"—is organizing among one of the most isolated and oppressed
groups of workers. Household workers, which include housecleaners,
cooks, child-care workers, gardeners, and workers who care for the ill and
the elderly, are usually women, predominantly nonwhite, and often non-
English-speaking and/or undocumented aliens. Often working alone and
for traditionally low wages, they find it hard to escape exploitation. Organizer Joyce Maupin explained that "the live-in workers are the most
oppressed: they are often treated like pieces of furniture."

In 1979, Maupin and several others were active in achieving the first
explicit protection under California law for household workers. San Fran-
cisco-based Household Workers Rights began from a campaign to publicize these rights to minimum wages, overtime, rest periods, and meal
periods. Free Speech Messages were prepared and broadcast on every
major television and radio station, with the themes: "Do You Know Your
Rights?" and "Household Workers are Entitled to Dignity on the Job."
The new organization got hundreds of calls in response to these broad-
casts.

In addition to continuing the Free Speech messages, there are monthly
meetings and monthly newsletters in Spanish and English. Workshops
are planned on health and safety and work techniques; questionnaires
found that burns, back injuries, and skin irritations were widespread
problems. Another core of activity is a referral service, which places
members without charging any fee, since most private agencies take
one-half of what the employer pays. A model contract is suggested, which
includes proration of vacation, sick leave, and other benefits; some employers, especially union people, have been responsive. These first organizing steps with a scattered workforce are already leading to better
working conditions.

ORGANIZING FOR SAFER WORKPLACES

Paul Crawford is a welder in Steamfitters Local 342 and chairperson of
his local's Welfare Committee. His union family tradition gave him the
feeling that "it's important to look out for your brothers, to make sure
that the environment is clean and healthful and there are the best working
conditions possible."

Local members work mostly on-call from a hiring hall as their services
are required in refineries and chemical plants in Contra Costa and
Alameda Counties in California. They are also called to situations where
radioactive leaks must be repaired. Crawford comments:

It's pretty scary when you get a dispatch and they [the hiring hall dispatchers] say, "This is a hot job!" You report and they want you to dress up like a monkey and go inside, with no explanation of the hazards you'll be exposed to.

Among more mundane health threats is uncontrolled release of hydrogen sulfide gases, in both the refineries and the chemical plants. Although the technology is available to control and recover the emissions and to provide proper ventilation for workers in the area, employers have resisted spending the money. To date, the most effective tactic has been brief walkouts when the fumes get too bad; members who have complained to the Occupational Safety and Health Administration (OSHA) have suddenly found themselves laid off or fired on a pretense. Proof of retaliation is difficult. OSHA has fined one refinery only $1,000 for gas releases, which is cheaper than taking proper precautions. The same refinery added insult to injury by demanding that workers shave so that safety air masks could be worn if necessary; upon inquiry, union members learned that the company had purchased two masks for five hundred people.

The northern rim of Contra Costa County, where these industries are located, has one of the highest rates of birth defects, asthma, allergy, and cancer in the nation;[9] Crawford has had cancer, and in the three months preceding his discussion with the editor, three of his union's one thousand active members were diagnosed as having cancer. Another frequent hazard is skin irritation. The mental stress of worrying about the dangers also takes a heavy toll, causing some to quit their jobs. Crawford and his wife (whose environmental health organizing in the same community is discussed in Chapter IX) recently moved after an eight-inch pipe at a Shell refinery exploded and caught fire a quarter of a mile from their home:

You have to go and work in it all day, and go home and smell it all night, and you don't really know what you're smelling. Our two kids went to school downwind from Shell, which was releasing gases all the time. I thought they could be doing a little better job of keeping it out of the atmosphere.

Crawford considers his health and safety organizing to be at an early stage, and he hopes to form alliances with other union locals to address the overall problem. So far, local members have voted to tax themselves seven cents per hour to provide supplemental income for members who become disabled long-term with cancer or other serious problems, and the thirty-person Welfare Committee is gathering detailed information about the substances they are working with and the legal and technical possibilities for control (see Chapter VIII discussion and references on this). Crawford is hopeful for significant improvements:

I think people will stick together once everybody gets educated. I realize I'm going to encounter some dangers, but by working together we can make our workplaces safer.

DISCRIMINATION

Federal and state laws prohibit job discrimination based on race, religion, sex, age, or national origin, and some state and local laws provide additional protections. But an antidiscrimination clause in your union contract can often provide an easier and quicker remedy than proceedings before an administrative agency or a court. Protection can also be broader than that provided by existing law, as is illustrated in this contract clause from the Electrical Trades Credit Union and Service, Office and Retail Workers Union of Canada:

The Employer agrees that there will be no discrimination against an employee or prospective employee by reason of age, race, creed, color, national origin, political or religious views, sex or sexual orientation, marital status, appearance or whether she/he has children.[10]

A union can also negotiate a plan with an employer to eliminate the effects of past discrimination. This was done, for example, in a nation-wide contract negotiated between the United Steelworkers and Kaiser Aluminum and Chemical Corporation, where Kaiser agreed to establish an in-plant, skilled-craft training program instead of hiring experienced craftspeople from the outside. Kaiser further agreed to admit 50 percent black employees into the program until parity was reached with the racial balance in the workforce, and the legality of this agreement was upheld in a landmark U.S. Supreme Court case.[11] The Kaiser plant in question was located in Louisiana, and only 1.83 percent of the skilled craftworkers were black, although the local labor force was 39 percent black. The training program, incidentally, provided in-house training opportunities for the first time to white employees of Kaiser. A less comprehensive, but more common affirmative action measure that has been negotiated both at union and nonunion workplaces is in-house job-posting of all vacancies before they are advertised outside a company.

In Chapter IV, the Willmar 8 and a film made about them were discussed as an example of the community that grew out of the first bank strike in Minnesota history. The strike issue was sex discrimination: the tellers and bookkeepers were consistently kept at low-pay while newly hired men were trained for higher status and higher-paying positions. The last straw came when the bank hired an inexperienced young man for a management position and asked the senior teller, with eighteen years of experience, to train him. She and the bookkeeper were both refused the opportunity to apply for the position.

The film and an excellent accompanying study guide explore many important issues besides "straightforward" sex discrimination. One is the concept of "comparable worth": the main reason women in this country are paid only fifty-nine cents for every dollar earned by white men is because certain jobs have traditionally been classified as "women's work" —and paid accordingly. Several strikes have addressed the issue of "comparable worth," in demanding reclassification of jobs by skill evaluation.

Another issue raised is that of attitude toward conflict, almost inevitable when dealing with workplace changes. In the documentary, two Willmar residents make the following statements: "I think they should call it off. After all, this is a Christian town and it would be nice if we had peace" and "We hesitate to discuss it too much for fear that there might be some ill feeling." The study guide asks: "How important is maintaining peaceful and tranquil relationships to you? Has the fear of confrontation, of unpleasantness, of causing a disruption ever prevented you from confronting a situation which bothered you? Did you find it easier to let the problem slide? Was it easier? What was disturbing about the possibility of a confrontation? What was the price paid for not confronting the problem?" This issue is especially important for women to explore, who have been traditionally socialized to smooth over conflict.

In High Point, North Carolina, the AFSC's Women in the Work Force project is helping women learn about and stand up for their rights. Most women in High Point work in the furniture manufacturing industry, where they are exposed to chemical fumes and wood dust. The project has created a support network and offered education on these hazards. A pamphlet series, *What Every Woman Worker Should Know About . . .* , provides information on discrimination, minimum wage and overtime laws, the National Labor Relations Act, unemployment compensation, job safety and health, and sexual harassment. The project has supported women in winning back-pay where employers have engaged in race discrimination, pregnancy discrimination, or where the women were denied unemployment benefits, as well as organizing to ensure hiring of women and minorities at federally funded construction projects.

New Ways to Work

At some traditional companies, workers have secured the right to vary their work hours. Two examples are the use of "flex-time"—where starting and stopping times can vary between workers—and a four-day week with ten-hour days. But part-time jobs are still very hard to find, especially those that do not penalize workers with lower pay and complete lack of benefits.

An unusual alternative is found at the Rolscreen Company of Pella, Iowa, which manufactures a variety of rolling screens, doors, and windows. Rolscreen has a job-sharing program, started at the request of one woman in 1977 who wanted an alternative to working fulltime. The company has had as many as forty job-sharing teams working on its assembly lines; each member works Monday, Wednesday, and Friday one week, and Tuesday and Thursday the next week. Job sharers receive the same hourly pay as other workers, as well as full health and dental benefits, though the life insurance benefit is prorated at 50 percent of full-time coverage. One drawback from the workers' point of view to this generally fair program is that job sharers must agree to work up to full-time when there are emergencies. A management official told the editor that "this doesn't happen often"—but at the time of the conversation, all job sharers were working full time to fill a backlog of orders.

Management feels that there are a number of business advantages to the job-sharing program: absenteeism has been "virtually eliminated," job performance evaluations have improved for 36 percent of job sharers over their full-time evaluations, and 78 percent of all job sharers are rated "high proficient" to "superior."

To date, workers have been more successful at convincing white-collar and professional employers to accept job sharing, according to Charles Renfroe of New Ways to Work, a San Francisco–based organization. The group provides extensive written and film resources to assist those interested in job sharing, some of which are listed in the Bibliography. A particular current focus is on nursing, which is a job with both "high burn-out" and a higher-than-average wage, a prime candidate for job sharing. In addition to workshops and counseling, the office keeps a "partners-in-search-of-partners" book, which can be consulted for a three-dollar yearly fee.

If one can find part-time work that pays a living wage (with or without a sharer), this is of course another alternative within traditional work parameters for those who wish more time in their lives to do their nonpaid work.

CHANGE WITH ALTERNATIVE WORK SITUATIONS

A Working Community

Alpha Farm is an eleven-year-old living and working community of fifteen located in Deadwood, Oregon. It takes its origin and inspiration from activist Quakers, though it now has members of many backgrounds. Their work combines a 280-acre farm with a rural mail route; Alpha-Bit, a cafe/book-and-craft store; a hardware store; and a construction contracting business. One member works full time as a newspaper editor in Salem, Oregon, and spends weekends with the community; another works part-time as an assistant midwife and woman's health practitioner at a local clinic.

Members can join Alpha after a year in residency (and new members are always welcome!). At the point of joining, all personal financial resources are turned over to the community for investment (to be returned if a decision is made to leave at any point). In return, all income is shared in common: the community pays for all food, clothing, shelter, health needs, and group recreation. As of fall 1983, the community was financially able to give each member a $15 per month personal allowance, twenty vacation workdays per year, and $150 plus a car to use for the vacation (with adjustments possible according to individual situations—one member is currently on an extended leave visiting her grandchildren in various parts of the country).

Work at Alpha is organized by teams and committees, such as hardware store, dairy, housekeeping, and fields. All decisions are made by consensus. Once a year at the end of October, the community begins an elaborate work-planning process, which results in an annual plan by February 1 of new and adjusted dreams, projects, and priorities, tempered by financial realities. During this planning time, each member has the opportunity to indicate how she or he would ideally like to spend his or her working time. The goal is to give each member work that she or he ideally wishes to do 50 percent of the time, as well as to keep a balance between special talents and versatility.

The core of Alpha is the farm, where members raise most of their own vegetables and fruit organically, as well as some of the cafe's requirements. They keep milk cows, milk goats, and chickens for eggs, maintain a wood lot, and grow dahlias for sale of cut flowers and tubers.

Caroline Estes, a founder of Alpha, explained that the rest of the members' occupations are

chosen for service, not just for the money. Mail delivery is a necessary government service; local residents and travelers are rejuvenated at Alpha-Bit; the community needed a hardware store; it also needs the services of people who can do high-quality construction work. We don't do anything just for the money.

Alpha's successful bid ten years ago to carry the local rural delivery route (two hundred miles, recently reduced to seventy miles) was a fortunate chance that helped break down the community's initial image of them as "those hippies." Three members drive the route two days each and thus come in regular contact with every person in their region. Each year at holiday time, the Alpha mail carriers leave a homemade gift for their neighbors in every mailbox—cookies, candy, or fruitcake.

Another early "outside occupation" was Alpha-Bit, started six months after the farm was founded. Alpha-Bit serves meals, snacks, and a ten-cent cup of coffee at tables surrounded by new and used books and a quality craft selection. A newer venture is the Mapleton Country Mercantile and Hardware, about two years old, which sells "the highest quality for a price we feel is fair. We don't try to sell junk to get a fast turnover." Mapleton is a town of about one thousand, and the hardware store has brought Alpha into contact with additional area residents who have never felt comfortable with alfalfa sprouts or yogurt smoothies at Alpha-Bit.

Cash return is not the standard that defines "work" at Alpha. As Caroline Estes explained:

Each day's work is equal to every other day's work. If you're delivering the mail, that's work. If you're baking bread, that's work. If you've just had a baby you're caring for, that's a day's work. We don't differentiate by how much money is brought in.

Another way to look at the difference between Alpha and the way work is ordinarily viewed in our society is expressed in a statement by one member about what Alpha means to her, included in the 1982 Christmas letter sent to friends, family, and acquaintances:

To be able to stop during the middle of a work day to take in a rainbow, a flower in bloom, a hug, a few moments of laughter, or even taking a nap before one falls on one's face.

VEGETABLES IN THE CITY

Veritable Vegetables is a nine-year-old produce distribution collective in San Francisco, run and owned by the people who work there. Mary Jane Evans, who joined the collective in 1976 when it was composed of two women and two men, explained that "as we grew, we wanted to offer a workspace for women in a male-dominated field." Veritable Vegetables is now an all-women's collective of seven full-time and two part-time warehouse workers, and two truck drivers.

Supporting a system of sustainable agriculture is a "major priority" of the collective. They provide a market for small farmers, including many organic farmers, and give local farmers purchasing priority when they have the same crop available as those further afield. Veritable's customers are community food stores, other warehouses, and health and whole food stores.

All decisions are made by consensus at weekly collective meetings. Job assignments are rotated among the five departments: warehousing, order-taking, order-making, books, and trucking. More recently, the collective has been reducing the frequency of job rotation because suppliers and customers have expressed a desire to talk consistently with the same person. A consideration that pulls in the opposite direction is the stress and life disruption engendered by being regularly assigned to the "early morning" (all-night) shift, a necessity that the collective has tried to share equally.

Why does Evans work in a collective? She answers:

Working in a worker-owned business is very satisfying. We have control over the business, and a say-so over decisions. Everyone is willing to struggle through problems together. You don't have the pressures of having a boss, and I feel the evaluation of an individual's work is a lot fairer. We also have the freedom to work cooperatively with other collectives and to throw business each other's way—but we do have to be viable as a legitimate business and not just as an ideal structure.

Veritable Vegetables has sometimes felt isolated because there are no other produce collectives in the area to share experiences with. They have also had problems typical of many collectives where few members had any background in the aspects of running a business usually taken care of by a boss—and bringing in outside advisers can be expensive. They are now able to pay members a living wage, but the collective has been almost completely "capitalized by labor" over the past nine years: except for truck financing, they received no loans or grants of any sort.

Evans spoke of Veritable's long-term dream of being able to work with an affiliated farm and retail store. "In the short-term, however, we hope to achieve financial stability, while continuing to provide a marketplace for the small farmer."

COOPERATIVE CHEMICALS?

In the early 1950s, a Quaker, pacifist owner of an English manufacturing plant that makes polyester, among other things, decided to turn over ownership of the business to a "commonwealth" governed democratically by the company's workers. E. F. Schumacher's description of Scott Bader Company provides an interesting example of the kinds of "business decisions" made possible by both a worker-orientation and an ethics-orientation, rather than a profit-orientation.

What do you do if suddenly trade slumps, and your competitors lay off 50 percent of their work force and you have to carry the whole thing? . . . It leads to quite a different kind of management. . . . We have to think ten times before we expand at the start, because we know once they are with us we belong together. . . .

We imposed upon ourselves a number of what I call "self-denying ordinances." One of them is, being of Quaker origin, we will not knowingly sell any of our products if we have reason to believe it will be used for armaments. . . . Another is that we are determined not to grow beyond the size of 400. . . . Just as in nature a cell doesn't expand and expand, but when there is a requirement of growth it splits and makes a new cell, so we have, under great pressures of growth, split and have put into being three new companies, totally independent. . . . But the primary concern is to keep the human touch.

When there are profits . . . for every pound that we distribute to ourselves, we set one pound aside for some external noble purpose. . . . The idea was that with this money we wanted to get involved with the requirements of the neighborhood. But [recently] within 50 miles, we couldn't find anything that needed doing. I mean in this little firm, only 400 people, over the course of almost 30 years, everything that other regions are crying out for has been looked after. The old people are looked after: they get their regular parcels. The boys' club wanted a baseball diamond: they've got it. The association of the blind wanted help with their Braille: they've got it. . . . So we have to go further afield, but just to hand it over to some national charity is witless: we don't want to do that. It's a big job. . . .

Scott Bader is more than an experiment, it's a life-style. Yet, in our primary purpose, which had been the humanization of the work process, in all these years we've not made much headway. We are hooked there on a technology—as the English schoolchild says of the chemistry lesson, he says it "stinks," and a chemical factory stinks. And it is a process that cannot be humanized. We might one day say, Well, then, we won't make polyester; we will do something quite different. . . . But meantime, we thought, we can't humanize the 38 hours a week that people work for their living, but what about the other more than 100 hours a week?

We said, Surely the community can develop activities, useful activities, for utilizing their spare time. . . . They then built themselves a community motor-car repair shop. We got two old-age pensioners to look after it; they're happy, they've got something to do, thank God. And when a car breaks down, they take the car to their own garage and repair it, and the cost is just the cost of materials. . . .

The next thing is, every Englishman has a little garden, so we had a simple idea: really good gardening tools and machines. . . . We . . . created a gardening-machine pool, again run by a number of old-age pensioners, and everybody has access to really superlative tools and they've all become passionately interested in growing things, not just keeping their lawns shorn.

The next thing that is now in the planning stage is a commonwealth woodworking shop, because they say, We can make our own furniture; we can even go further and make a surplus of furniture for local sale . . . a new life-style is gradually developing, which may in fact take off the pressure on the need to earn wages, so that we could reduce the working hours, and perhaps we can leave it free to people to choose. . . . I think if it were 20 hours [wage work] would be just a chore, for a few hours every day, and human nature can stand that.[12]

THE "MOVEMENT JOB"

If you have ideas about societal changes that need to be made, you may want to try to get paid for working on making them happen. Some of the people mentioned elsewhere in this book—Frances Moore Lappé in Chapter II and Bob Dunsmore in Chapter IX—found their initially unpaid political work expanding to create new organizations that provide the means for full-time jobs. Another possibility is to work for an already existing organization.

Valerie Blake is a program staff member at the San Francisco office of the American Friends Service Committee (AFSC). Now thirty-four years old and a black single mother, she has worked with AFSC-related programs since she was eighteen.

Valerie's political involvement was influenced by her aunt, who organized "The Group," an organization designed to deal with housing and food problems in their neighborhood, when she was a teenager. At age eighteen, she got a part-time receptionist job with the Hayes Valley Education Project, a program partially supported by AFSC. The program taught adults—mostly older blacks who had received no education in the South—how to read and write. She doesn't recall making a political choice in taking that job, beyond satisfying her desire "to work with people, not with machines."

With her attention directed toward the literacy issue, she noticed that many ten- to eighteen-year-olds in the neighborhood couldn't read, write, or do arithmetic, despite years of compulsory school attendance. Starting what has become a lifetime focus, she wrote a program proposal and became youth coordinator of the project, which changed its name to the Harriet Tubman Community Education Center.

Valerie felt that "the kids weren't learning because they couldn't apply school to their daily lives—we go to school and are expected to just store up the information until we're eighteen." So she set up a program where the young people themselves, all voluntarily recruited, chose and ordered household products and sold them door-to-door. Each student was responsible for her or his own bank account in dealing with customers and suppliers. When the students made profits, a system was set up at neighborhood stores where they could charge clothing, shoes, and other necessities against the profits, thus taking a burden off their parents. To succeed in this program, the students had to be able to read, write, add, and talk intelligently about their products.

The project continued for three years, despite chronic lack of funds. To help sustain it, Valerie donated back her salary and took night jobs as a bartender, cook, and waitress to support herself, while working in the center during the day. When the project finally folded due to financial problems, she took a job as afternoon receptionist at AFSC's regional office. She says the three years had helped her clarify her personal values —that "youth were people" and that she "wanted to provide guidance for those who had trouble making it in the regular school system."

After only three months as receptionist, Valerie heard about a staff opening in AFSC's high school program. The program, which focused on student rights and responsibilities, was intriguing to her. She and another staff member traveled all over Northern California making speeches on the subject to high school students. After the novelty wore off, though, she began to feel a lack of focus and to wonder whether she was really helping the kids.

After the loss of the other staff member due to budget cuts and some internal AFSC reorganization in 1976, Valerie worked on developing the Youth Advocate Project. The project focused more on the needs of poorer and Third World students—the ones whose first response was: "I'm being suspended—great!" rather than, "I'm being suspended—my rights are being violated." The project has evolved through the years as more experience has been gained and as rapport has slowly been established with school officials, who first tended to view Valerie as an "enemy" when she stuck up for students' rights.

Valerie's work is now at an interesting crossroads: "I am trying to transfer the knowledge and skills that I have, and my ability to make changes, to students and to their parents." The knowledge and skills are those she uses in working on a demonstration project focused on one San Francisco high school. Students come to her if they feel their rights have been violated—anything ranging from an unjust suspension to a feeling that they are just not learning enough. She also gets involved when she hears of problems through students who are working with her. For example, in the case of a fight, she tries to go to the scene, get the story from both sides, and then confer with the dean, attempting to get the students put on her "caseload" rather than just let them be suspended. She'll talk with the students, find out about their family situations, where they sleep, where they do their homework, why they hate school. She makes home visits and talks with their parents—her goal is to see that the students get an education.

Valerie has been doing this for a while, with sporadic student and parent participation. The new twist is that halfway through this school year, the whole operation is to be turned over to a staff of six ninth- and tenth-grade student advocates, supported by seven volunteer parents she has been training. These students and parents will recruit and train replacements when they and their children become eleventh graders. If the idea works, she hopes the San Francisco school board will approve an expansion of the program to more San Francisco high schools, and in the longer term, she will be able to turn her attention to a new issue.

The AFSC pays more than the bare-subsistence variety of "movement job," but the pay is not high, and the San Francisco Bay Area has among the highest cost of living in the United States. In addition to participating in all the extra-hours committee meetings that invariably come with "movement work," Valerie has even worked a second job, until exhaustion forced her to make a choice:

The kids I work with—mostly black and Chicano—live across the street and around the corner. That's what has kept me going. There were many times I was going to quit because I needed more money. It was easy to do this kind of work when it was "just me"—but then my kids needed things, and I wondered if they'd start to steal like some of the kids I work with, because I couldn't buy them what other kids had. Then I'd see a kid I talked with one week become a prostitute on the corner the next week, or strung out on drugs. I live in it, and I can't walk away from it. I have to do something to change it.*

CHANGES AT HOME AND IN THE COMMUNITY

If you are thinking about long-term changes in your work life, there may be gradual steps you can take to make the transition both possible and easier.

First, think about what skills you already have, and what skills you might develop, that would give you a more significant work choice. Community colleges provide a wealth of low-cost or free training, often during non-work hours; if you can reduce your material outlays enough, part-time work combined with education for new work may be your best alternative. Another way is barter and skills-sharing: you might trade gardening for mechanical knowledge or set up an informal apprenticeship that provides free (initially unskilled) labor to a skilled neighbor in exchange for training. If you were able to quit your job and kids and go to school full-time, new skills might be learned in one year instead of three, but it is better to commit three years to making necessary changes than to go the rest of your life without making them!

---

*On June 27, 1984, as this book was going to press, Valerie Blake died suddenly at the age of 35. She will be deeply missed.

Often, the sort of job we'd like to leave pays a lot more than the sort of job we'd prefer. Making the adjustment can mean doing more of our work at home and reducing the need for cash. Gardening, home maintenance, sewing, self-help health skills—all reduce our need for cash outlay. It would be utopian to pretend that such activity does not require a significant investment of time—and a lot more time when you are just learning new skills. The question is whether you'd rather be sewing instead of keypunching to earn the money to buy clothes or playing in the community orchestra instead of writing detergent ads to earn the money to be entertained. Since most work around the home has been viewed traditionally (at least in this century) as "women's work," this is an important issue for families to watch when adding new home-work tasks. On the other hand, construction-related skills carry the opposite bias. Who would enjoy a particular type of work most? How is the burden of mutually disliked work allocated?

For household-centered work, or for smaller-scale craft production, we should definitely look to small-scale machinery that can assist with relieving drudgery. Scott Bader Company, described above, provides a good example of the shared use of excellent gardening tools, car repair tools, and furniture-crafting tools. Gandhi once suggested a standard for the evaluation of the worth of a machine:

The craze is for what they call labor-saving machinery. Men go on "saving labor" till thousands are without work and thrown on the open streets to die of starvation. I want to save time and labor, not for a fraction of mankind, but for all. . . .

Take the case of the Singer Sewing Machine. It is one of the few useful things ever invented, and there is a romance about the device itself. Singer saw his wife laboring over the tedious process of sewing and seaming with her own hands, and simply out of his love for her he devised the sewing machine in order to save her from unnecessary labor. . . . It is an alteration in the condition of labor that I want. This mad rush for wealth must cease, and the laborer must be assured, not only of a living wage, but a daily task that is not a mere drudgery. . . . The sewing machine had love at its back. The individual is the one supreme consideration. The saving of labor of the individual should be the object, and the honest humanitarian consideration, and not greed, the motive. Replace greed by love and everything will come right.[13]

THE POLITICS OF EMPLOYMENT AND UNEMPLOYMENT

In Chapter I, we discussed the long-term necessity of people regaining the power to do important work and to decide what kinds of work are done in our society. Right now, most decisions about what will be produced and who will produce it are made by large corporations.

When they can, corporations replace human labor with machines. Machines do not go on strike, demand higher wages, or require fringe benefits. For the jobs that are left, a growing problem is union-busting. During the last decade, an increasing number of corporations have been employing professional union busters. In 1979, an estimated $100 million was paid to these firms.[14] Testimony before the House Subcommittee on Labor-Management Relations in December of that year revealed extensive use of undercover agents and lawyers who brag they can keep the issue of unionization tied up in court for at least five years. Perhaps the most outrageous information to come out was that a group of Boston hospitals had billed the cost of their union-busting services to Medicaid, and that Rockwell International had included over $1 million in anti-union consultant fees in its "cost-plus" billing of the Department of Defense for aerospace contracts.[15]

Less well-heeled employers are provided with less sophisticated strategies, either at group seminars or by purchasing various "package deals," according to how much they want to spend. One company hands out a checklist of twenty-six "Early Warnings" at its seminars, including such questions as:

- Are groups of employees forming to include individuals who normally do not associate with each other?
- Have new terms become apparent in the vocabulary of various employees? Have employees inquired whether the company has an arbitration procedure? A seniority list? Pays area standard wages? A bumping system?
- Are employees usually following other employees or a stranger after leaving the company premises?
- Are complaints being made by a delegation, not single employees?

Another company provides a day-by-day anti-union campaign plan, complete with seven canned letters to be sent to employees' homes, eleven canned posters for company bulletin boards, texts of speeches to be delivered by supervisory personnel to meetings of employees, and suggested contents of personal visits by supervisory personnel with each employee.

Sexism and racism are used as explicit tools by the union busters. A consultant at one seminar advised participants: "It's absolutely legal to scare the bejesus out of your female employees with threats of strikes, violence, and picket lines, and I suggest to you that is a very good way to scare the hell out of them."[16] In North Carolina, a company sent its mostly white workers a tape recording of faked radio news coverage of a "Teamsters strike," complete with gunshots, screams, and breaking car windshields. All of the union "supporters"—professional actors—speak with heavy, black ghetto accents. The Teamsters lost the election 1,272 to 883.[17]

Another tactic is to move. In California, Simpson Dura-Vent Company, the nation's third-largest manufacturer of metal chimney pipe for wood stoves and gas furnaces, solicited and was offered $2.5 million in tax-exempt financing by the City of Vacaville toward building a new plant. Vacaville is beyond commuting distance from Redwood City, the plant's location for the past twenty years. It is also a low-wage, nonunionized area: Dura-Vent's one hundred full-time and one hundred and ten seasonal employees, 90 percent minority, are represented by the United Electrical, Radio and Machine Workers of America (UE) and earn an average of $7.50 per hour. The company's owners rejected consideration of an alternative site, located by the union, available at the same price and financing terms, but within commuting distance for present employees. Management has also refused to offer present employees the right to transfer to the new site.[18]

UE, together with the Plant Closures Project, filed a lawsuit against the City of Vacaville to challenge the use of redevelopment funds for union-busting purposes. A settlement established strong municipal policies governing companies that accept such funds: affirmative action hiring, a requirement of recognition of the union that represented workers at the company's old plant, and a one-year notice of future plant closure. The city also agreed to provide financial assistance to workers who wish to transfer to a plant moving from another California location and to forgo use of tax-exempt financing to attempt to attract a company from another California city. The Plant Closures Project hopes to make such rules statewide in the next legislative session. Dura-Vent claims it still plans to move to Vacaville, even without the tax-exempt financing, but five months after the lawsuit's settlement, it had not taken steps to do so, and its workers planned to oppose any building permit application in Vacaville.[19]

According to the Bureau of National Affairs, Inc., 2,700 U.S. plants closed in 1982 and 1.2 million workers lost their jobs. Six hundred of these closures were permanent, affecting 215,000 workers.[20] The plant closure situation is often described as one of "runaway shops"—but, according to Ralph Nader's Corporate Accountability Research Group, very few companies actually shut down their U.S. operations to expand similar operations overseas:

People concerned about unemployment and the power of multinational corporations [should] concentrate on a more pervasive phenomena: the export of capital from the U.S. in the form of technology, U.S. aid, bank loans and direct foreign investment. It is this process, rather than individual companies running away, that is responsible for the gradual shift in production work from the U.S. to the Third World. . . .

The reason these countries [Japan, South Korea, Brazil] have built modern, competitive steel, auto and textile industries is not because American firms have "runaway," but because American corporations and banks have made decisions *not to invest* in these industries in the U.S., and have encouraged export-oriented development policies overseas. . . . U.S. Steel didn't close its plants in Youngstown, Ohio, and "run to" Japan or Korea; it simply operated them until they were no longer competitive—and reinvested the profits in Marathon Oil. And now one of its subsidiaries is building an office building in Seattle utilizing imported Japanese steel processed in South Korea.[21]

As another example:

Much of the capital generated from the harvest of Northwest timber has been invested in countries such as Indonesia and the Philippines (and, after 1973, Chile), where government policies have encouraged corporate investments by companies like Georgia-Pacific and Weyerhauser. Most attractive to the companies were loose environmental regulations, which allowed the companies to harvest timber without replanting, and government repression of labor, which kept wages low.[22]

Ralph Nader's organization is not the only one with this analysis. The Canadian Conference of Catholic Bishops agrees:

The present recession appears to be symptomatic of a much larger structural crisis in the international system of capitalism. . . . We are now in an age, for example, where transnational corporations and banks can move capital from one country to another in order to take advantage of cheaper labor conditions, lower taxes, and reduced environmental restrictions. . . . The consequences are likely to be permanent or structural unemployment and increasing marginalization for a large segment of the population in Canada and other countries. . . . Through these structural changes, "capital" is reasserted as the dominant organizing principle of economic life. This orientation directly contradicts the ethical principle that labor, not capital, must be given priority in the development of an economy based on justice. . . . As long as technology and capital are not harnessed by society to serve basic human needs, they are likely to become an enemy rather than an ally in the development of peoples.[23]

How can we fight against this trend? One way is an actual or threatened consumer boycott. This tactic was successfully used by the Save Nabisco Action Coalition (SNAC), formed when Nabisco announced a shutdown of its plant in Pittsburgh, Pennsylvania. A letter-writing campaign that threatened a nationwide boycott of Nabisco products changed the company's mind.[24]

Another way to keep jobs and capital at home is to increase community and worker participation in plant shutdown decisions. An unusual strategy was implemented by Local 1357, United Food and Commercial Workers Union (UFCWU) when the A&P—majority owned by a West German conglomerate—announced plans to shut down at least forty-four of its Philadelphia-area stores, a move that threw about two thousand UFCWU members out of work. With pledges of $5,000 each from six hundred union members, UFCWU offered to buy a block of the stores.

The resulting negotiations led to an interesting agreement:

- A&P reopened twenty stores immediately, with most of the others to follow, under a new subsidiary, Super Fresh.
- Rehired union members were given a voice in store operations.

- Workers accepted temporary pay-cuts averaging 20 percent and vacation and overtime pay reductions.
- A&P agreed to put 1 percent of the gross annual sales of each store into an employee-controlled trust to provide capital for future store buyouts and starting up employee-owned enterprises.
- A&P gave the workers an exclusive option to purchase any of the reopened stores they might decide to close in the future, at a "fair market price."

In addition, A&P sold two stores directly to employees to be run as worker-owned cooperatives—Employee Owned and Operated Supermarkets (O&O). This was accomplished by the sixty employees who chose to scrape together $5,000 each to provide about 20 percent of the amount needed to purchase and open the stores: with this basis, the rest of the money was obtainable from a bank with a guarantee from the Small Business Administration. After almost a year of operation, the two stores were financially viable, with weekly sales up 20 percent and 40 percent.[25]

Crucial to the feasibility of such alternatives is adequate notice of a company's intent to close. This notice gives workers time to formulate plans and to obtain financing. Activists in almost every state are lobbying for legislation that would require varying amounts of notice, and there have been some successes.

Another place where change in governmental policy is crucial is in setting limits on the export of capital by banks and multinationals. In addition to seeking regulatory legislation, unions with some control over joint employer-union pension funds have begun to assess investments of that vast amount of money on "social" criteria. Responding to a critical report written for the U. S. Department of Labor by an anti-union consultant, Robert Georgine, president of the AFL-CIO Building and Construction Trades Department, observed that union employees' pension funds are often "invested in ways which have sacrificed the jobs of their participants." He felt that investments must be considered for their impact on "the participants and the beneficiaries of their plans," including workers, retirees, and communities.[26]

Perhaps the most serious governmental policy problem is our government's political, economic, and military support to repressive regimes. Governments in Central America, Chile, South Korea, and Taiwan maintain cheap labor for American corporations, making it more economically advantageous to transport raw materials and finished products vast distances than for each nation to produce mostly for its local markets.

Unemployment organizing is a rapidly growing area of activism. In June 1983, the National Unemployed Network was formed, the first such coalition of unemployed councils and committees since the 1930s. The network plans to work on issues of plant closing, job retraining, government-funded jobs or extended unemployment compensation, utility shutoff and home foreclosure moratoriums, universal health care, full use of surplus food, and "money for jobs, not war."

Another new organization, the Interreligious Economic Crisis Organizing Network (I/ECON), formed in February 1983. Initially consisting of seventeen national and regional denominations, faith groups, and ecumenical bodies, I/ECON planned to focus its work on alternatives to plant closing stopping mortgage foreclosures, encouraging corporate accountability, providing support groups for unemployed people, education of the religious community, and international networking on these issues.

The formation of these national groups reflects extensive, creative, local organizing. The United Citizens Organization of East Chicago (UCO), a coalition of nine churches and two United Steelworkers locals, persuaded local merchants to offer an "Unemployed Discount Program" to unemployed individuals.[27] In Minnesota, a coalition of citizens, labor and farm organizations accomplished the passage in May 1983 of the nation's first mortgage foreclosure moratorium. The legislation allows unemployed or underemployed homeowners to obtain a six-month grace period; farmers who face low commodity prices can obtain up to a one-year grace period.[28] In Philadelphia, Energy for Employment organizes support groups for unemployed people in churches, senior citizen centers, and community organizations. The ten-session support groups discuss job search skills, stress management techniques, and provide personal support for unemployed people to "come out of the closet" in a positive, caring atmosphere.[29]

These broad efforts to counter unemployment, along with the alternative discussed elsewhere in this chapter, may begin to shift control of the U.S. economy back to the people with whom it belongs.

WHAT YOU CAN DO

1. To clarify your personal and vocational goals, make a list of what you would like to do for the next five, ten, twenty, or more years. Be imaginative and complimentary. What do you really want to do? Please dream! Having described what you want to do, examine what skills, abilities, and experiences you have and need to carry out your vision, as well as who might be good people to work together with on these goals.
2. Make an inventory of the skills you presently have—things you do well and enjoy. Write an autobiography that describes the activities, both paid and unpaid, in which you have participated. Include in your description what you did and did not like about each activity. Were some of the activities for which you were not paid more meaningful than some for which you were paid?

After identifying your long-range and short-range personal and vocational goals and inventorying your skills, try to identify what new skills you will need to achieve your goals. Assess each new skill according to the time and effort it involves. Make a five-year plan for the changes you want to make.

3. Obtain copies or summaries of basic federal labor law protections, your state's wage, hour, and working condition laws for your industry, your union contract. Read them. Are there any surprises? Try comparing union contracts with friends, too.

4. See Chapter VIII for a discussion of where you can start on occupational safety and health issues.

5. Have a potluck discussion about the kinds of long-term changes of job distribution and structure you could envision happening in your community. Try to find out if there are worker-owned collective or cooperative enterprises, and make a point of patronizing them. Are there other ways you and your friends can support such changes?

6. Have a household meeting to discuss what work is already done in the household, what other work could be done, and who is or will be doing it.

7. Discuss with your family and friends the racial and sexual composition of your workplaces. Who has which jobs? What about the composition of the workforce of the businesses you patronize—banks, food stores, retail shops? Are there ways you can support changes? Examples: (1) Change your bank to one with a more balanced work force, informing your previous one of why. (2) A black male firefighter told the editor that he noticed that the first woman to qualify for training in his department was struggling with certain tasks, unaided by the instructor or other males. He showed her that when she knew the necessary technique, much less physical strength was needed and she was thus able to meet the rigorous physical tests.

8. Turn to Chapter I and items 3 and 9 in the "What You Can Do" section.

NOTES

1. Aaron Back et al., *Occupational Stress: the Inside Story,* published by Institute for Labor & Mental Health, 3137 Telegraph Avenue, Calif. 94609 (1981).
2. Barbara Garson, *All the Livelong Day: The Meaning & Demeaning of Routine Work* (Garden City, N.Y.: Doubleday & Company, 1975), pp. 13–14.
3. Back, *Occupational Stress,* p. 47.
4. Garson, *All the Livelong Day,* p. 68.
5. Back, *Occupational Stress,* p. 19.
6. Garson, *All the Livelong Day,* p. 26.
7. Back, *Occupational Stress,* p. 62–67.
8. Mary Ellen Hombs and Mitch Snyder, *Homelessness in America: A Forced March to Nowhere* (Washington, D.C.: Community for Creative Non-Violence, 1982), p. 39.
9. *Contra Costa Times,* November 15, 1981; *San Francisco Examiner/Chronicle* (Sunday), December 6, 1981.

10. *Bargaining for Equality* (San Francisco: Women's Labor Project, 1981).
11. *United Steelworkers vs. Weber,* 443 U.S. 193 (1979).
12. E. F. Schumacher, *Good Work* (New York: Harper & Row, 1979), pp. 77–83.
13. Quoted in *All Men Are Brothers,* from *Young India,* November 13, 1924.
14. Richard Kazis, "Anti-Union Firms Step Up the Pressure," *In These Times,* December, 19, 1979, p. 7.
15. Ibid.
16. *Newsweek,* January 28, 1980, p. 9.
17. Ibid. The editor has heard this tape-recording, which is lengthy and incredibly racist. Many of the company's workers reportedly believed that this recording represented excerpted news coverage of an actual strike.
18. Information from a factsheet distributed jointly by the Plant Closure Project and the union.
19. Information from Henry Weinstein, "Vacaville Job Development Policy May Set Precedent," Part I, *Los Angeles Times,* July 14, 1983.
20. "1982 Plant Closures Affect 1.2 Million Workers," *Multinational Monitor* 4, no. 4, p. 7.
21. Tim Shorrock, "Editorial," *Multinational Monitor* 4, no. 4, p. 3.
22. Fred Miller, "Seeing the Forest *and* the Trees," *Multinational Monitor* 4, no. 4, p. 21.
23. Excerpts from "Ethical Reflections on the Economic Crisis," January 1983, Episcopal Commission for Social Affairs, Canadian Conference of Catholic Bishops, 90 Parent Avenue, Ottawa, Canada K1N7B1. Quoted in *The Interreligious Economic Crisis Organizing Network Newsletter* 1, no. 1 (April 1983).
24. *National Unemployed News* 1, no. 1, (July 1983), p. 5.
25. Information from John Egerton, "Workers Take Over the Store," *New York Times Magazine,* September 11, 1983.
26. *Catering Industry Employee,* magazine of the Hotel Employee and Restaurant Employee International Union (HEREIU), August 1983, p. 1.
27. *U.C.O. Perspective* 2, no. 1 (January 1983).
28. "Foreclosure Alert VII," published by Center for Community Change, 1000 Wisconsin Avenue N.W., Washington, D.C. 20007, p. 2.
29. *I/ECON Newsletter* 1, no. 1 (April 1983).

SOURCES OF FURTHER INFORMATION

Groups Mentioned in Chapter

Alpha Farm. Deadwood, Oreg. 97430.

Household Workers' Rights. 330 Ellis Street, Room 501, San Francisco, Calif. 94102.

Interreligious Economic Crisis Organizing Network (I/ECON). 15 State Street, New York, N.Y. 10004.

National Unemployed Network. 116 5th Avenue, McKeesport, Pa. 15132.

New Ways to Work, San Francisco. 149 9th Street, San Francisco, Calif. 94103.

Plant Closure Project. c/o Catholic Charities, 433 Jefferson Street, Oakland, Calif. 94607. Coordinates a national network.

United Food and Commercial Workers Union, Local 1357. 210 East Courtland Street, Philadelphia, Pa. 19120.

Veritable Vegetables. 233 Industrial Street, San Francisco, Calif. 94124.

Willmar 8. Film available from: California Newsreel, 630 Natoma Street, San Francisco, Calif. 94103.

Additional Resource Groups

Center for Community Economic Development. 1878 Massachusetts Avenue, Cambridge, Mass. 02140. Small-scale, democratically owned industry.

Comparable Worth Project. 488 41st Street, No. 5, Oakland, Calif. 94609.

Distributing Alliance of the North Country Cooperatives (DANCE). 530 Kasota Avenue, Minneapolis, Minn. 55414. Consumer-owned, worker-managed food distribution.

Economic Rights Project: Feminization of Poverty Conference, American Friends Service Committee, New York Regional Office. 15 Rutherford Place, New York, N.Y. 10003.

Gender-Fair Education Resource Center, American Friends Service Committee, Dayton Regional Office. 915 Salem Avenue, Dayton, Ohio 45406.

Institute for Labor and Mental Health. 3137 Telegraph Avenue, Oakland, Calif. 94609. Also runs a labor-consciousness club program for children.

The Midwest Center for Labor Research. 4012 Elm, East Chicago, Ind. 46312. Plant closings, union busting, community destruction.

National Council for Alternative Work Patterns. 1925 K Street, N.W., Suite 308, Washington, D.C. 20006

Neighborhood Youth Employment Program, American Friends Service Committee, New York Metropolitan Regional Office. 15 Rutherford Place, New York, N.Y. 10003.

New Ways to Work, Palo Alto. 457 Kingsley Avenue, Palo Alto, Calif. 94301. A work-issues center that offers books, conferences, speakers, and films.

Bibliography

General Commentary on Work

Back, Aaron, et al. *Occupational Stress: The Inside Story.* Oakland, Calif.: Institute for Labor and Mental Health, 1981.

Garson, Barbara. *All the Livelong Day: The Meaning and Demeaning of Routine Work.* Garden City, N.Y.: Doubleday, 1975.

Illich, Ivan. *Tools for Conviviality.* New York: Harper & Row, 1973, 1980.

New Ways to Work, Palo Alto. Offers the following resources (for postage add 75¢ under $2.50; $1.25 over $2.50; 10 percent over $12.50.): Dollars and Sense, *Shifting Sands,* 1982 (on U.S. job trends), $1.50; Corporate Action Project, *Corporate Action Guide,* 1974, $3; Institute for Labor Education and Research, *We Are Not the Problem! A Short Course on What's Wrong with the American Economy.* 1983, $1; Popular Economics Press, *What's Happening to Our Jobs?,* 1978, $2.30; Alice Kessler-Harris, *Women Have Always Worked: A Historical Overview,* 1981, $6.95.

Schumacher, Ernest F. *Good Work.* (New York: Harper & Row, 1979).

Terkel, Studs. *Working: People Talk About What They Do All Day and How They Feel About What They Do.* New York: Avon, 1982.

Cooperatives, Collectives, Worker's Control

Brandow, Karen, Jim McDonnell, and Vocations for Social Change. *No Bosses Here! A Manual on Working Collectively and Cooperatively,* 2nd ed. Philadelphia: New Society, 1983.

Case, John, ed. *Workers' Control: A Reader on Labor and Social Change.* New York: Random House, 1973.

Community Publications Cooperative. *A Guide to Cooperative Alternatives.* 1979. Available from: Box 426, Louisa, Va. $5.95.

Honigsberg, Peter Jan, et al. *We Own It: Starting and Managing Co-ops, Collectives and Employee Owned Ventures.* Laytonville, Calif.: Bell Springs Pub., 1982.

Lindenfeld, Frank, and Joyce Rothschild-Whitt. *Workplace Democracy and Social Change.* Boston: Porter Sargent, 1982.

Phillips, Michael, and Salli Rasberry. *Honest Business: A Superior Strategy for Starting and Managing Your Own Business.* New York: Random House, 1981. Includes cooperatives and collectives.

Sketchley, Peter, with Frances Moore Lappé. *Casting New Molds: First Steps Towards Worker Control in a Mozambique Steel Factory.* 1980. Available from: Institute for Food and Development Policy, 1885 Mission Street, San Francisco, Calif. 94110. $3.95.

Zwerdling, Daniel. *Workplace Democracy.* New York: Harper & Row, 1979.

Job Skills, Work Changes, and Work Time

Bolles, Richard N. *What Color Is Your Parachute? A Practical Manual for Job Hunters and Career Changers,* rev. ed. Berkeley, Calif.: Ten-Speed Press, 1983.

Hewes, Jeremy Joan. *Worksteads: Living and Working in the Same Place.* Garden City, N.Y.: Doubleday, 1981.

Job Sharing Through Collective Bargaining. San Francisco: New Ways to Work, 1982. $2.50. Write for complete list of publications to address above.

Olmsted, Barney, and Suzanne Smith. *The Job Sharing Handbook.* New York: Penguin Books, 1983.

Reader's Digest, eds. *Complete Guide to Sewing.* New York: Random House, 1976.

Unions, Collective Bargaining, Legal Rights

Alliance Against Sexual Coercion. *Fighting Sexual Harassment, An Advocacy Handbook.* Available from: Box 1, Cambridge, Mass. 02139. $3.50.

American Federation of State, County, and Municipal Employees (AFSCME). *Sexual Harassment on the Job: What the Union Can Do.* Available from: 1625 L Street, N.W., Washington, D.C. 20036.

Handy Reference Guide to the Fair Labor Standards Act (Federal Wage-Hour Law). Available from: U.S. Government Printing Office Washington, D.C. 20402, or from local U.S. Department of Labor Offices.

A Layman's Guide to Basic Law Under the National Labor Relations Act. Available from: U.S. Government Printing Office and National Labor Relations Board, Washington, D.C. 20402, or from local NLRB offices.

Union for Radical Political Economics. *Women Organizing the Office.* Available from: 41 Union Square West, New York, N.Y. 10003. $2.

Union WAGE, 330 Ellis Street, Room 501, San Francisco, Calif. 94102 offers the following publications (add 65¢ postage): ORGANIZE! *A Working Women's Handbook,* $2.50; *You Can't Scare Me: Stories of Women Activists and Organizers,* $1.50; *Labor Heroines: Ten Women Who Led the Struggle,* 75¢; *Talking Union* (definition of terms used in negotiations, organizing and meetings), $1.25; *Working Women and Their Organizations—150 Years of Struggle,* $1; *Jean Maddox: The Fight for Rank and File Democracy,* $1.

Women's Labor Project. *Bargaining for Equality,* 2nd ed. 1981. Available from: Box 6250, San Francisco, Calif. 94101. $5 ppd.

Women's Worth: Valuing Our Own Worth—Realizing Our Own Value. 1982. A resource manual for use with "The Willmar 8" film. Available from: California

Newsreel, 630 Natoma Street, San Francisco, Calif. 94103. $3.50, or free
with film rental.

A Working Woman's Guide to Her Job Rights. Washington, D.C.: U.S. Government
Printing Office. $1.60.

Unemployment and Plant Closings

Southern Neighborhoods publishes several manuals on unemployment organizing, including: *Fighting the Root Causes of Unemployment,* $3; *Training Unem-
ployment Fighters; Manual for Trainers,* $10. Available from: 915 24th Ave-
nue North, Nashville, Ten. 37208.

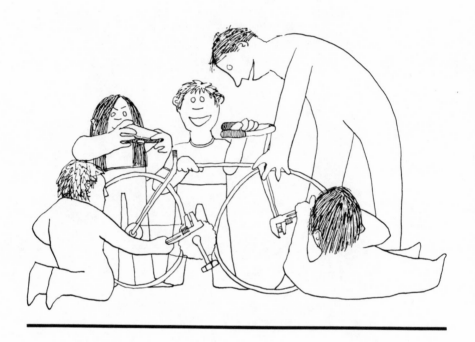

CHAPTER VII

Children

QUERIES

1. What do our daily lives teach our children about our responsibility in the world? Am I working at an unpleasant or destructive job in order to make payments on a bigger house or to buy my children fashionable clothes? Do I have time to prepare nutritious foods, help them with a learning project, or protest injustices that I perceive? Have I discussed these conflicts between buying and doing with my children?

2. Do I feel guilty that I am economically unable to buy my children what "other children" have—clothing, toys, bigger allowance for amusements, summer camp? Do I discuss with my children how much money I get paid, how much some other people get paid, and why? Do I discuss with them the difference between economic values and human values? Or do I think they are too young to understand? Do we listen to what children can tell us about these values?

3. Are we creating a home environment that helps people grow—children and adults alike? Is it a growing place (or as B'rer Rabbit calls it, a "laughing place")? Are we trying to raise our children in a vacuum? Are there good role models from which parents and children can learn?

4. How welcome are children in our community? What does our community offer in the way of broadly available day care, family counseling, and health services? What are we doing about making our community more responsive to the needs of children and families?

5. What kinds of games and toys do our children play with? What skills and values do our recreations teach? What materials go into the playthings? What toys can we make instead of buy?

6. Do I help my children realize—and play with—the diversity of the natural environment? Do I help them understand issues relating to air quality, water quality, and the place of nonhuman life in our communities?

7. Is there a program that welcomes parent participation in our children's school? If not, why not? Are we letting the "experts" do it?

8. How do we divide labor in our homes? Are we extending our families —giving and receiving help? Are we allowing enough unstructured time to just be together?

9. How do we deal with conflict in our homes? Do we express our feelings and ideas openly and work to resolve differences or find workable compromises?

10. Outside school, what activities involve most of our children's time? Are these activities active or passive?

11. Do I feel I have to be the "perfect parent"?

The Cynics

- "Simple living is taking away the TV set."
- "It's having your mom brainwash your dad into not buying comic books or records anymore."
- "Simple living. We never did start."
- "It's eating really healthy, awful stuff for a while, which nobody eats anyway except your parents. Then it's their breaking down and fixing hamburgers."
- "Simple living is feeding your cat dry cat food."
- "It's having Kelley's mouth zipped."

The Converts

- "Simple living means our whole family in front of the fire instead of the TV."
- "It's playing games or doing improvisational theater."
- "Simple living means not having crud to eat, like candy and sugary cereal."
- "It's the simplest problem . . . problems like figuring out how to make things."
- "We don't spend as much. Mom used to sort of butter us up."
- "It's doing it ourselves . . . like when we see advertisements on TV, it's making what I want myself instead."
- "Simple living is not having my mouth zipped. That's quiet living."

THE CONCEPT OF CHILD CARE

This chapter is not only for parents and children. It is written for all of us who have alive in ourselves the wonder and fear of our own "child-person."

This child-person is not the way you remember yourself as a child, but the way you are now when you are excited or creating something new and spontaneous, when you have abandoned your adult habituation and gone off to do something you've always wanted to do, or when you are angry and hurt. Most likely this child-person is who you are before you fall asleep at night, the quiet, feeling person who puts you back together again after a hard day or a hard lifetime of experience (even if your lifetime is only three years so far).

In childhood are the beginnings, the roots, of who each of us becomes. Yet the child-person is not a product, a has-been, but rather a being who needs nuture, an ongoing process. We are all involved in "child care," whether we recognize it or not, as we care or fail to care for the child within day by day.

While everyone may be involved in child care, not everyone is a parent. Becoming a parent can now be largely a matter of choice. Many people are choosing not to be parents, for reasons such as population, professional involvement, or personal preference. Among those who are, some opt for adoption or caring for foster children. We know of people in group living situations who have developed special part-time "godparent" relationships with children in their groups.

Yet, however much experimentation may be going on with its shape and function, the family still remains the basic social unit of our society. It is the preserver and transmitter of traditions and values—the place we came from, return to, or try to escape from for a while. As they grow, children build relationships outwardly, one circle at a time: from parents to relatives, to people in the community, to the rest of the world.

Because of this key role, the American family is the centerpiece of the overdeveloped consumer society. Families are also consumers of such things as food, clothes, automobiles, entertainment, and packaged recreation. Indeed, economists regard the number of new housing starts as one of the most sensitive indicators of the "health" of our economy, because with each new family dwelling will come a whole houseful of expensive manufactured goods—the upkeep, repair, and replacement of which keeps the families occupied and the whole system turning. Through media like television and the attention paid to them by parents, the attitudes of consumerism are taught to children often for as many hours a week as they spend in school. And very young children, as *Washington Post* columnist Colman McCarthy has pointed out, think the television is a friend; they don't realize it is a stranger in the living room trying to sell them things!

In this consumerist family setting, though, we believe much that is of value is lost: the family ceases to be a center of life and learning in its own right, and is turned instead into a receiver and consumer of values, mostly economically based, that come from institutions outside it and beyond its control. How much of the much-discussed "generation gap" is based in the fact that programing and advertising are aimed separately at children, teenagers, mothers, fathers, and older people in the home, and that they exploit the differences of outlook of each? We think a great deal. There is also a whole outlook on life being taught, one centered on novelty, the importance of packaging, and the idea that meaning and fun are to be found only in mass, passive activities.

In contrast, simple living can mean working to reclaim and reassert the centrality of the family itself, however structured, as a primary area for living and growing. In this reclaimed environment we are attempting to articulate, live out, and pass on to the children we nurture a set of values that stress the importance of conservation and fair distribution of resources, self-reliance in work and play, cooperation with others across age and gender lines in mutual assistance and constructive social action, and resistance to injustice and oppression, both near at hand and far away.

Different families have undertaken this task of reclamation and simplification in different ways: sharing, extending family structures, and drawing some of our community's institutions, such as workplaces and unions, into co-responsibility for quality child rearing. Parents are finding many ways to pool resources and ease their burdens through cooperation—anything from renting a big old house and stocking it with toys, books, and buggies, to settling into a neighborhood together. Nuclear families, too, can benefit from shared child care, co-op housekeeping and cooking, or weekends off occasionally. Choosing to be a parent doesn't need to mean martyrdom or a life sentence to drudgery.

The varieties of parental sharing are endless. Two women we interviewed have worked out a barter system arrangement where one cares for their combined four small children three days a week while the other spends that undivided time developing her craft skill as a carpenter. The child-care mother participates with her friend's children as well as her own in a morning co-op nursery school. In the afternoons she takes all the children on errands, to the park, or on small excursions. She is a born educator who can take a child's simple "what if" and help her or him develop it into a day-long project or a playtime involving many different materials and friends. The other four days of the week both mothers spend special at-home time with their own children. The carpenter mother pays for her time without child-care responsibility by doing carpentry work for her friend—neither her friend nor her spouse have that talent. She also keeps her friend's car tuned.

In a group living situation, and in neighborhoods with a strong sense of community, parents, nonparents, and children all have more opportunity to learn from each other. Living together in community can also permit sharing of responsibility. This not only allows adults to have time and space for themselves, but also to give full energy to children. In these settings, childless people can also explore the parent role on a temporary basis.

One single parent extended her family by sharing her home with an older friend. She told us:

At the beginning, my four sons, whose ages span from twenty to fourteen, were a little unsure of how our household would be changed to accommodate an older person with serious health problems. Nevertheless, in spite of their doubts, they knew they wanted to try it. Little by little they began to let their guards down, and their lives, as well as mine, have become richer. Our friend is becoming a dear grandmother who enjoys and prizes their exploits and explorations. I have a companion who has a wealth of experience and who is willing to let us become part of her life. She enjoys the exchange of ideas with the boys, watching their active lives, meeting their friends.

Another small group that seems to be working hard at building a new life-style for themselves consists of three single parents and their eight children.

We share an old house within walking distance from town. All but one of our children are preschool or elementary school age. The younger kids bunk together. The older ones have converted huge walk-in closets into neat little private hangouts. The adults have a room that is a quiet room where we can read or carry on a conversation with a degree of coherence.

At first, life was really chaotic with all of us. The kids fought over their toys, competed for adult attention, and refused to cooperate in the running of the house. As parents, we found we had to make a lot of adjustments, too. We had to get over the "She pinched *my* son," or "They broke *our* record player." We discovered that it is really important to work out a common set of expectations regarding child rearing. Even with some guidelines, our old images, habits, and patterns still can get in the way.

One of the things we did was set up a *nurturing schedule.* Each of us adults works with all the younger kids one day in rotation. This nurturing schedule frees each adult to have two days we're not "on" with the kids.

There are other good things about living together aside from the shared work part. No one, child or adult, feels isolated anymore. And we do have truly *free* time now when someone else is taking care of things. By encouraging everyone to assume more responsibility, we all can be "mother" sometimes—the kids, too. We're learning to say what we need in a way that can be heard.

I've really come to respect how open kids are when we meet them halfway. They instinctively know what they need and their feelings are not easily hidden. As single parents, we have found it easier to relate to those feelings with the support and help of other adults and children. I don't have to say in frustration, "I can't do everything!" anymore. Instead I can say, "Ask Connie, she knows about animals," or "I can help you build it, if Tom will help us figure out how much wood to buy."

Sharing the joy is the best part. Not a day passes that somebody doesn't do something that jars us out of our rut and makes us laugh at the world or ourselves. The big problems look so much smaller when they're shared. The love is there for the asking and the giving. The thing I ask myself is, "Why haven't we done this before?"

It is also important to have our unions and our workplaces recognize their responsibility for the care of children in our communities. One

union, the Baltimore Joint Regional Board of Amalgamated Clothing
Workers of America, operates six child-care centers for over thirteen
hundred of its members' children. The centers are near parents' workplaces and are open ten to twelve hours per day, five days a week. Cost
is shared by approximately seventy employers and the served parents.
Another approach, won by a Canadian union, is to have the employer
contribute 50 percent of an employee's day-care costs.

Unions have successfully bargained for other provisions that help parenting remain on at least an equal footing with work: use of sick leave for
the care of a sick child or to take the child to the doctor (District 65, UAW)
and the absolute right to refuse overtime (St. Louis Automotive Association and Machinists, IAM). Even more common is the right to refuse
overtime except in emergency situations. This last provision, while especially important for parents, is important for all of us who have other
priorities in our lives besides our jobs.

FACING PROBLEMS AND FINDING SOLUTIONS AS A FAMILY

Several families we visited use a "family meeting"* process as their way
to air and share feelings, set up work schedules, discuss money, and make
plans together. These meetings are not just times to hear complaints, but
regular get-togethers. Some begin with "excitement sharing," when individual family members tell about what happened that day or what's coming up. Then perhaps others will want to hear more about a new project
or will begin discussing a controversial topic.

One family of five decided to have every person, even the seven-year-
old, cook dinner one night a week. The two unclaimed weeknights are
"surprise" nights, when people either fend for themselves or elect to
cook again. Fasting has also been tried! This family is exploring vegetarian cooking by making Monday night rice night, Tuesday cheese, and
Thursday beans. Wednesdays and Fridays are usually fish and chicken.
The schedule goes for a month, so at the end of that time, each member
has a repertoire of four or five dishes of a type. One Christmas each
person received a card file (with a patchwork cover of his or her favorite
old fabrics) in which to record some of the innovative recipes that each
cooks up.

Another family sees their family finances as the arena to practice shared
responsibility. They list all their sources of income, even the kids', and
all the month's expenses; it's a real discipline to remember where all that
small change goes! The kids like doing the arithmetic and finding out how
much they're behind or ahead. If there is extra money at the end of the
month, they talk about how to use it. Usually any surplus money is
earmarked for the next month's expenses, like insurance. The family feels

---

*See Chapter IV for suggestions that may help with the meeting process, even in a group
as small as a family!

that this is a tremendous way to see what the family values are: when it's everybody's money, somehow each feels more responsible. Wanting something becomes a matter of dollars and sense as well as desire. Strangely, the kids seem more flexible in this respect than the adults!

Another family used the family meeting as a way to learn not only about their home economic picture, but about world economics. After learning about world hunger, they decided to have a meal of rice, tea, and fruit one night a week and to donate the money they would have spent on the meal to UNICEF. A ten-year-old suggested the project, so he takes care of the money and mails a check off every month or two to the UNICEF offices in New York.

WHAT TO DO FOR RECREATION?

TV OR LIFE?

Families can learn to create a sense of joy in being together without depending on any outside helpers. Time spent watching television or playing computerized war games on the TV screen is *not* the same as time spent talking, reading, cooking, inventing something, sewing, gardening, playing hard outside, sitting around on the porch, *and* many more things that you, the reader, can think up. Moreover, television becomes a chief focus for entertainment only if we let it. If our children are watching it too much, perhaps we need to ask ourselves, and them, "What need is this fulfilling?" Are the children seeking security, or even community, in the world of television because their own world is too adult-oriented or too chaotic or too boring? Are the adults quietly ignoring the problem, choosing not to come to terms with it at all? Can we appreciate the good programing but also encourage our children to be discriminating?

What kind of activities could we involve our children in doing with us? How about their helping us to prepare the next meal, plant some seeds, or do some simple carpentry? Children like to feel useful and learn new skills. It gives them a sense of worth to be involved in "real" projects that benefit everyone in the family. The movement and excitement of a project is much healthier than the passive response that television evokes. There are many idea books (see Bibliography) available that give directions for making playthings and that outline educational projects. Making your own toys not only saves money, but can be fun. Biking not only saves gas, but can make you independent of a "chauffeur" and able to see and feel the world more directly. Sewing or redesigning old clothes not only saves resources, but is also more expressive of an individual's uniqueness.

WAR TOYS IN A HUNGRY WORLD

Commercial advertising often pushes toys on our children that we would rather they didn't play with. The year of 1982 saw the reintroduction of "GI Joe" and other war toys that had been pulled from most store shelves during the Vietnam War. This new onslaught of war toys includes the latest in hi-tech weapons: mobile missile systems, lasers, sophisticated tanks, espionage systems, "good guy" male and female action figures, "bad guy" action figures—some of which have Russian, Chinese, and Arab features, and some of which are deliberately designed so that a child can, according to one toy company official, "pick his nationality."

"Toys are Teaching Tools," the official brochure of Toy Manufacturers of America, Inc., states: "Today's toys are tomorrow's adult tools. . . . Toys help children to assume adult roles and to experiment with the objects, machines and technology of adult society." By their own admission, then, toy companies are preparing our children for war. They are also teaching children to be comfortable with the very "adult tools" that are directly responsible for lowering the quality of children's lives: more money for defense means less money for education, social services, and medical care.

It is difficult, but crucial, for parents to deal rationally and positively with their children and peers about this issue; even the most protected children learn to want symbols of physical power. But it is possible to deal intelligently with this whole issue and to feel that we have some control over arms proliferation on the home front.

One effort occurred in late 1982, when a small group of parents, enraged by television commercials for the GI Joe Mobile Missile System —the "MSS"—mailed a few petitions threatening a boycott of all Hasbro products to local children's organizations in San Francisco. A few weeks later, hundreds of signatures began pouring in from as far away as Idaho. People had taken it upon themselves to make more copies of the petitions, to collect signatures in front of toy stores, and even to put anti-MX stickers on MSS packages sitting on shelves. As a result, in early 1983, Steven Hassenfeld, president of Rhode Island-based Hasbro (one of the two *Has-bro*thers), met with the San Francisco parents for three hours to try to justify this toy. The discussion ended with his agreeing to "see about" removing the decal that symbolizes radiation danger from the MSS package. He was informed his action was inadequate, and the group planned to continue its campaign during the 1983 Christmas season. They have a large task ahead of them: the *New York Times* reported that the GI Joe series was the number-one seller of the 1982 Christmas season.

We can help children develop acceptable ways of expressing their anger and frustrations: punching bags, drawing funny pictures in effigy, making up nonviolent names like "banana bean." Humor can quickly deflate anger. Aggression can also be channeled into sports, pounding sets, carpentry, action games, music. There are board games, as well as "new games" that stress cooperation, which are exciting and full of action.

One way we can motivate our children—and ourselves—to face up to the issue of war and war toys is to recognize explicitly what preparation for real war does to children all over the world. In a June 1983 high school commencement speech, Marian Wright Edelman, president of the Children's Defense Fund, reminded her listeners of a few of the correlations:[1]

- Forty thousand young children die from malnutrition and infection each day worldwide.
- In the United States, poor children die at three times the rate of nonpoor children.
- More children in the United States thus die of poverty each five years than the total number of U.S. battle deaths in Vietnam.
- In 1981, the Reagan Administration and Congress cut $9 billion from children's disease-prevention programs and from lifeline support programs for poor families. In 1983, $3.5 billion in new cuts were proposed by the Administration.
- The cost of nine B-1 bombers would finance a year's Medicaid for all pregnant women and children living below the poverty level.
- When President Reagan took office, the United States spent $18 million *per hour* on defense. In 1983, it spent $24 million per hour. For 1984, the administration proposed $28 million per hour.
- One day's worth of U.S. defense spending would pay for a year's free school lunches for half a million children. (This year, after school lunch funding was cut, one school district started feeding hungry children leftovers from the trays of their wealthier peers.)[2]

Our children must be helped to understand that B-1 bombers and MX missiles are *not* toys. Even when they are not used, they still cause needless suffering and death to children in their school classes and children around the world.

PEER PRESSURES

If a family's efforts to simplify their life together mean that they have a different life from that of their friends, won't the children complain? Budgets, schedules, and consensus aside, don't kids resist doing work that other kids' moms do? Won't they be resentful of not buying a new back-to-school wardrobe, of not having a regular department-store Christmas, of not buying into the American Dream? Especially if they've had these things before, but even if they haven't—how do we convince our children that living simply, if it means giving up such things, is living better?

Peer pressure is not such an obvious challenge to the parents of small children. Because their world view is still quite narrow, they look to their parents to explain things. Interaction with other children and adults is limited. The family value system is not questioned severely. Depending on the neighborhood, everybody may seem pretty much alike. However, children learn early to spot the differences. "Because my daddy said so" soon yields to "Mark's dad lets him." Television, the nursery school or day-care center, church, the local grocery store, or the street corner offer opportunities for the preschooler to collect data that either support or challenge his world view.

Children seek to feel at home in the world—more than that, they seek some kind of mastery of it. Sometimes that means having a special, even magical, way to grasp it, to touch it, or to belong in it. Many of the clothes, cars, and houses that adults own or covet seem magical to children. Certainly, teenage fads reflect this desire for affiliation. The haircuts (or lack of them), the jeans, pop art T-shirts, expensive bicycles, and so on —these are valuable not only because they are functional or beautiful, but also because of what they symbolize: power and tribal identity. The same is true for young children. Their toys, clothes, and games can be a statement that they belong. Talking about what was on television last night is like adults exchanging comments about the ballgame or the weather. It is all part of a common reality and a sign of status. Children aren't the only people who confuse what a person *has* with what a person *is*.

If a family that is working to simplify their life begins cutting down on things and getting away from the television culture, they may feel at first as though they are handicapping themselves. Not buying can be like saying, "You are different"; not going to Mcdonald's can be like saying, "You can't belong." There is no hard-and-fast rule about being different. It's more often *how* something is done than *what* is done. However, when a child's sense of worth seems to be involved, then it is important to be able to be flexible whenever possible, to be willing to bend, to negotiate. Simplifying our lives does not mean taking things away, but rather clearing away whatever is not of value in order to replace it with something that is truly valuable. It means finding better alternatives.

Sometimes people need to experience the cruddy TV show, the platform shoes that kill the feet, and the toy that breaks. Of course, it hits home harder if they have paid for these things themselves. Each person eventually develops his or her own value system. The point is not to resist all popular fashions or fads just because they're popular, but to learn to be *selective*. Know what you want and why—and then take the consequences. By being free to pick and choose, to go along with the crowd or not, we can show others what it is to be a responsible consumer and citizen.

THE SIMPLIFICATION PROCESS

In seeking to simplify our lives, we are not seeking to deny our children access to the twentieth century or to the way the world operates (or does not operate). If anything, we are trying to remove the confusion that comes from such denial. By learning to be creators as well as competitors, conservers as well as consumers, we are practicing the making of choices: sometimes saying yes, sometimes no; sometimes controlling, sometimes letting go of control. While learning to be more self-reliant, we are also learning to be more involved.

The more self-reliant life is not a life of convenience—especially for those who have had enough money to pay someone else to do simple repairs or to entertain their children with an assortment of home video games. On the other hand, those of us who have felt trapped outside looking in at the goodies may suddenly feel a whole new range of exciting possibilities open to us that we never realized we had the "resources" to accomplish.

It is important to experiment with these new ways gradually. Busy parents may already feel stretched to the limit, and things always take twice as long as you planned when you're just learning how. If a family agrees that their recipe for living creatively should include sewing, carpentry, gardening, bread-baking, financial planning, and thrift shopping, these all take know-how, energy, and time.

Helping kids become more self-reliant is often very messy and frustrating. Your nerves may be on edge while you are learning to do something you've never done before, making mistakes, taking the consequences, convincing others to help, resenting change. The compost heap needs attention—and the goat, if you've gone that far, needs milking.

Sure, it's easier (and sometimes necessary) to open a can of pineapple-grapefruit drink and a package of graham crackers for snack time than to help the kids bake zucchini bread from the zucchini they've planted and cared for themselves. Sometimes the bread doesn't even turn out (someone forgot the baking powder), but when it does, the satisfaction is truly wonderful. The bother, if it isn't always half the fun, is certainly half the point. Confrontation, not escape, is what this life is all about. Involvement, not comfort.

Being a parent is like being a twenty-four-hour-a-day teacher. We are the primary sources, the first reference, the givers of permission. Still, how many of us have yet to give ourselves that permission to be involved, to be different, to resist, to suffer even? How many of us say what we believe by the way we live our lives?

We can begin to live full lives, less dependent on material resources when we ask ourselves seriously what it is we want and need out of family life and how we can achieve our goals with minimal harm to ourselves, our children, and other people. For many of us, answering these questions may mean we will need to face up to the mess, recycle the bottles and cans, and learn how to repair and renovate old clothing, toys, and furniture. It may mean selecting food that is nourishing and economical and cutting down on our use of electrical energy and fossil fuels. It may mean involving ourselves in the mainstream of our community, participating in local politics, following through on what we believe, whether we can win or not. Most of all, we must become aware of and responsible for our decisions, begin to model the behavior we expect of others, and approach each day ready to learn from ourselves and our children.

Beyond focusing in on our homes and neighborhoods, we need to give our children hope in this nuclear age, to help them feel that they have some real power and purpose in their lives. Child suicide and drug abuse have soared during the past decade. Introduction to other cultures can help them to develop a global consciousness and a sense of responsibility and belonging. Any natural interest, from gardening to music to computers, can serve as an entrée for meeting diverse cultures. And these interests can be encouraged as skills for the future. We can also encourage our children to get involved in their own right in community on broader political activities, as well as with youth-oriented projects, such as the Youth Advocacy Project. described in chapter VI, or the Detroit Anti-Hunger/Youth Advocacy Center, described in Chapter II.

We are now faced with some of the greatest challenges ever faced by humankind, challenges caused by astounding technological advances. How do we prevent our annihilation, reverse the arms race, and reallocate resources to solving problems of starvation, disease, and pollution? What will be our ethical mores vis-a-vis creating and prolonging life? Our children, by responsibly taking charge of their own lives, will be learning the skills they will need to tackle these problems as adults.

Pearl Buck, the American novelist who lived much of her young life in China, described the importance of her family experience in an address given at a joint session of the National Conference on Family Relations and the New York State Conference on Marriage and the Family:

We did not merely learn, we learned that we had something to do with all we learned—that nothing human was alien to us, because we, too, were human. We learned this not by hearing it said, but simply by seeing our parents deeply involved in action. They were so interested in what they did that they made themselves interesting to us. We were not left outside of their activities or left to ourselves while they came and went—we came and went, too. Yes, we saw things and did things that many of us here would not consider suitable for children—I came to adulthood ready for life.

I believe the problems of the world must first be met in the home before we will have men and women sufficiently educated for the world, and that we do our children the most grave injustice when we do not fit them in the home for the world they will find waiting at their door when they step outside. If [the child's] home has shielded and denied him the knowledge and practice of life he will be terrified. The child prepared in the home through all the life of the home for the life of the world steps forward a self-confident and integrated creature. He will be afraid of nothing because he will say, "I know about this—I know what to do."

WHAT YOU CAN DO

SOME TOOLS FOR INTRODUCING KIDS TO SIMPLE LIVING

- Sturdy carpentry tools, real but child-size.
- Lumber.
- Nails, screws, nuts, and bolts.
- Sturdy gardening tools, real but child-size.
- Seeds, cuttings.
- Compost.
- Planters (might be made with sturdy carpentry tools).
- Old machines, junk.
- Old magazines, clippings, scraps of all kinds.
- A handcrank ice cream maker for home ice cream, fruit sherbets.
- Sewing supplies.
- Trunk filled with thrift-shop finery.
- Scarves, flimsy material for dancing, illusion, make-believe.
- Musical instruments, homemade as well as manufactured.
- Old sheets, blankets, clothespins.
- A cupboard at child level with cooking and clean-up supplies.
- Your child's own tested recipe file.
- Lots of cleaning stuff, child-safe, child-manageable.
- A bike with tools and oil to care for it.
- A bus schedule with well-used routes marked.
- Band-Aids and disinfectant.

EXERCISES FOR CHILDREN AND ADULTS

1. Help your child make a family scrapbook. Include familiar people unrelated by marriage or blood. Exchange children for a weekend. Plan a neighborhood potluck. Celebrate a favorite holiday by including single people and people over age fifty.

2. Make an inventory of what your child owns. Help your child develop the categories and system for accounting (you'll learn how he or she thinks). Are there things that are no longer used? Can your child think of someone who *would* use them? If they need repairs or mending, can you help your child restore these unused items before passing them on?

3. Do all the things your child owns have a place? How does your child order space? Are tools—crayons, clay, hammers, nails, and books—readily accessible? Can your child take charge independent of you? Using old boxes, pegboard, or similar materials, can you help your child organize his or her space? (Be prepared, this may take days. Take long walks or water your yard when it gets too intense.)

4. In a nonjudgmental way, discuss with your child what she or he wants for Christmas or for her or his next birthday. How did this desire

arise? How will the gift be used? Who makes it? Where do the materials come from? What happens to it when it gets broken or old?

5. Pack lunches and take an all-day walk around your city or town. Take money for carfare home; you'll be surprised how the miles fly by. Share your feelings about what you see. What decisions have been made in your town or city about the use of space? Is there a "poor side of town"? Is there a "rich side of town"? Who has the most available recreation, transportation, libraries, clinics?

6. Check out your neighborhood thrift stores with your child. Take along three dollars each. Another day, compare what you paid with the retail prices of the same things new.

7. Try using the family meeting when a serious problem comes up. All members should have an opportunity to state their views and feelings *uninterrupted.* Resolution might not come in one meeting. Ask some member to state where things rest at the end of the time allotted. Appoint another time when you can all meet to continue your discussion.

8. Investigate what resources your city has available free or for very little cost—in entertainment, educational activities, health services, and other areas. Make your own "people's yellow pages" directory, including the people in your neighborhood to see about fixing a sink, planting a garden, flying a kite. Check out the libraries for story hours, puppet shows, records, and films.

9. Use children's response to high-powered advertising of war toys as an opportunity to discuss peace: how people are working to prevent wars, and who are some peace heroes? There are "superheroes" in many areas of our lives, such as sports, space, medicine, literature, and art. Discuss these people, as well as the heroes in our families and communities.

10. In North America, north of Mexico, there are about 700 species of birds, 100,000 species of insects and spiders, 700 species of butterflies, 865 species of trees, 180 species of amphibians (frogs, toads, and salamanders), 278 species of reptiles (turtles, lizards, snakes, and crocodiles)—not to mention mammals, rocks, flowers, bushes, fish, mushrooms, and ferns. There are many more subspecies of astonishing variety: broccoli, cauliflower, green cabbage, red cabbage, and brussels sprouts are all varieties of one plant species. How can we and our children play with these "educational toys"? (Try not to be *too* squeamish about bugs!) What outlets are there for natural exploration in the area that can be reached by walking, bicycle, public transportation? Are there programs for adults and children at local parks? Are there programs for adults and children at local chapters of such organizations as the Sierra Club or the Audubon Society?

11. Could a school or youth group find ways to explore environmental issues? Project Ecology of the Highline Public Schools (Box 66100,

Seattle, Washington 98166) developed a series of elementary school projects that are still available in varying quantities, though the project has been defunded. One project, for example, helps children collect and identify polluting substances in their community's air, explores their effects and their sources.

NOTES

1. "Notes and Comment," *The New Yorker*, June 27, 1983, p. 26.
2. Mary Ellen Hombs and Mitch Snyder, *Homelessness: A Forced March to Nowhere* (Washington, D.C.: Community for Creative Non-Violence, 1982), p. 40.

SOURCES OF FURTHER INFORMATION

Groups Mentioned in Chapter

Children's Defense Fund. 1520 New Hampshire Avenue, N.W., Washington, D.C. 20036.
Disarmament Project—Safe Toys. c/o AFSC, 2160 Lake Street, San Francisco, Calif. 94121.

Additional Resource Groups

Children's Campaign for Nuclear Disarmament. Box 550, RD #1, Plainfield, Vt. 05667. Direct letter-writing campaign.
Children's Creative Response to Conflict Program. c/o Fellowship of Reconciliation, Box 271, Nyack, N.Y. 10960.
Children's Public Policy Network. 122 C Street, N.W., Washington, D.C. 20001.
Day Care Council of America. 1602 17th Street, N.W., Washington, D.C. 20009.
Fair Housing for Children Coalition. Box 5877, Santa Monica, Calif. 90405.
Housing Rights for Children Project. 6501 Telegraph Avenue, Oakland, Calif. 94609.
Parenting in a Nuclear Age. c/o Bananas, 6501 Telegraph Avenue, Oakland, Calif. 94609.
Peace Resource Center of San Diego, Alternatives to War Toys Program. 5717 Lindo Pasao, San Diego, Calif. 92115.

Bibliography

Background Books on Children and Family

Bartz, Wayne, and Richard Rasor. *Surviving with Kids: A Lifeline for Overwhelmed Parents.* San Luis Obispo, Calif.: Impact Publishers, 1978.
Blessington, John P. *Let My Children Work.* New York: Doubleday/Anchor, 1975.
Boston Women's Health Book Collective, Inc. *Ourselves and Our Children: A Book by and for Parents.* New York: Random House, 1978.
Breitbart, Vicki. *The Day Care Book—The Why, What, and How of Community Day Care.* New York: Alfred A. Knopf, 1974.
Cohen, Dorothy H. *The Learning Child.* New York: Vintage/Random, 1973.
Erikson, Erik. *Childhood and Society.* New York: Norton, 1963.

Faber, Adele. *How to Talk So Kids Will Listen and Listen So Kids Will Talk.* New York: Avon, 1982.

Faber, Adele, and Elaine Mazlish. *Liberated Parents, Liberated Children.* New York: Avon, 1975.

Fraiberg, Selma H. *The Magic Years.* New York: Scribner's, 1959.

Gordon, Dr. Thomas. *P.E.T.: Parent Effectiveness Training, The Tested New Way to Raise Responsible Children.* New York: New American Library/Plume Book, 1975.

Hallett, Kathryn. *A Guide for Single Parents.* Millbrae, Calif.: Celestial Arts, 1974.

Holt, John. *Teach Your Own.* New York: Delacorte/Lawrence, 1981.

Moustakas, Clark E., and Cerela Perry. *Learning to Be Free.* Englewood Cliffs, N.J.: Prentice-Hall, 1973.

Satir, Virginia. *Peoplemaking.* Center City, Minn.: Hazelden, 1975.

Idea Books

Animal Town Game Company Catalog. Available from: Box 2002, Santa Barbara, Calif. 93120. Offers board games such as "Save the Whales" and "Dam Builders (Beavers *vs.* Army Corps of Engineers!)."

Auerbach, Stevanne. *The Whole Child.* New York: Perigree/Putnam, 1981.

Caney, Steven. *Playbook.* New York: Workman Publishing Company, 1975.

Cardozo, Peter. *The Whole Kids Do-It-Yourself Scrapbook.* New York: Bantam, 1979.

Carr, Rachel. *Be a Frog, a Bird, or a Tree.* New York: Harper & Row, 1977.

Gregg, Elizabeth, ed., and the Boston Children's Medical Center. *What to Do When There's Nothing to Do.* New York: Dell, 1970.

Growing Without Schooling Newsletter. ed. John Holt. Available from: 308 Boylston Street, Boston, Mass. 02116. $10/six issues.

Kelly, Marguerite, and Elia Parsons. *The Mothers Almanac.* New York: Doubleday, 1975.

Koch, Kenneth, et al. *Wishes, Lies and Dreams: Teaching Children to Write Poetry.* New York: Harper & Row, 1980.

Mander, Jerry. *Four Arguments for the Elimination of Television.* New York: Morrow Quill Paperbacks, 1978.

New Games Resource Catalog. Available from: New Games Foundation, Box 7901, San Francisco, Calif. 94120. $1.

New Ways of Learning Newsletter. ed. J. Blankenship and S. B. Nelson. Available from: Box 1161, Liburn, Ga. 30147. $10/six issues.

Project Ecology Instruction Materials Catalog. Available from: Highline School District, 15675 Ambaum Boulevard, S.W., Seattle, Wash. 98166.

Robertson, James, and Carolyn Robertson, eds. *Brown Paper School (1961–82).* Boston: Little, Brown & Company, 1982.

Shettel, Doris. *Lifestyle Change for Children.* United Presbyterian Program Agency, 1981. Suitable for grades 3–6. Available from: Alternatives, Box 1707, Forest Park, Ga. 30051. $4.

Sierra Club Kids for Nature Yearbook. San Francisco, Calif. Annual daily journal and calendar for kids, full of projects and information.

Thomas, Marlo, and Ms. Foundation, Inc. *Free to Be You and Me.* New York: McGraw-Hill Book Company, 1974.

Children and Nonviolence

Brethren House Team. *Peacemaking Activities for Children.* 1981. Available from: Alternatives, Box 1707, Forest Park, Ga. 30051. $3/copy + 15 percent postage.

Coerr, Eleanor. *Sadako and the Thousand Paper Cranes.* New York: Dell, 1977.

Fisher, Roger, and William Ury. *Getting to Yes: Negotiating Agreement Without Giving In.* Boston: Houghton Mifflin Company, 1981.

Friends Peace Committee and Stephanie Judson, ed. *A Manual on Nonviolence and Children.* Philadelphia: New Society, 1977.

Magic Mouse. Box 44141, Tucson, Ariz. 95733. Makers of children's series stressing peace, nonviolence, sharing. Order tapes direct or request through your local PBS station.

McGinnis, Kathleen, and James McGinnis. *Parenting for Peace and Justice.* Maryknoll, N.Y.: Orbis Books, 1981. *Program Guide* also available for study group leaders.

Orlick, Terry. *The Cooperative Sports and Games Book: Challenge Without Competition.* New York: Pantheon, 1978.

Orlick, Terry. *The Second Cooperative Sports and Games Book.* New York: Pantheon, 1982.

Peachey, J. Lorne. *How to Teach Peace to Children.* 1981. Available from: Alternatives, Box 1707, Forest Park, Ga. 30051. $1/copy + 15 percent postage.

Prescott, Susan. *If Kids Shouldn't Fight, Why Do Grown-Ups?* Port Townsend Peace Coalition, 1982. Coloring book suitable for grades 1–6. Available from: Alternatives, Box 1707, Forest Park, Ga. 30051. $3.

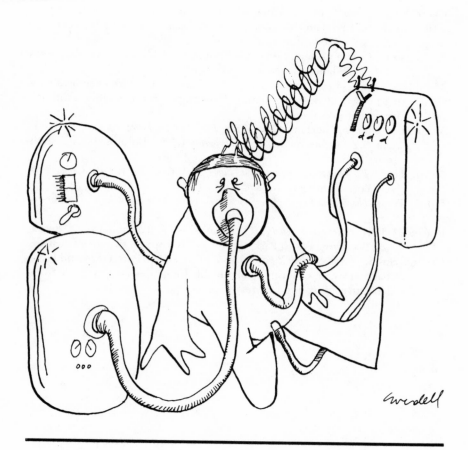

CHAPTER VIII

Health Care

QUERIES

1. How can we begin to take charge of our own physical and mental health? Are there ways to challenge the health-care system's control over us?

2. How well are my family and I covered in case of sickness? Have any of us needed medical care but done without it because of the cost? Does anyone presently need it?

3. How do I choose the medicine I take? Do I understand its side effects and do I use it correctly?

4. Do I ask the health-care provider to explain fully all advice and treatment? Have I ever asked about a nonmedical alternative, sought a "second opinion," or, after consideration, disregarded a provider's advice?

5. Do I feel capable of handling health crises until professional medical help arrives? Do I know basic first aid and Cardio-Pulmonary Resuscitation (CPR)?

6. Do I get enough physical exercise to keep my body well toned? Do I heed the messages it sends me and take preventive measures before getting sick?

7. Do I realize my life-sharing potential through blood donations? Or through donations of my body organs to the living when I die (recycling myself)?

8. Am I aware of health hazards at home and at my workplace? Do I know how to find out?

9. Am I aware of sources of environmental pollution in my community? Is anything being done about them?

10. Am I aware of alternative approaches to health care? Have I, my family, or my friends tried any?

Health: from the same Anglo-Saxon root as *heal, hale, holy,* and *whole.* Broadly, any state of optimal functioning, well-being, or progress.

—*The American Heritage Dictionary of the English Language*

The World Health Organization defines *health* as "a state of complete physical and mental well-being and not merely an absence of disease or infirmity." Health, then, is a positive condition of harmony of body, mind, and spirit. In *The Best Health Ideas I Know,* Robert Rodale, editor of *Prevention* magazine, describes health as a "talent" that we can develop in ourselves through study, practice, and effort. A key factor in this process is our attitude toward health. Do we expect someone to cure us or do we assume responsibility for our own well-being? Do we have the desire to be healthy? According to Richard Carlson, author of *The End of Medicine,* "Health is a dynamic state, one the individual can actively pursue." How actively are we pursuing better health for ourselves?

Our physical and psychological environment is a major determinant of health. Since our lives depend on nature, preserving and enhancing the environment are very important health-related tasks. Among the environmental problems that concern our health are: contamination of food, air, and water; excess noise and congestion; and substandard housing. Stress of unemployment, poverty, race and sex discrimination, and the fear of war continue to undermine our health. In addition, the sheer complexity of our modern lives and the overabundance of choices and opportunities that we face today often lead to stress and confusion.

Individual habit and group activities are as important to health as the environment: our diets; our exercise; our tobacco, alcohol, or drug use; the safety of our driving habits; the stress generated by earning and spending our money; the way we relate to our families, neighbors, and communities. We can consciously work to create a more healthful "inner environment." Some aspects, such as diet, are within our immediate control; others, such as employment and community, involve a longer process. It is healthier to choose the kinds of changes we want to make than to be overwhelmed by the stress of external, seemingly uncontrollable changes. A commitment to simpler living will lead to sounder nutrition (junk food is expensive) and healthier recreation (exercise and celebration don't cost much).

THE POLITICS OF HEALTH

The United States is the only industrialized nation in the world, with the exception of South Africa, that does not have a national health program for its people. . . . 11 nations have lower infant mortality rates; 14 nations have longer life expectancy rates for both men and women. . . . Yet we spend [about] 10 percent of our GNP on medical care.

—*Congressman Ron Dellums, Congressional Record,* June 7, 1983.

America's health-care system focuses on treating disease rather than promoting health. It could be more correctly called a "disease-care system," for it emphasizes illness, drugs, and surgery at the expense of primary and preventive care. Comparatively little time, effort, and money are allocated to teaching people how to maintain good health. Instead, health care has become a commodity one buys rather than something one does. Unnecessary tests and procedures, overtreatment, and "iatrogenic disease" (disease introduced by the medical-care system itself, such as drug side effects) use up much of our medical resources. In his book *Medical Nemesis: The Expropriation of Health,* Ivan Illich argues persuasively that modern medicine sickens more than it cures and that the medical establishment is a major threat to health.

A dubious distinction of our health-care system is specialization. No longer does the family doctor deliver babies, make house calls, counsel us, and care for our everyday health needs. Instead, we frequently get shunted from specialist to specialist, feeling more like objects than human beings as we pass down the assembly line, paying a fee-for-service at each stop. Another important factor here is that hospitals have become the major location for providing medical care. The increasing sophistication of medical procedures, along with the fact that most insurance plans pay only for in-hospital care, has reinforced this central role of hospitals.

How has this unhealthy situation come about? Health care is big business in America. Our profit-motivated, "medical-industrial complex" is an enormous concentration of wealth and power, rivaling that of the defense industry. Hospitals and medical schools have joined forces to pursue teaching and research, often focused on unusual or advanced symptoms of disease, while common diseases and public health problems get less attention. Hospital and drug suppliers and private insurance companies have all allied themselves with the big hospitals in order to look after each other's business interests.

Power, money, and decision-making in our medical-industrial complex operate in a pyramid from the top down, leaving little room for participation by the people most immediately affected by health care—the patients. The traditional licensing system controlled by the American Medical Association also leaves little room for exercise of the important skills of any health-care provider "below" the rank of doctor and attempts to stifle "competition" from alternative health-care workers, such as nurse practitioners, acupuncturists, or nutrition experts.

The medical-industrial complex wants our health-care money to be spent on drugs, high physician fees, and extremely expensive and often unnecessarily duplicated diagnostic machinery. This situation is only magnified in Third World countries, where companies often push the choice of one fancy machine in a city hospital at the expense of pure water or basic inoculations for thousands of people.

The average American family works about one month out of every year to cover the family's medical bills—which are the number-one cause of personal bankruptcy! Medicare and Medicaid used to provide a "floor" for poorer Americans to rely upon for needed medical care, but that is no longer the case with the cutbacks that started in fiscal year 1982. Here is one example:

James Wilson is a 63-year-old totally disabled man on Medicaid who lives alone in a back-woods South Carolina shack without plumbing, telephone, radio, or television. According to his physician, Mr. Wilson needs seven different medicines to stay alive and out of pain. But the new regulations limit Medicaid patients to three prescriptions a month at government expense.

According to his doctor, Mr. Wilson "is facing the decision of whether to take his medicine for his heart and high blood pressure this month or wait until next month and take his medicine for gout and arthritis instead."[1]

Money in this country can also determine whether one is considered "crazy" or simply "having some difficulties":

Upper middle class women enjoy the boutiquing of psychiatry and engage in private therapy; they are labeled neurotic. Lower class women are commonly diagnosed as schizophrenic, incarcerated in state hospitals, administered electroconvulsive treatment (shock therapy) and tranquilized into a stupor. . . . A welfare mother, overwhelmed by environmental and economic stress, falls into a depressed stupor—involutional melancholia or urban stress fatigue? Is she mentally ill or a social casualty?[2]

Proposals for national health insurance continue to appear on the American political scene. Most remain grounded in a partnership between the federal government and the private insurance companies, which leaves unresolved the more basic issues of priorities and power in the health-care delivery system. These proposals incorporate profits to all sectors of the medical-industrial complex as a major feature. One exception is the Health Services Act introduced by Congressman Ronald Dellums. This act would establish a publicly funded national health service that would provide health care for all Americans as a matter of right. It would be staffed by salaried health workers whose services would emphasize the maintenance of health as well as the treatment of illness. The act has many interesting provisions, including: decentralized, community-based control through local elections; democratic management of health-care facilities by their workers; strong emphasis on occupational and environmental health problems; free education of health-care workers; and an attempt to "expand the roles of health workers by enabling them to participate in health-care delivery to the maximum extent consistent with their skills and permit alternative approaches to healing" (section 303). The estimated total cost of providing good health care to all Americans under the National Health Service would be 20 percent less than the total now being spent on health care without accomplishing this goal. In addition to the very personal and small-scale approaches to health discussed in the rest of this chapter, we need to be looking at approaches such as the Health Services Act, which would modify the distorted manner in which health care is delivered in this country.

STEPS TOWARD HEALTH

FINDING OUT ABOUT YOURSELF

Traditionally, doctors have had the aura of magicians. A first step toward breaking this spell is to educate ourselves about how to keep our bodies healthy and what the healing process is once we get sick. We must take responsibility for healing ourselves and view health workers as our assistants rather than as our healers.

A wide range of self-help health books are available. A popular example is *The Well Body Book,* which advocates treating the *causes* of common diseases (preventive medicine) rather than the *effects.* It includes a physical self-examination and basic diagnostic questions to assist the reader in determining what ailments really require outside medical attention. Another book, published by the Boston Women's Health Book Collective, is *Our Bodies, Ourselves,* which helps women learn practical health information and skills from the personal experiences of other women. Information on women's medical problems, the United States health-care system, and the changes needed to make the system more just for everyone are clearly presented.

Which symptoms are important to assess in which situations? Knowledge is especially important for parents of small children, who have been trained by our system of medical ignorance to run to the doctor for every health problem. Self-care books and classes can teach recognition and treatment of childhood ailments and accidents. Parents can learn to use simple medical equipment, such as an otoscope, to check for early signs of ear infections. Most important, self-care knowledge gives confidence in one's own ability to be responsible for the health of one's children. Self-care skills can be used in partnership with a cooperative health practitioner; symptoms can be described on the telephone, and parents can be talked through treatment instructions or be advised to bring in the child, if necessary.

Elders are also especially vulnerable to lack of basic medical knowledge. Classes such as those described in Chapter V should be available in every community and do not necessarily need an "expert" to teach them.

It is important to figure out a way to put your new health knowledge together with action. One medical researcher expressed frustration with the all-too-human tendency of smokers to "point toward some fat, jolly, chain-smoking neighbor who is seventy-five years old"—to the degree where "even a medical school pathologist has been seen smoking during a lecture to medical students in which he was describing the relationship between lung cancer and cigarette smoking."[3]

If, for example, you decide that your body needs an exercise program, stick with it! It takes at least two months of exercise three or more times a week to get "over the hump" of shifting from a sedentary to an active life. Start out slowly and work your way into it. Expect to feel some soreness or tiredness during the first month or two—take it as a sign that you are on the right track. Soon you will feel much better than you thought you could!

If you become seriously ill, it is especially important not to ignore what you can do with your own body's regenerative powers, in addition to seeking medical attention. In *Anatomy of An Illness,* Norman Cousins describes his self-engineered recovery in 1963 from a rare, painful, "irreversibly degenerative and fatal" nerve disease. With the cooperation of an unusual physician, Cousins removed himself from a hospital setting and prescribed laughter—readings from funny books and screenings of funny movies—and literally laughed himself to recovery. Today, based at a major medical school, Cousins works with support groups in which seriously ill people explore their self-healing potentials together through a variety of methods.

LEARNING ABOUT MEDICINES

We live in a drug-oriented society. Drugs are overprescribed, overconsumed, often useless, and sometimes dangerous. Drug companies bombard doctors with millions of dollars' worth of advertising each year. For every dollar brought in by drug sales, about twenty-five cents goes toward advertising expenses and only ten cents goes into research. Medical journals are supported by drug company advertising, which aims at so familiarizing doctors with the brand names of the advertisers that prescribing them will become an automatic response.

What can we do when we get a prescription from a doctor? Ask her or him to prescribe a generic formula. Prescription drugs have two names —a brand name popularized by advertising and a *generic* name giving the drug's chemical identity. Generic drugs are generally cheaper (sometimes very much so) and comparable in quality and strength to their more expensive brand-name counterparts. If you have difficulties with doctors or pharmacists in your community about getting generic prescriptions filled, you may need to join with others to solve the problem. The campaign conducted by the North Coast Gray Panthers, described in Chapter V, is one such example.

It is important to keep careful records of all drug purchases—including nonprescription, "over-the-counter" drugs—and any reactions you may have. Call the person who prescribed the drug *immediately* if you have any adverse reactions. Be suspicious if a drug is prescribed for every ailment. Always ask that the drug's name, correct dosage, and instructions for use be recorded on the container. Drug companies are required to include a labeling leaflet for each drug they produce. Ask for this leaflet, which includes a full chemical description of the drug, its purpose and the hazards involved in its use. It is also important to ask your health-care provider or pharmacist about possible interactions between drugs you are taking as well as about food or drink that might interact with the drugs. For example, one commonly prescribed family of drugs that includes tetracycline is neutralized if dairy products are also in your stomach when it is taken.

Groups, such as elders, who tend to use a lot of drugs, and the health-care personnel who treat them, need special awareness of drug issues. Education programs such as SRx, described in Chapter V, are important assets for every community to consider incorporating as part of its health-care system. For library or home reference, *The Essential Guide to Prescription Drugs* or *People's Pharmacy #2* are books that can give you detailed information about drug prices, composition, side effects, and comparative efficacy.

Along with the movement toward natural foods and simpler living, there seems to be a revival of interest in the "tried and true" home remedies some of us recall our grandparents using to heal us—for example, hot apple cider vinegar and honey tea to soothe sore throats or camomile tea to calm one's tummy. Some people feel that many health problems created by synthetic drugs could be eliminated by relearning and relying more upon these folk remedies. This is a field worth exploring. At the same time, it is important to remember that "natural" drugs are still drugs, and that some naturally occurring herbs can produce dramatic reactions in the human body. With these remedies, it is important to obtain advice from a knowledgeable herbal practitioner and to take as much care with regards to dosage and frequency of use as you would with drugs prescribed by a conventional practitioner.

Sticking Up for Your Rights

We have the right to have the causes, prevention, and treatment of our medical complaints explained to us in words we can understand. Often doctors use "medi-code" to explain things to us either because they hope to discourage us from asking further questions or because they are not skilled in explaining medical problems in ordinary language.

As a patient, you should insist on "informed consent"; no health-care practitioner or hospital can perform a surgical procedure or medical treatment on you without your consent. Before you say yes or no, you have a right to know what treatment is being proposed and why, what other treatments are possible, whether this treatment is for *your* benefit or for research, how risky it will be, how much it will cost, and whatever else you need to know to make a considered, informed, uncoerced decision.

Many medical workers feel that unnecessary procedures and surgery are often performed for financial gain. Dr. Mary Howell of the National Women's Health Network states: "Of the 800,000 hysterectomies performed in this country in just one year recently, one-third of them were unnecessary, 1,000 of them were fatal."[4] Some medical insurance plans pay for second opinions. Even if yours doesn't, you should try to find the means to get one if your doctor has recommended major surgery.

Confidentiality is a patient's right. Your medical records are strictly private, and the health-care worker, hospital, or your workplace cannot legally release them without your consent. You also have a right to privacy while you are in a hospital. Hospital workers should treat you with respect and dignity. It is often difficult to insist on being treated properly when you are sick. Many hospitals now have patient advocates, whose job is to explain and support you in sticking up for your rights and to act as a liaison between patients and health-care workers. You can ask your family and friends to assert themselves and do the same.

You should not feel shy about going elsewhere next time, or asking for different people to treat you in a publicly or privately paid group health facility. But it is worth remembering that medical personnel can learn to respect a patient's needs and right to participate in health-care decision-making. If you feel you have been treated as "a hip" rather than as a whole person by your doctor, treat the doctor as a whole person and let her or him know, even if you don't clarify your feelings about the situation until after you have recovered. Medical personnel can also benefit from "preventive care." Ruth Dreamdigger, in her sixties and a member of the Philadelphia Life Center (described in Chapter IV), participates with a group of women who volunteer their time and experience to train medical students in doing pelvic examinations. She explains that "we help doctors to be less frightened, to be aware of the comfort of the patients —physically and psychologically—and to remember and respect the woman."

Supporting Alternative Health Systems

Neighborhood-based health centers that attempt to reorient us toward community health care are always under pressure due to financial difficulties and the challenge they pose to the medical establishment. Some have "gone under," but some of the many clinics that started to service primarily "street people" successfully expanded their services to the broader community to include working people, elders, minorities, and the unemployed. One local, nonprofit health center that is surviving well despite the constant scramble for funds is the Country Doctor Community Clinic in Seattle, Washington. "Country Doc"—as it is called by the local people —was founded in 1971 on the belief that health care is a human right, not a privilege of the wealthy. Serving the Capitol Hill and Central Area neighborhoods of Seattle, the Country Doc staff welcomes twenty thousand patient-visits a year from a clientele which, as of fall 1983, was 97 percent within the federal government's low-income guidelines and 64 percent unemployed (and their families).

The clinic has a staff of twenty, including several doctors, nurse practitioners, physician assistants, a mental health counselor, a social worker, a lab technician, a pharmacist, a community health nurse, clinical assistants, and administrative staff. They are assisted by volunteers in providing a unified system of health care, which includes health promotion, day and evening clinics, and specialty clinics, such as foot care for elders and home visits for the disabled. Clinic Administrator George Parker explained that most of the staff work at Country Doc because "here they are capable of dealing with a person as a whole." For example, if the medical practitioner is presented with a complaint of pain and she or he suspects that it is emotionally based, the mental health counselor would then see the patient. If the mental health counselor finds that the emotional pain is due to having no job and no food on the table, the Country Doc staff take steps to deal with the underlying problem. Or if a patient who has been found to need prescription medication has no money, she or he is not simply sent out the door with a prescription blank. The prescription is filled free-of-charge at Country Doc's own pharmacy, which then bills the "Assistance Fund," that exists to supply medications, food coupons, or transportation to those patients who need these essentials to complete their treatment plans.

Parker feels it is especially important to understand that a basic change has recently taken place in United States health policy which is making it more difficult for clinics such as Country Doc to survive and for the poor to get decent health care. "During the 1960s and 1970s, the health policy of this country focused on three areas: quality, accessibility (geographic and economic), and on the fact that everyone deserves basic health care. Now, cost containment is the only criterion being used by the federal and many state governments."

He explained that some states are now giving Medicaid care contracts to the lowest bidder to save money without regard to the quality of care. At the same time, private companies have held discussions with group health-care providers, with the goal of lowering the costs these companies have to pay in health benefits, with minimal concern for quality of care. In return, they would grant to a particular group practice exclusive access to compensated medical treatment of the company's employees.

If implemented, the results will squeeze into the middle a section of the population who will have limited or no access to health care. These people will be squeezed out of the Medicaid system by cost cutting and out of the private sector by preferential agreements between purchasers and providers of health care. For these people, fortunately, there is the community clinic system. But this system can offer no financial security that it will *always* be there when needed.

Country Doc finds that only 20 percent of its patients have any sort of medical coverage (including Medicare and Medicaid) or can afford to pay on a sliding fee scale. The rest is made up by a complicated and changing set of contracts with the city, county, state, and federal governments that must be renegotiated every year. For the past five or six years, their full-time doctor was paid for by the National Health Service Corps, which is in the process of being abolished in urban areas. They have managed to get replacement funds from another source, but an increasing number of unemployed have at the same time put heavier demands on the clinic.

One approach to survival is unity. Instead of competing for funds with other neighborhoods' health facilities, Country Doc is part of a coalition that looks at itself as a community health system and approaches the funding agencies as such. In the fall of 1983, this coalition joined with food banks and emergency housing groups to form a new "Survival Services Coalition." This coalition's purpose is to acquire needed funds for these three basic needs of the City of Seattle. Director Parker explained how the need for this broader coalition has become increasingly obvious to Country Doc: "We are seeing the effects of cuts in nonmedical programs, such as children's food and help for the aging. People with no food or housing wind up here in need of health care."

Another "alternative" approach to health care is the use of nontraditional therapies. If you have not been completely satisfied with conventional medical professional treatment, try looking elsewhere. Take the opportunity to first explore this when you have a relatively minor illness, rather than when you find yourself in a serious or frightening situation. Maribeth Riggs, an herbal practitioner, suggests that you interview the alternative practitioner in some detail and make sure you feel comfortable with the answers. What kind of formal or informal education does the practitioner have? What system of diagnosis does she or he use? What is the method of healing (not just the name of it, but a full explanation)? Perhaps most important, are there other clients you can talk with? Riggs points out that we rarely think of asking these kinds of questions—especially the last question—of a conventional hospital or doctor, although we know that all doctors and hospitals are not of equal quality.

The Berkeley Holistic Health Center is an example of healing centers in various parts of the country where practitioners trained both in traditional medicine and in other approaches have come together to offer an integrated approach to healing. The Berkeley Holistic Health Center began in 1975 as an educational project and, in 1981, expanded to a full range of clinical services. A group of thirteen in-house practitioners (including seven women), together with twenty associate practitioners, offer care that ranges from a family medical practice to reflexology to acupuncture to art therapy. The center serves a broad economic, racial, and ethnic cross-section of the Berkeley/Oakland area and includes special services aimed at meeting the needs of women, gays, and lesbians. All practitioners charge on a sliding scale, with a conscious aim of serving low-income people. They are handicapped in accomplishing this goal by the fact that most health insurance plans, Medicaid, and Medicare do not cover most alternative therapies.

In addition to clinical care, the center offers a broad range of education. Friday night free lectures introduce various alternative therapies; typical topics are "Introduction to Acupuncture," "Addictions, Our Bodies and Our Lives," and "Preventive Vision Care." There are also paid workshop series, including classes that offer nurses continuing education credits. The center has published a newspaper that reached a circulation of fifty thousand, and it plans to resume this publication in January of 1984. Support groups are sponsored to deal with a variety of problems, including AIDS, drugs, alcohol, food, and premenstrual syndrome.

Merrill Featherstone, a counselor at the center, explained that the center hopes to offer an alternative health-maintenance insurance plan to small workplaces. It is also expanding its work beyond pure education and clinical services. One goal is to help people with assessment of the health effects of their environment. Another is to expand the center's networking with the community as a whole—in order to be involved actively with the issues that affect the overall quality of life.

In addition to seeking out treatment from alternative practitioners, it is important to explore, when needing treatment for a minor condition or a long-term one (such as chronic pain), whether there is an approach that leaves the control of treatment in your own hands, that may use fewer drugs and treatments from or visits to a health practitioner. As an example, the Bibliography lists several books that offer alternative pain therapies that can be explored at home by you and your family or friends.

Yet another important development in health care is the hospice movement, which offers an alternative to the extreme medicalization of death. In many communities, paid and volunteer hospice workers help dying persons and their families to come to terms with approaching death and to make dignified individual choices concerning their remaining time on earth. In addition to working with people at home or in the hospital, some communities have hospice centers or homes that offer an alternative to hospitalization. These centers reduce the financial burden of health care and, for those who cannot remain at home, give people a place to die in dignity within a supportive environment. Hospice facilities and organizations have different sponsorships and philosophies, and, as with all medical treatment, you should ask enough questions initially to ensure that you will feel comfortable with the particular approach taken.

INSISTING ON OCCUPATIONAL HEALTH AND SAFETY

Pottstown is the center of the manufacture of pottery, porcelain, enamel, and similar wares. Here, when the weather is murky, the smoke from hundreds of stacks settles down on the towns like a blanket. I visited some of the factories [in 1911] where I saw the workers dipping the wares into the lead glaze that after firing makes china white. These men after a very few years, became so poisoned with the lead and its fumes that their teeth fall out and their joints are locked as if with the worst attacks of rheumatism. I was told that these workers did not live longer than 28–33 years old. The sacrifice of their lives was only one of the demands of capitalism.

—*The Autobiography of Big Bill Heywood,* 1927.

How much has really changed since 1911? The Department of Health and Human Services estimated in 1979 that every year 400,000 people develop occupational diseases, which subsequently cause 100,000 deaths per year.

It took Congress until 1970 to address the occupational health issue and to pass the Occupational Safety and Health Act, which ensures the right to "safe and healthful working conditions for working men and women." This act, the Toxic Substance Control Act of 1976, and the Federal Mine Safety and Health Act of 1977 are the only federal health regulations that govern our workplaces. Individual states have also adopted local occupational safety and health laws, some of which are stronger than federal law. However, little funding has been appropriated for their enforcement.

In July 1982, federal enforcement was weakened when the Occupational Safety and Health Administration (OSHA) implemented "Voluntary Protection Programs" in about 75 percent of covered workplaces. The stated purpose was to "promote cooperative labor-management health and safety efforts." Those worksites in the voluntary compliance program are now exempt from scheduled inspections and surprise visits. Workers at these sites must first bring their complaints to a worksite committee, which, unlike OSHA, is not required to protect the anonymity of the worker. This leaves the "complaining" workers especially vulnerable to intimidation. We must organize to make occupational safety and health laws stronger and to demand funding for enforcement of these laws. But why?

None of us are exempt from occupational hazards. Thousands of chemicals used in modern industry cause surface skin problems, systemic disease, and genetic changes. Stress, noise, vibration, unguarded blades and presses, insufficient safety barriers or warning signals, heat, cold, bad light, X-rays, other radiation, and dusts also can be severe occupational hazards; *Work Is Dangerous to Your Health,* by Stellman and Daum, can help you identify and act on these hazards. Many of these cause multiple cancers, sterility, deafness, blindness, miscarriage, heart disease, respiratory failure, and death. Even the arts can be hazardous. Photographers are heavily exposed to toxic developing chemicals, and potters can get lung damage from silica-laden clay or fume-producing kilns and are exposed to lethal metals in some glazes.

In the past, women have been barred from some workplaces that use toxic chemicals. The attempts of women to end such exclusion raised the issue of health and safety of pregnant women and women of childbearing age. A few companies have required that women be sterilized prior to employment, but now men also are experiencing changes in sexual function, fertility, and genetic damage to sperm. Spouses and children exposed to work clothes can also develop "occupational" diseases. It is time to question whether substances that can cause such extreme damage are truly beneficial to our lives.

There is a great deal you can do to bring about healthier workplaces. At work, you can:

- Join with your co-workers to identify the hazards in your workplace.
- If a health problem manifests itself with many workers, try to isolate the source and determine whether it is workplace-induced.
- Learn what precautions are necessary for working with hazards in your workplace—exhaust systems, protective gear (do you use it?), safety instructions and inspection of machines, breaks for operators of video-display terminals (VDTs), special cleansers/lotions, sanitary facilities, showers, appropriate chairs.
- Investigate what alternative processes may be available that do not dictate such hazardous working conditions.
- Find out who makes and enforces health and safety regulations in your workplace.
- Learn your rights under OSHA regulations and your state's laws, learn what educational and support organizations exist in your area to help you.
- Help maintain a healthy workplace—watch for leaks and accidental spills, keep dangerous materials covered, wash toxic materials off skin, avoid unnecessary exposures.
- Find out what occupational health services are available to you at work and in your community: if you have questions about occupational exposures, ask your supervisor, union safety steward, nurse, doctor, or health and safety engineer.
- If you find that a problem remains undealt with at work, write or call OSHA or your state's health department.

At home, you can:

- Isolate contaminated work clothes and wash them separately.
- Identify hazards from artwork and hobbies—and use protective gear as needed and keep chemicals stored away from children and pets in spillproof containers.
- Go see what solvents are stored "under the kitchen sink" (should they be there?).

Most of all, you can share what you have learned with others and encourage them to identify their own occupational health hazards. Organize for improved health and safety conditions. (One example is discussed in Chapter VI.) We must start asking ourselves: What am I exposed to? Should I or anyone else be exposed to it? What do I need to do to protect myself and others? What should the employer do to protect us? Do we need to organize to change the situation?

Working for a Healthy Environment

We must seek to control environmental health hazards, both those known to affect human health directly and those that upset the balance of entire ecosystems and bioregions. Many toxic substances unnecessarily contaminate our air, water, and land.

Citizens often feel unable to begin addressing this issue because of the perceived scientific complexity. To break through this barrier, the Sierra Club has published *Training Materials on Toxic Substances: Tools for Effective Action.* This 550-page book includes such topics as "The Science of Toxic Substances," "The Politics of Toxic Substances," "Case Studies of 'Citizens as Detectives,' " an "Organizer's Handbook" on how to put together a task force in your community, "Designing a Community Research Program," nineteen steps in "Choosing and Planning a Project," as well as copies of over one hundred articles and brochures on a variety of toxic substance problems from many points of view. This is an important tool that can turn frustration into empowerment!

What is an "unnecessary" environmental health hazard? Elin Crawford of the Delta Drinking Water Defense Fund (Contra Costa County, California) became interested in environmental health issues when her thirty-three-year-old husband, Paul, became ill with cancer that they believe stems from a childhood spent downwind from the Nevada nuclear weapons test site. (Paul Crawford's work on occupational hazards in the same community is discussed in Chapter VI.)

In her reading about "atomic veterans," Elin also learned of veterans made ill by Agent Orange—a herbicide sprayed in Vietnam. Contaminants contained in Agent Orange have been shown to be acutely toxic, as well as causing both cancer and birth-defects. She was therefore shocked to read of plans to spray the herbicide 2-4-D—which often contains the same contaminants—to "control" water hyacinths near the county's drinking water intake site. Upon investigation, she learned that the spraying was to take place mainly because of complaints from a commercial marina owner about interference with recreational boating.

Feeling that the marina owner was "holding the county's drinking water hostage," Elin joined with several others to bring a lawsuit that successfully prevented the spraying in 1983 and petitioned the court to require an Environmental Impact Report before any future spraying would be allowed. She also helped organize other actions to deal with the water hyacinths, including hand-harvesting by about two hundred local residents.

The story was not over, however. At preliminary hearings, the state argued that it should be allowed to spray two other chemicals. One of them was diquat, which is usually contaminated with ethylene dibromide

(EDB). EDB-contaminated substances had recently been banned by Fresno County, California, following the deaths of several farmworkers from contaminated drinking water. The other chemical was Rodeo, a nonselective herbicide Elin describes as "killing everything it touches." The state subsequently decided against spraying Rodeo, but the marina owner purchased it over-the-counter and sprayed it himself in July of 1983. After the judge refused an injunction at the preliminary hearings, the state sprayed diquat in the same area in September of 1983. Upon inspection after the spraying, Ellen found damaged but living water hyacinths —and mile after mile of dead tule grass, an endangered plant species that forms a vital part of the general health of the marsh, providing food and shelter for its nonhuman users and minimizing wave erosion. Elin also received a number of phone calls from unwarned local residents whose children developed rashes after swimming in the waters near the time of the spraying. Her group plans to go through with a full court trial to stop future sprayings.

Research has shown other ways to control water hyacinths. Mechanical harvesting is possible, as well as several forms of biological control that are in wide use in Florida and Louisiana. The concern about "control" is also ironic in light of the fact that scientists in the People's Republic of China have been investigating the purposeful cultivation of water hyacinths in order to provide organic fuel for biogas generators in areas without much waste vegetation.[5] (See pp. 201 and 234 for information on biogas.)

Elin Crawford firmly believes that:

We have to stop thinking of the "easy solution," which is chemicals. They've been looking only at the short-term cost, but we have to budget for the long-term cost. We're finding out it's a lot more expensive in the long run as we start to die.

TAKING CHARGE OF YOUR WHOLE LIFE

Our psychological health is affected by work and environmental stresses. It is also affected by actual or perceived lack of control over the important decisions that touch our lives.

In his book *Helplessness,* Martin E. P. Seligman argues that "learned helplessness" is responsible for much mental illness—both in humans and in experimental animals. "Learned helplessness" is produced "when an animal or a person is faced with [and learns that] an outcome is independent of his responses."[6]

To summarize the theory: In extensive experiments with both humans and animals, Seligman and his associates have shown that once helplessness has been learned in one situation, a high percentage (around two-thirds) of subjects will not try to affect the outcome in a new situation that occurs soon afterward—even though the person or animal now objectively has control. If the person or animal has many experiences with helplessness, it takes correspondingly longer and longer for this effect to wear off. On the other hand, if the person or animal first has positive experiences with control, one or a few subsequent experiences with helplessness will not have the same, action-inhibiting effect.

In "speculations" based on his experimental and clinical findings, Seligman observes:

Having an annual income of $6,000 a year, instead of $12,000, does not automatically produce helplessness. The lives of poor people are replete with instances of courage, of belief in the effectiveness of action, and of personal dignity. But a low income restricts choices and frequently exposes a poor person to independence between outcome and effort. . . . A child reared in such poverty will be exposed to a vast amount of uncontrollability. . . . If poverty produces helplessness, then effective protest—changing one's conditions by one's own actions—should produce a sense of mastery.[7]

To maintain the health of ourselves and our communities, we need to challenge existing institutions and make them more responsive to our needs. We need to work toward a society in which nutritious food is available for everyone, pollution is controlled, consumer products are made safe, and drugs and cigarettes are not pushed by advertising. We need informed consumers of health care, who can take care of themselves as much as possible and demand quality care if they need it. Finally, we must take charge of our whole lives—perhaps the most important thing we can all do for our mental and physical health.

WHAT YOU CAN DO

1. Have each person in your discussion group explore one book mentioned in the text or in a Bibliography area and share the usefulness and limits of this resource with your group.
2. Take a "health inventory" of yourself, your family, your friends, or your community. Consider general physical fitness, stress factors, environmental pollution, work and home hazards, nutrition, creativity, emotional expression and community involvement—in addition to any obvious health difficulties. What improvements can you make?
3. Join with your friends, neighbors, co-workers, or family in identifying the two to five most serious health hazards in your surroundings. What can you do about these?
4. Next time you are mildly ill, or an illness drags on and on, find out what alternative treatments are available. Try one and discuss your reactions with your family, friends, or discussion group.

NOTES

1. Mary Ellen Hombs and Mitch Snyder, *Homelessness: A Forced March to Nowhere* (Washington, D.C.: Community for Creative Non-Violence, 1982), p. 40.

2. Anthony Colletti, "Psychiatric Oppression and Class," *WIN* Magazine, August 2 and 9, 1979.
3. James J. Lynch, *The Broken Heart: The Medical Consequences of Loneliness* (New York: Basic Books, 1977), p. 88.
4. Mary C. Howell, M.D. (co-Founder of National Women's Health Network, formerly associate dean of Harvard Medical School), correspondence dated September 1983, p. 1.
5. Chen Ruchen, Ziao Zhiping, and Li Nianguo, "Putting Biogas to Work," *Asia 2000* 1 (1981) 1:14.
6. Martin E. P. Seligman, *Helplessness* (San Francisco: W. H. Freeman and Company, 1975), p. 46.
7. Ibid., pp. 159, 165.

SOURCES OF FURTHER INFORMATION

Groups Mentioned in Chapter

Berkeley Holistic Health Center. 3099 Telegraph Avenue, Berkeley, Calif. 94705.
Country Doctor Community Clinic. 402 15th East, Seattle, Wash. 98112.
Delta Drinking Water Defense Fund. Box 1067, Martinez, Calif. 94553.
National Women's Health Network. 224 7th Street, S.E., Washington, D.C. 20003.

Additional Resource Groups

Bakersfield, Lamont, and Arvin Organizing Project, American Friends Service Committee, Pacific Southwest Region. 980 North Fair Oaks Avenue, Pasadena, Calif. 91103. Successfully organized a campaign for medically indigent adults.
Black Women's Health Project, 450 Auburn Avenue, N.E., #157, Atlanta, Ga. 30312.
Clean Water Project. 1341 G Street, N.W., Washington, D.C. 20005.
Friends of the Earth. 1045 Sansome Street, San Francisco, Calif. 94111
Health Policy Advisory Center (Health/PAC). 17 Marie Street, New York, N.Y. 10007.
Health Security Action Council. 1757 N Street, N.W., Washington, D.C. 20036.
Labor Occupational Health Program, 2521 Channing Way, Berkeley, Calif. 94720.
Occupational Health and Safety Project, Urban Planning Aid. 120 Boylston Street, Boston, Mass. 02006.
People's Medical Society. 33 E. Minor Street, Emmaus, Penn. 18049.
Planetree Health Resource Center. 2040 Webster Street, San Francisco, Calif. 94115. Offers packets of information ($5/packet) on many health topics; in-depth research done on request; one in-depth research packet included in $35 membership fee; book catalog includes many books listed here.

Bibliography

Books About the System

Bullough, Vernon L., and Bonnie Bullough. *Health Care for the Other Americans.* New York: Appleton Century Crofts, 1982. Discusses class and race barriers to adequate health care.

Ehrenreich, Barbara, and Deirdre English. *Complaints and Disorders: The Sexual Politics of Sickness.* Old Westbury, N.Y.: Feminist Press, 1974.

Ehrenreich, Barbara, and Deirdre English. *For Her Own Good: 150 Years of Expert's Advice to Women.* New York: Doubleday, 1979.

Ehrenreich, John, ed. *The Cultural Crisis of Modern Medicine.* New York: Monthly Review Press, 1979.

Epstein, Samuel S., M.D. *The Politics of Cancer.* San Francisco: Sierra Club, 1978.

Fuchs, Victor. *Who Shall Live: Health, Economics and Social Choice.* New York: Basic Books, 1974.

Illich, Ivan. *Medical Nemesis: The Expropriation of Health.* New York: Bantam, 1976.

Kotelchuck, David, ed. *Prognosis Negative: Crisis in the Health Care System.* New York: Vintage Books, 1976.

Source Collective. *Organizing for Health Care: A Tool for Change.* Boston: Beacon Press, 1974.

Drugs, Herbs

Consumer Reports, *The Medicine Show,* rev. ed. New York: Pantheon Books, 1980.

DeBairacli-Levy, Juliette. *Nature's Children: A Guide to Organic Foods and Herbal Remedies for Children.* New York: Schocken, 1978.

Graedon, Joe. *People's Pharmacy #2.* New York: Avon, 1977.

Long, James W., M.D. *The Essential Guide to Prescription Drugs.* New York: Harper & Row, 1977.

Panos, Maesimund B., M.D., and Jane Heimlich. *Homeopathic Medicine at Home: Natural Remedies for Everyday Ailments and Minor Injuries.* Los Angeles: J. P. Tarcher, 1980.

Spoerke, David G., Jr. *Herbal Medications.* Santa Barbara, Calif.: Woodbridge Press, 1980.

Tierra, Michael. *The Way of Herbs: Simple Remedies for Health and Healing.* New York: Washington Square Press, 1983.

Self-Help Resources

Baulch, Evelyn M. *Home Care: A Practical Alternative to Extended Hospitalization.* Millbrae, Calif.: Celestial Arts, 1980.

Berkeley Holistic Health Center. *The Holistic Health Handbook: A Tool for Attaining Wholeness of Body, Mind and Spirit.* Berkeley, Calif.: And/Or Press, 1978.

Berkeley Holistic Health Center. *The Holistic Health Lifebook: A Guide to Personal and Planetary Well-Being.* Berkeley, Calif.: And/Or Press, 1981.

Boston Women's Health Book Collective. *Our Bodies, Ourselves: A Book by and for Women,* rev. 2nd ed. New York: Simon and Shuster, 1976.

Consumer Reports, ed. *Health Quackery: Consumer's Union Report on False Health Claims, Worthless Remedies and Unproved Therapies.* New York: Holt, Rinehart & Winston: 1981.

Cousins, Norman. *Anatomy of an Illness; As Perceived by the Patient: Reflections on Healing and Regeneration.* New York: Bantam, 1981.

Fenwick, R. D. *The Advocate Guide to Gay Health.* Boston: Alyson Publications, 1978.

Ferguson, Dr. Tom. *Medical Self-Care: Access to Health Tools.* New York: Summit Books/Simon and Schuster, 1980.

Henderson, John, M.D. *Emergency Medical Guide,* 4th ed. New York: McGraw-Hill, 1978.

Huttman, Barbara, R.N. *The Patient's Advocate: The Complete Handbook of Patient's Rights.* New York: Penguin, 1981.

Julty, Sam. *Men's Bodies, Men's Selves: The Complete Guide to the Health and Well-Being of Men's Bodies, Minds and Spirits.* New York: Delta, 1979.

Laws, Priscilla W. *The X-Ray Information Book: A Consumer's Guide to Avoiding Unnecessary Medical and Dental X-Rays.* New York: Farrar, Straus & Giroux, 1983.

Lifchez, Raymond, and Barbara Winslow. *Design for Independent Living: The Environment and Physically Disabled People.* Berkeley: University of California Press, 1979.

McGuire, Thomas, D.D.S. *The Tooth Trip.* New York: Random House/Bookworks, 1972.

Orbach, Susan. *Fat Is a Feminist Issue II: A Program to Conquer Compulsive Eating.* New York: Berkley Books, 1982.

Pantell, Robert H., M.D., James F. Fries, M.D., and Donald M. Vickery, M.D. *Taking Care of Your Child: A Parent's Guide to Medical Care.* Reading, Mass.: Addison-Wesley, 1977.

Rosenfeld, Isadore, M.D. *Second Opinion.* New York: Bantam, 1982.

Ryan, Regina Sara, and John W. Travis. *The Wellness Workbook.* Berkeley: Ten-Speed Press, 1981.

Samuels, Mike, and Nancy Samuels. *The Well Baby Book.* New York: Summit Books, 1979.

Samuels, Mike, and Nancy Samuels. *The Well Child Book.* New York: Summit Books, 1982. Also, coloring book version.

The Self-Care Catalog. Self-care books and tools. Available from: Box 717, Inverness, Calif. 94937. Free.

Watt, Jill, and Ann Calder. *I Love You But You Drive Me Crazy: A Guide for Caring Relatives.* Fforbez Publications, 1981. Available from: Planetree Health Resource Center, address above, $5.95 + $1.50 shipping.

Werner, David. *Where There Is No Doctor: A Village Health Handbook.* Palo Alto, Calif.: Hesperian Foundation, 1977.

Death and Dying

Duda, Deborah. *A Guide to Dying at Home.* Santa Fe, N. Mex.: John Muir Publications, 1982.

Kubler-Ross, Elisabeth. *Death: The Final Stage of Growth.* Englewood Cliffs, N.J.: Prentice-Hall, 1975.

Kubler-Ross, Elisabeth. *On Death and Dying.* New York: Macmillan, 1969.

Morgan, Ernest. *Dealing Creatively with Death: A Manual of Death Education and Simple Burial,* 10th rev. ed. Burnsville, N.C.: Celo Press, 1983.

Workplace Health

Bacow, Lawrence. *Bargaining for Job Safety and Health.* Littleton, Mass.: MIT Press, 1982.

Center for Science in the Public Interest. *Household Pollutants Guide.* Garden City, N.Y.: Anchor, 1978.

A Handy Reference Guide—The Steiger-Williams Occupational Safety and Health Act of 1970. Washington, D.C.: U.S. Government Printing Office, 20402. $.20.

How to Use OSHA: Worker's Action Guide to the Occupational Safety and Health Act. Available from: Urban Planning Aid, 120 Boylston Street, Boston, Mass. 02006.

Hricko, Andrea, and Melanie Brunt. *Working for Your Life; A Woman's Guide to Job Health Hazards.* Available from: Labor Occupational Health Program, 2521 Channing Way, Berkeley, Calif. 94720. $5. Also available: *A Worker's Guide to Documenting Health and Safety Problems* (compiled from union health and safety committee experiences), $2; *Workplace Health and Safety: A Guide to Collective Bargaining,* $3.50; *California Negotiated Clauses for Health and Safety,* $2; *The Monitor* (bimonthly magazine), $8/year.

Makower, Joel. *Office Hazards: How Your Job Can Make You Sick.* Washington, D.C.: Tilden Press, 1981.

NYCOSH. *Health Protection for Operators of VDTS/CRTS.* Available from: 32 Union Square, Room 404, New York, N.Y. 10003. $1.

Shaw, Susan. *Overexposure: Health Hazards in Photography.* 1983. Available from: Friends of Photography, Box 500, Carmel, Calif. 93921.

Stellman, Jeanne Mager. *Women's Work, Women's Health; Myths and Realities.* New York: Pantheon, 1977.

Stellman, Jeanne M., and Susan M. Daum. *Work Is Dangerous to Your Health.* New York: Vintage Books, 1973.

Environmental Health

Environmental Defense Fund and Robert Boyle. *Malignant Neglect: Known or Suspected Cancer-Causing Agents in Our Environment and How by Controlling Them We Can Control the Spread of Cancer Itself.* New York: Alred A. Knopf, 1979.

Epstein, Samuel S., M.D. et al. *Hazardous Waste in America: Our Number One Environmental Crisis.* San Francisco: Sierra Club, 1983.

Gofman, John W., M.D. *Radiation and Human Health.* San Francisco: Sierra Club, 1981.

Nader, Ralph, et al., eds. *Who's Poisoning America: Corporate Polluters and Their Victims in the Chemical Age.* San Francisco: Sierra Club.

Samuels, Mike, M.D., and Hal Zina Bennett. *Well Body, Well Earth: The Sierra Club Environmental Health Sourcebook.* San Francisco: Sierra Club, 1983.

Sierra Club. *Training Materials on Toxic Substances: Tools for Effective Action.* 1981. Available from: 530 Bush Street, San Francisco, Calif. 94108. $11.50 for citizen action groups; $15.50 for individuals or public institutions; $19.50 for businesses; postage included.

Van Strum, Carol. *A Bitter Fog: Herbicides and Human Rights.* San Francisco: Sierra Club, 1983.

Self-Help Pain Therapies

Bierrman, June, and Barbara Toohey. *The Women's Holistic Headache Relief Book.* Los Angeles: J. P. Tarcher, 1979.

Feldenkrais, Moshe. *Awareness Through Movement: Health Exercises for Personal Growth.* New York: Penguin, 1972.

Gach, Michael Reed. *Acu-Yoga: The Acupressure Stress Management Book.* Japan Publications (distributed by Harper & Row), 1981.

Lorig, Kate, R.N., and James F. Fries, M.D. *The Arthritis Helpbook: What You Can Do For Your Arthritis.* Reading, Mass.: Addison-Wesley, 1980.

Prudden, Bonnie. *Pain Erasure.* New York: Ballantine, 1982. Uses myotheraphy, a muscle pressure-point technique.

CHAPTER IX

Energy

Civilization in this country, according to some, would be inconceiva-
ble if we used only, say, half as much electricity as now. But that is
what we did use in 1963, when we were at least half as civilized as
now.

—AMORY B. LOVINS [1]

QUERIES

1. In what ways do I use more than a small amount of nonhuman energy?
2. Do I have some direct control over the energy consumption level in our society, or is it the result of large-scale governmental and corporate policies?
3. Even if large quantities of energy were available at a reasonable price, would continued increases in our society's use of it benefit me and society?
4. If the energy companies in my area are privately owned, do I know how their rates compare with those charged by publicly owned utilities with similar energy supplies? Are there ways I can affect the energy investment decisions of my area's energy companies, whether publicly or privately owned?
5. Does public transportation in my area provide a real alternative to automobile travel? If not, what effective policy changes could be made?
6. Are there noneconomic dangers connected with continued reliance on nonrenewable energy sources?
7. Have I explored which renewable energy sources could be feasible in my community and my household?

Today Americans use more energy per person than anyone else on earth—even though most Americans have already made efforts to cut down somewhat on energy consumption. As of 1979, Americans still used twice the energy of the average European, who had a comparable standard of living.[2] This difference in energy use can be found in all aspects of our lives: in the home and in the workplace, in clothing fibers, packaging, transportation, agriculture, and in the military.

We waste energy in many ways that are not obvious. For example, it takes an enormous amount of energy to bring aluminum ore out of the ground and to process it. Throwing out an aluminum can instead of recycling it is roughly like throwing out half that can full of oil.[3]

Though farming has supposedly become more efficient, the energy involved in producing food has grown, too. In 1910, it took an average of one calorie of energy to produce, prepare, and put on the table one calorie of food in the United States. It now takes an average of ten calories of energy to put one calorie of food on the table.[4] This astounding figure is attributed mainly to the energy now devoted to fertilizer production, manufacture and use of farm machinery, long-distance transportation, and food-processing technology.

The growth of the military since 1940 has also contributed to our increased energy use. We maintain a vast arsenal and garrison all over the world. A larger percentage of the government's tax revenues goes into the *development* and *procurement* of weapons than into any other single item.[5] Even without the vast amounts of waste that have been reported, military spending would require tremendous quantities of energy.

In our transportation system, the most efficient modes of freight and passenger traffic—the railroad and intracity trolleys—have been systematically eliminated during the past 40 years and replaced with trucks and cars, which require much more fuel and capital and which have much more devastating effect on the environment. People are also traveling farther between their homes and jobs.

In the area of manufacturing, important changes have taken place. Shirts and dresses are now often made of petroleum-based synthetics rather than cotton or wool; shoes, luggage, and purses are made of petroleum-based plastic instead of leather; food and consumer goods are more packaged, and the packaging is made of plastic rather than of paper, wood, or cloth. All of these changes have required more energy and done more damage to the environment. They have also meant increased profits for the manufacturers.

There are many changes that can be made to reduce energy use without fundamentally affecting Americans' life-style, and many conventional analyses stop there. In the long run, however, if Americans are to reduce consumption to our fair share of the world's energy resources, we must separate our definition of "the good life" from practices that consume large quantities of energy. The sooner the family begins to learn to share a small, warm part of the house for its winter activities, the more energy resources will be left for other uses and the less pressed the family will feel when new shortages suddenly force them into unfamiliar contact in the living room. The sooner workplaces and schools in hot parts of the United States adjust their activities to the day's cooler hours, the less miserable people will feel when the air conditioning shuts off. Both of

these examples have important implications for life issues discussed elsewhere in this book.

Energy is a subject that is very vulnerable to mystification. Very few
people have seen a solar collector, a nuclear power plant, or an oil rig
close up. Within the space available in this chapter, it is impossible to
explain the technical specifications of a solar collector or a nuclear power
plant, but we will first try to give you a very brief idea of what the
conventional energy sources are, what alternative sources of energy exist,
and the relative financial and human costs of the two. We will then
explore what changes can be made by individuals and communities to
reduce energy use and to bring about direct change in the source of our
energy from nonrenewable to renewable. Finally, we will look at some of
the political struggles that are underway to curb the power of the energy
companies, which are continuing to push us toward energy suicide.

WHAT'S THE PROBLEM?

The problem, to state it simply, is the continued reliance on nonrenewable forms of energy to sustain our everyday lives. While this is more
profitable in the short run for large energy companies that are exploiting
these resources, it is not beneficial to us now or to future generations.
The exploitation of most sources of nonrenewable energy is also dangerous and damaging to the environment. Even if nonrenewable energy
supplies were much greater, their continued use could not be justified on
this ground alone—in the face of the fact that cost-effective technology
to implement alternatives exists now. Another common factor nonrenew-
ables share is the great centralization of their production and distribution, which tends to keep decisions that affect their use in the hands of
a small elite.

Oil and Gas.

Oil, gas, and coal are the compressed and transformed remains of
prehistoric plants and animals buried under layers of sedimentary rock.
These hydrocarbon fuels have been valuable because long, slow chemical
change, over millions of years, has concentrated great energy in a relatively small volume of material. They have also been abundant and readily obtainable. Now, however, it appears that the known supplies of natural gas and oil will run out in fifty to sixty years at current levels of
consumption. If demand increases by only 4 percent per year, that estimate drops to twenty-five years!

As the more accessible supplies run out, we have developed new ways
to get at previously protected supplies. Serious pollution and environmental disruption have thus increased with off-shore oil drilling, oil spills,
and exploitation of reserves in vulnerable ecosystems such as Alaska's
North Slope.

Coal.

The known coal reserves are likely to last up to a century longer than oil and gas, but much of this reserve is contained in deposits that must be strip-mined, with familiar environmental effects. Much of this coal is also low-grade, considering both energy content and polluting contaminants. If the world makes a massive conversion to a coal economy, we can expect atmospheric carbon dioxide to double by early in the next century.[6] The exact effects of this on the world's climate are disputed, but most theories accept that there would be massive changes, such as the melting of the polar ice caps or the triggering of a new ice age.

Synfuels.

Coal and oil shale can be converted into synthetic gas by high technology methods that use massive amounts of water.[7] Suitable deposits for this conversion are mainly located in dry Western states, which use the same scarce water for agriculture. There is not enough water for both.

Nuclear power.

Nuclear power plants produce electricity the same way conventional power plants do: by spinning turbine generators, which convert mechanical energy into electrical energy. In nuclear plants, these turbines are spun by the steam that results when water is heated by the splitting of uranium nuclei. The temperature of this nuclear reaction is at a wasteful millions of degrees, when the consumer end-uses usually require temperature differences of only tens of degrees—"like cutting butter with a chainsaw."[8]

After the Three Mile Island near-melt-down, numerous "smaller" accidents, careless handling of radioactive wastes, design errors, and the construction of nuclear power plants near earthquake faults, no American needs to be told that there are safety and environmental problems with nuclear power. But Americans have been told that there are no viable alternative sources of energy and that if they don't accept nuclear power, then they must expect to return to a "primitive" way of life. In fact, nuclear power, which produces only electricity, cannot supply nonelectrical energy demands now satisfied by dwindling oil, gas, and coal supplies.

RENEWABLE ENERGY TO THE RESCUE?

Renewable energy is energy that will never be depleted as long as the sun shines. Unlike the advocates of nuclear power and other nonrenewable technologies, no advocate of renewable energy claims that any one technology can solve most or all energy problems. There are two reasons that renewable sources are a good solution to our energy dilemma. First, a variety of technologies can be optimally fitted to a variety of end-uses.

For instance, bath water can be heated by the sun to 140 degrees, leaving the hydro-electric dam free to produce electricity capable of powering much higher-temperature industrial processes. Second, locally variable conditions can be used as appropriate—wind, waves, unusually clear skies, and so forth.

Most of us have already put on one to three sweaters in the winter to cut down on energy bills, but few of us have a solar collector or windmill next door. So here is a brief description of the major energy technologies we may expect to encounter in a shift toward a renewable energy future.

Human Energy.

Human energy, fueled by food calories, can power a bicycle or chop a carrot. Much of our addiction to high energy use stems from our failure to distinguish between drudgery and reasonable human activity. Wouldn't it make more sense to save our nonhuman energy for transporting the backbreaking loads?

No energy.

This, of course, is conservation. The Harvard Business School study, "Energy Future," showed that U.S. energy consumption could be reduced by 40 percent through conservation—an amount of energy equal to the output of fourteen hundred nuclear power plants.[9] And if all new houses for twelve years were built to employ passive solar heating and cooling methods, as much energy would be saved as is expected from the entire Alaskan North Slope.[10] In addition to insulating our homes and using public transportation, some special kinds of conservation, such as recycling, cogeneration, and composting, are separately described below.

Passive Solar.

Passive solar is a term that can refer to any solar system that does not generally require outside power for its operation—cooling by shade trees, for example. It also describes a type of building that is itself the heating and cooling system. A passive solar building collects, stores, and distributes heat by itself because heat storage material and a collecting method (such as a greenhouse on the south wall) has been incorporated into its structure. The warm air may or may not be transmitted throughout the house by the use of ducts and small fans.[11]

Active Solar.

Active systems are generally what people think of when they think of solar energy—solar collectors, tanks, and pumps. Solar collectors are placed on a roof, and the energy collected is used to heat hot water. This hot water may be used for heating the house as well as for domestic hot water.[12] Solar collectors do presently rely to some extent on nonrenewable metals, such as copper and aluminum—but isn't this a better use for our limited aluminum supplies than, for example, nonrecycled soft drink cans?

Photovoltaics.

Photovoltaic cells convert the sun's energy directly into electricity. They are now economically practical for household locations at least one mile from the nearest power line, and the cost has been dropping rapidly.

Hydro-electricity.

Hydro-electricity is a clean, renewable form of energy, produced by river water flowing through a hydro-electric turbine. Large dams do have major impact on the surrounding ecosystem, and nearly all potentially useful and economically and environmentally feasible large dam sites in this country have already been exploited,[13] though further such development has been pushed by the government and by large energy companies. However, small dam sites that had fallen into disuse are now being replaced and rebuilt in places such as New England, sometimes even on an individual household scale.

Wind.

People have been using windmills for energy for hundreds of years and have let them fall into disuse as fossil fuels have become more accessible. Wind energy systems have good potential in windy areas, and an offshore wind generator system has been designed that theoretically could produce enough electricity to supply all of New England.[14] At the moment for most locations, other energy sources are more economically practical.

Alcohol Fuel.

Renewable alcohol fuel already has been used to replace gasoline, particularly in the form of gasohol. It is an alternative that excites car-fascinated Americans, and arguments can be made about its being a good renewable energy source. On the one hand, a large portion of U.S. grain is now fed to livestock. If this grain were used for alcohol production, the residue, called "distillers dried grain," can in turn be fed to cattle. Because of the yeast in the fermentation process, the residue actually has a higher protein content than the original grain.[15] On the other hand, J. Baldwin, the *Next Whole Earth Catalog*'s Soft Technology Editor, makes a strong case against the use of alcohol:

Many reports show that it takes rather more than one BTU of fossil fuel to make one BTU of alcohol fuel—a net energy loss. Some papers show net energy break even, especially when using otherwise "worthless" biomass. These papers usually ignore the fact that "worthless" substances suddenly acquire worth when there is a demand for them, and that such substances often have ecological roles to play in ways that are not yet well understood.

Most large-scale alcohol schemes include corn. Corn, in addition to being useful food in a world where millions starve, is a notorious user of fossil fuel-based fertilizers, water (50 gallons per plant), and topsoil (typically, nine tons per acre of corn per year!). . . .[16]

Methane/biogas.

Biogas is an organically generated fuel gas that results from the anaerobic (without oxygen) decomposition of vegetation and human and animal wastes by micro-organisms. It is being extensively used in China and India in individual household installations. Several U.S. cities have been using biogas technology on a larger scale. In China, where biogas digesters are fed with animal manure, human wastes, and crop wastes, the only by-product is organic fertilizer, which is created from the fermentation procedure. Waste from U.S. cities is unlikely to be quite so pure. Very little of the key organic plant nutrients, such as nitrogen and phosphorous, are wasted in the digestion process.[17]

Composting and biological pest control.

With careful composting of all organic waste (human, animal, and vegetable), our dependence on fertilizer from petroleum could be greatly reduced. Similarly, concentration on methods of pest control that use good farming practices and predators to control insect pests and plant diseases could reduce or eliminate our dependence on petroleum-based pesticides.

Wood.

As of 1977, 54 percent of the houses in Vermont had wood stove heating capabilities, with about 40 percent having been backfitted with wood stoves during 1974–1976.[18] Wood makes a lot of sense as an alternative energy source in areas where wood is plentiful, though stoves that adequately reduce pollutants are still in developmental stages. But simply burning wood does not turn it into a renewable source of energy. J. Baldwin asks: "How many of you who burn wood plant trees? . . . A great many woodburning civilizations have completely destroyed their forests (old China, for example) and many others are well on the way (India and many South American countries). . . . Wood may be renewable, but it isn't inexhaustible unless managed."[19]

Wood may also offer a more important energy alternative than providing heat. "If the object is to use wood to save the greatest amount of energy, the highest and best possible use of wood would be in structures. Steel floor joists require 50 times more energy to manufacture than joists made of wood. Aluminum siding uses 20 times more energy than wood. Bricks are 25 times more energy intensive to make than boards and shingles."[20]

Cogeneration.

Cogeneration, used extensively by European industry, is actually a form of energy conservation—the use of waste heat from industrial processes to produce on-site electricity. In 1975, a Dow Chemical study found that, through use of cogeneration, U.S. industry could meet half of its own electricity needs by 1985, as opposed to the one-seventh currently being met by this means. Cogeneration would have saved $20 to $50 billion in energy investment and eliminated the need for more than fifty large reactors.[21] U.S. industry is increasingly utilizing cogeneration, but optimal usage has not been aggressively pursued.

Recycling.

Making a can from recycled aluminum uses only 5 percent of the energy required to make it from aluminum ore. Making paper from recycled materials uses only 25 percent of the energy necessary to make it from wood.[22] Recycling without refabricating an item is even better: in Iowa, which has a law that requires bottle recycling, refillable beer bottles are reused an average of twenty-five times.[23]

Some U.S. cities have developed waste conversion facilities, where metals and aluminum are removed by magnets and hand-picking after being collected together with the rest of the trash. Remaining combustibles are burned for energy. This is not a very efficient or nonpolluting energy source, and the quality of recycled material is not too good either. Another defect is that these plants *require* a certain amount of garbage in order to be economical, which encourages garbage production and discourages recycling. A better approach is that of Islip, Long Island, a community of three hundred thousand where residents separate newspaper, cardboard, glass, and metal from other household wastes before they are collected.[24] If food wastes are composted, there is indeed very little "garbage" left for collection.

Transitional Technologies.

No renewable energy advocate thinks we can instantly stop using fossil fuels. Rather, we should save the fossil fuels we still have for making the transition to renewable energy sources over the next twenty-five to fifty years. Organic farming methods are better developed for certain crops than for others. Why not save the petrochemical sprays for limited use where we haven't yet found anything else that works or for the thirteen-year rotation of locusts? Why not use natural gas only as a backup fuel for home heating, as solar technologies become more efficient? This requires an approach to our energy needs that assesses all the costs involved, and not just the profit and loss figures on an energy company's annual balance sheet.

WHAT DOES IT COST?

DOLLAR COSTS

To have any meaning, the productivity and efficiency of any energy source must be expressed in terms of *net* energy—the amount of energy delivered minus the amount of energy used to produce and get it there. If the energy cost of delivering one kilowatt of electricity is one kilowatt, then we're like guinea pigs on treadmills—getting nowhere.

It takes energy to make energy. Research, exploration, development, delivery, and cleanup all require an investment of energy. The coal has to be mined, shipped to the power plant (which itself has to be built), converted by furnaces and generators to electricity, carried along power lines to substations, and distributed to consumers, who must have their own capital plants (wiring, switches, appliances, and so on) to be able to use it. On top of these energy costs of production, about two-thirds of the electrical energy generated is lost in transmission before it arrives at the light bulb or toaster it's intended to power.

The concept of net energy is essential for evaluating the future of our energy resources, because as oil, coal, uranium, and other nonrenewable fuels become scarcer, we have to work harder and use more energy to get them, whether by offshore drilling, extracting oil from shale, strip-mining coal (which also involves restoring the land after the coal has been taken out), or developing energy-intensive ways of recycling uranium. These nonrenewable technologies are also highly centralized, a situation that heavily reduces their transmission efficiencies: the farther energy flows from its original source through a series of transfer steps, the less of it will be available at the end of the chain to do the work we intend it to do. One advantage of a decentralized energy system is that the energy is used more efficiently, because it doesn't have as far to travel.

There is yet another efficiency factor: after the energy gets to where it is intended, how efficient is our use of it? Do we feed our electricity to a self-defrosting refrigerator that uses much more energy than an ordinary one? Do we use our gasoline in a gas guzzler, a small car, a carpool, or a bus? Finally, as Amory Lovins points out, "how much function we perform says nothing about social welfare, which depends on whether the thing we did was worth doing."[25]

As the guinea pig runs faster to stay in the same place, producing energy from nonrenewable sources fuels inflation as much as our cars. As Barry Commoner explains, because the most accessible supplies have been used first, "it is inevitable that the cost of produc[tion] will rise faster and faster as you continue to use it. And the chief reason for inflation now is the rising price of energy."[26]

But what does producing energy from renewable sources cost today, as compared with producing energy from nonrenewable sources? Amory Lovins, of Friends of the Earth, is one of the world's foremost experts on the economics and technical aspects of energy production. Lovins calculated the amount of *investment* money (expressed in 1976 dollars) necessary to build energy systems to deliver (or save with conservation) the energy equivalent of one barrel of oil per day, for a wide range of sources. Here are some comparisons:[27]

Technology	Capital Investment to Deliver Energy Equivalent of One Barrel of Oil Per Day
Heating and Cooling of Buildings U.S. coal, 1970s price:	$2,000 to $3,000
or	
Frontier oil and gas (such as Alaska) 1980s price:	$10,000 to $25,000
vs.	
Building new commercial buildings that incorporate all *passive* solar features:	*Negative* $3,000*
or	
Three levels of conservation in existing buildings:	
—Common leak-plugging:	$0 to $5,000
—Most heat recovery systems (pumps that keep heat or coolness from escaping):	$5,000 to $15,000
—Worst case, very thorough building retrofits:	$25,000
Home Heating and/or Electricity Nuclear electric, mid-1980s price:	$200,000 to $300,000
or	
Large conventional coal-electric plant, with scrubbers for air quality, 1980s price:	$170,000
vs.	
Retrofitted 100 percent solar space heating, with no backup required, using costly traditional flat plate collectors and seasonal storage (the most expensive possible solar), mid-1980s price:	$50,000 to $70,000
or	
200kW wind-electric, late 1970s price:	$200,000

*In other words, the builder has to spend *less* to construct the building than otherwise would have been necessary to include a conventional heating/cooling system.

Factors other than capital investment add to the consumer's price in oil, coal, or nuclear-powered energy systems. Conservation, solar or wind systems have minimal additional costs.

Another aspect of costs is the efficiency of the machine using the energy, which can be examined through *life-cycle costing.* A more efficient machine may cost a bit more new, but over its lifetime save immense amounts of energy. As one example, the Association of Home Appliance Manufacturers has issued figures that show the relative energy efficiency of refrigerators: over the anticipated lifetime for the same size refrigerator, fuel costs for the least efficient models range from $600 to $1,000 higher than the most efficient.[28]

On top of all this is the quite arbitrary pricing of nonrenewable fuels —considering that future generations are not bidding against us to preserve existing reserves for those uses for which they may be most ideally suited. It is especially disastrous not to consider this arbitrary pricing factor when making individual and societal decisions about energy policy: "Whether solar heat can compete today with a rapdily vanishing supply of artificially cheap gas is irrelevant and misleading."[29]

Some of this artificial cheapness comes not only from lack of consideration for future generations, but from direct and indirect government subsidies. Massive oil and gas depletion allowances are one example. Another is a shale oil synfuels plant being built by Union Oil Company in Colorado, which is backed by Department of Defense contracts to purchase its entire output of diesel and jet fuel for ten years at a *minimum* price slightly higher than the current market value.[30] The special problem with this sort of subsidy is that our society cannot afford the capital investment necessary for full parallel development of nonrenewable and renewable resources: a choice has to be made, and the wrong choice, based on short-term profit considerations, may well prove disastrous.

Another economic consideration is jobs. Jerry Gordon, of the United Food and Commercial Workers Union, estimates that solar technologies provide two to four times as many jobs as nuclear power plants.[31] Another way of looking at this issue is the effect of government spending on solar energy development versus government spending on military production. Using Lockheed Missiles and Space Company as the basis for its analysis, the Mid-Peninsula Conversion Project estimates that solar energy technologies could provide close to double the number of jobs that military technologies could for skilled craftspeople, factory workers, engineers, and architects.[32]

NONECONOMIC COSTS

Our dependence on consuming immense quantities of energy costs us our lifetimes—despite all the contrary beliefs we are taught that claim we are the happy beneficiaries of more leisure. Ivan Illich's analysis of the "captive tripper"—the typical American who must drive a car because there is no other way to get to work, obtain food, visit friends, and so forth —rings dramatically true on a gut level:

The typical American male devotes more than 1600 hours a year to his car. He sits in it while it goes and while it stands idling. He parks it and searches for it. He earns the money to put down on it and to meet the monthly installments. He works to pay for petrol, tools, insurance, taxes and tickets. He spends four of his 16 waking hours on the road or gathering his resources for it. And this figure does not take into account the time consumed by other activities dictated by transport: time spent in hospitals, traffic courts and garages. . . . The model American puts in 1600 hours to get 7500 miles: less than five miles per hour. In countries deprived of a transportation industry, people manage to do the same, walking wherever they want to go, and they allocate only three to eight percent of their society's time budget to traffic instead of 28 percent. What distinguishes the traffic in rich countries from the traffic in poor countries is not more mileage per hour of life-time for the majority, but more hours of compulsory consumption of high doses of energy, packaged and unequally distributed by the transportation industry.[33]

Another energy myth is that our centralized energy distribution system offers us greater convenience and reliability than we might expect from a decentralized, renewable energy system. The convenience question is similar to the issues raised by the automobile example above: Lovins questions whether people might not prefer making weatherization adjustments or regularly adjusting their solar plumbing to the convenience of paying high utility bills or living next to a nuclear reactor.[34] As for reliability, the bigger a system, the more wasteful backup is required to ensure uninterrupted service should there be a system problem:

Some opponents of soft technologies have suggested, for example, that in order to be as reliable from the user's point of view as electric heat, any solar heating system must be duplicated. But this argument stands reality on its head. The reason electrical grids are designed to such exemplary—and expensive—standards of reliability is that they must be, because so many people depend on them that a failure would be a social catastrophe. If your solar system fails (which, of course, it should not do, as there should not be much to go wrong with it), you can put on a sweater or go next door until it is fixed. But if the electrical grid fails, there is nowhere else to go and not much you can do about it.[35]

Not much you can do about it—are we going to be willing to continue to leave control of our energy future to large energy corporations? As the definitions of renewable energy technologies imply, and the examples that follow illustrate, there is the possibility of returning energy decisions to a local level. Individuals, neighborhoods, towns, cities, or counties can make a large impact on their own energy supply and use.

Renewables are not automatically decentralized, however. Solar could become big business and be built in centralized, inefficient ways. As of 1979, 90 percent of all Department of Energy funds available for solar development went to large corporations.[36] There is even less federal funding available today for local solar energy development. But continuation of dependence on nonrenewable energy leaves local democracy even less chance. A 1975 report commissioned by the federal government's Nuclear Regulatory Commission projected that security measures needed to protect nuclear materials from sabotage could mean the evolution of a nuclear police state in the United States.[37]

Beyond internal repression, war could become the ultimate price we pay for the convenience of private cars and a centralized electric grid. Richard Barnet, resource analyst, points out that

we are not going to be able to continue taking a third of all the oil that's used because it is not only the question of whether we can light our houses and heat them, but it really goes to the fundamental question of war and peace. We are now in the business of threatening war over access to resources in other people's countries. So what really we're looking for is a new mode of living with the majority of the four billion people on the planet.[38]

In choosing to reject going to war for energy, we must also reject nuclear power. Aside from the increased possibility of theft of the uranium mined and transported for nuclear power plants, the main source of nuclear weapons proliferation in the world today is nuclear power plants.

Six countries—the United States, the Soviet Union, the United Kingdom, France, China, and India—have exploded nuclear devices. At least ten countries—West Germany, Israel, Belgium, Japan, Italy, Argentina, Taiwan, Pakistan, South Korea, and Iran—have reprocessing facilities and materials sufficient to reprocess separable plutonium for three to sixty nuclear weapons. South Africa and Brazil have uranium enrichment facilities accomplishing the same purpose. India and most of these latter twelve countries have obtained their bomb fuel and reprocessing technology through nuclear power plants supplied by the United States and Western Europe. This puts them all into at least "near-nuclear" status—able to produce bombs within a short time if they choose.[39]

The United States has much of the ability and responsibility to stop this proliferation. Even for the reactors American companies do not sell "whole," American technology is relied upon in ways besides the supply of whole reactors:

Probably every light water reactor program and manufacturer in the world depends in some way on an intricate and little known network of U.S. licensing and technical support. . . . "Soviet reactors in Finland . . . are being built by the Soviet Government as a principal contractor. But the backup safety system is being supplied by Westinghouse Electric. . . . Thus, doing without the Americans is difficult even in the case of a Soviet-supplied reactor. . . ." Even the most outwardly independent European reactor program today requires U.S. licensed processes for manufacture or controlling water chemistry, U.S.-made instruments, U.S.-designed hardware of many kinds. Even the supposedly independent Canadian CANDU program exists only on U.S. sufferance: some 20–30 percent of the hardware is made in the U.S.[40]

Supposedly "safer" nuclear fusion reactors, now in experimental stages, present even more of a weapons proliferation problem. In association with a fusion reaction, inert Uranium-238 is easily converted into Plutonium-239, greatly simplifying the whole problem of isotope purification.

At the current rate of proliferation, it has been estimated that there will be sixty countries capable of exploding nuclear weapons by the year 2000. Clearly, a world that uses nuclear energy is not a safe one.

WHAT CAN WE DO?

INDIVIDUAL OR SMALL GROUP CHANGES

How can we begin to change our daily energy use patterns, alone or working with others? Personal habits can have more to do with this than we might guess at first. Here are a few general suggestions for starters.

Set a goal (but don't expect miracles).

First, you may want to set a goal for an "energy diet"—perhaps the average level of energy use in the developed world or in a particular country, such as Sweden, England, or France. Whatever diet you choose, don't expect miracles. There are just too many things beyond our immediate control, which is why we have to organize for larger changes as we go along. The energy required to collect and store and treat drinking water and to transport it hundreds of miles and pump it to a tap in a big-city apartment is vastly greater than that required by a farmer or peasant who gets water from a stream or well—but we could cut down on our water use. And although we may want to use a watch for a lifetime, the economics of a throwaway culture condemn us to replace the watch we can't afford to repair. The web in which we are caught is a tangled one indeed, not easily undone. But we need not wait for society to change; we can make changes now. There is no assurance that social and political reorganization will follow, but we believe personal change is a necessary part of creating new institutions.

Many of these possible personal changes can be summed up in three words: *pare, share,* and *care.*

Pare empty energy uses.

One of the first things you can look for are empty energy uses that add nothing to our lives—possessions that are a worry more than a joy, labor-saving devices that don't save labor, things that are larger or more than we need. How many electrical conveniences, from clocks and toothbrushes to dishwashers and pencil sharpeners do we own that could be eliminated or replaced with simpler mechanical devices? What are our real needs and how many of the things we buy and want would disappear from our lives if they were not advertised? Try to think of some nonobvious possibilities—one Palo Alto elder purchased an adult tricycle, with large baskets, for grocery shopping and other trips up to several miles. Buying at local farmers' markets and from stores that stock local produce also helps to cut down on food transportation energy costs.

People's needs vary, and not everyone has the luxury of choice. If I am poor and need a car, I may only be able to afford the secondhand gaseater that has depreciated rapidly to a bargain price.

Care for what you own and use.

An obvious way to invest less in material things is to cherish and care for them so that the energy investment involved in their manufacture is spread over as long a time as possible. If I *must* own a car, careful maintenance can extend its life up to ten years and spread the energy costs accordingly.

Share.

Sharing ownership or use of things with others can also help spread energy costs. Car pools can substantially reduce the energy spent on personal transportation and also help us get to know our fellow riders. The co-ownership of tools, garden implements, recreational equipment, and so on eliminates unnecessary duplication of possessions among friends and neighbors. A small use-fee can collect funds for repair and replacement and eliminate hassles. And, as a hidden benefit, sharing may help overcome one of the causes of unnecessary possessions—the lack of mutually satisfying and interdependent relationships with others. In addition to sharing possessions, modifying the ways we share our lives can also save energy. We can come out of our "own" rooms on cold days and learn to share the heated kitchen or living room, and we can make more friends within walking or bicycling distance.

Many other specific suggestions for eliminating empty energy uses, caring for the things we own, and sharing their ownership and use can be found elsewhere in this book.

Minor physical modifications to buildings can also go a long way toward energy saving, and successive changes can be financed by savings from the initial ones. Many neighbors have weatherization parties—an insulation blower that can help insulate three to four houses in one day could be rented by a group, for example. Tenants in a master-metered apartment building could negotiate with the landlord to receive rent reductions corresponding to the energy they save—and then use the money saved by habit changes to purchase water heater insulation and low-flow shower heads. A bit more research and volunteer labor might convince the landlord to make somewhat more costly modifications, with cost savings shared.

Homeowners, housing cooperatives, and businesses may want to make more major changes to existing buildings. As figures presented earlier on page 204 show, renewable energy technologies are generally more economic right now than nonrenewable technologies. So why isn't everyone doing it?

The problem is that most owners of residences and small businesses don't have easy access to the hundreds or thousands of dollars necessary to make major energy changes—it has to be borrowed and it is a large investment. Energy companies, on the other hand, can borrow large sums of money and charge us, month by month, on our utility bills. By the end of twenty years, we will have paid an energy company two, three, four, or five times the amount of money we would have otherwise spent on solar heating construction. Some communities, such as those discussed below, are making it easier for building owners to choose renewable energy solutions. Our federal, state, and local governments must also stop subsidizing the large energy companies and start making the installation of decentralized, renewable energy sources easier.

St. Francis Square, a large San Francisco housing cooperative, had thirteen sets of solar collectors installed, which heat, on a year-round average, 60 percent of their hot water. These were financed through a loan from the National Cooperative Bank. Despite San Francisco's fog and the fact that its utility rates are among the lowest of major American cities, this is an economic investment in the long term. Jerry Lax, of the Solar Center, the cooperative that installed the St. Francis system and hundreds of other large systems, estimates that this system will last around forty years and will pay for itself in twenty years. California has a solar tax credit, however, that reduces the payback time to about half that—a very important factor when we are talking about individuals, small groups, and small businesses making energy investment decisions.

COMMUNITY ENERGY

DAVIS, CALIFORNIA

Davis is a place where citizens became interested in energy long before the "energy crisis." In 1966, an election was fought over the city council's refusal to construct bicycle paths; the winners proceeded, over the next ten years, to construct twenty-eight miles of bicycle paths. In 1972, hundreds of people were involved in putting together a controlled growth and resource conservation plan for Davis, and in 1976, after extensive research and experiments, Davis became the first city in the United States to enact a comprehensive energy conservation code.[41]

Davis' energy code and other legislative policies strongly encourage both energy conservation and use of renewable energy sources. The code is based on experimental construction which showed that a carefully designed and oriented passive solar building could use as little as one-seventh of the energy of a building designed without consideration of sun angle or access. One builder who was initially vehemently opposed to the ordinance became one of its strongest advocates when he discovered that the specifications kept the buildings cool in the summer, warm in the winter, and cost only $35.10 more to construct to code specifications, according to his calculations.[42] New construction is an extremely important energy factor in Davis, whose population has risen from twenty-five thousand in 1976 to thirty-six thousand in 1983. In 1980, the "energy budget" new construction was required to meet was made stricter, but builders were allowed greater latitude for innovative designs. For example, apartment builders were no longer required to install flat plate collectors for hot water heating if they could otherwise meet the energy budget. In practice, almost all continue to use the collectors, which in an apartment complex can be centrally placed in the best sun orientation to provide efficient water heating for several buildings. As another innovation-encouraging approach, the city council recently leased unused sewage ponds to a private company that is experimenting with a method of cheaply concentrating the sun's rays on photovoltaic cells. A six-acre site could potentially supply 250 homes with electricity in this fashion. Other aspects of the energy policy include narrower streets heavily shaded with deciduous trees that let the sun through in the winter and the encouragement of home businesses to cut down on commuting energy costs.

There are a number of different statistics that attest to the results of all this energy activity. From 1973 through 1978, for example, residential electrical use dropped by 18 percent, and natural gas use by 37 percent.[43] Another study shows a 15 percent reduction in electrical use during the first forty-one months of the energy code, resulting from code requirements only, from January 1976 to March 1979.[44] In 1981, an incentive program sponsored by the local utility resulted in an electrical usage drop of at least 7 percent from the already lowered consumption, with effect from price changes controlled for. The actual drop was 22.3 percent in peak-load usage, with the average of fifty surrounding communities dropping 13 percent, and Davis received the $100,000 incentive "reward" to spend on its energy programs. In 1982, the same program, turned over by the utility to the chamber of commerce, resulted in a large drop in commercial energy consumption and another $100,000 reward.

Tom Tomassi, Davis City Council member and former mayor, is both approving and cautioning about the utility's conservation programs: "Conservation programs must ultimately be controlled by the cities or counties. If there were conservation and retrofitting to the extent possible, it would put PG&E [the utility] out of business."

According to Tomassi, the key to Davis's energy success has been citizen involvement—from the initial 1966 bicycle election, to the drafting of the growth ordinance and energy code, to the 1981 campaign that involved at least one hundred people going door-to-door to give their neighbors conservation information:

In Davis, energy conservation has become an everyday, everybody involved kind of occurrence. I find it startling to drive through other communities and to see new buildings constructed without energy use taken into consideration or without solar collectors. I think, what are they going to do in 20 years? They will have to go back and retrofit, and they could have been saving money all along.

COUNTY ENERGY PLANS

Not every community has as many bicycle-lovers as Davis, nor such an avid initial interest in energy issues. How can *your* community be helped to see the importance of energy in its day-to-day life?

One way is to make a county energy study. Franklin County, Massachusetts, a low-income, rural community of 65,000, found that if the county continued to use conventional energy sources, an average family would be spending $5,300 to $7,300 yearly on energy alone by the year 2000 —with much of that money leaving the county.[45] The amount Franklin County currently pays for energy equals the payroll of the county's ten largest employers.[46] By use of conservation and renewable energy resources, however, Franklin County could be largely energy self-sufficient by the year 2000.[47] This study helped spur the activities of official energy committees in twenty-two of the county's twenty-six towns, the production of a five-year county plan of energy goals and policy, and a number of other experimental energy programs.

Making a county energy analysis involves clever research and a lot of arithmetic. The Institute for Ecological Policies of Fairfax, Virginia, has produced two books, complete with detailed breakdowns and worksheets, that show you how to do it: *Energy and Power in Your Community* and *County Energy Plan Guidebook* (see Bibliography for ordering details). Where does your county's energy come from? Where is the consumer's energy money going? How could renewable energy change the picture? What would the situation look like in the year 2000? These are some of the questions these books help you answer.

SAN LUIS VALLEY, COLORADO

San Luis Valley, Colorado, is a rural, economically depressed area, with a ninety-day growing season. It is the largest alpine valley in the world, with the valley floor 8,000 feet above sea level. Winter nighttime temperatures go to 50 degrees below zero, but the valley is blessed with sun 300 to 330 days per year. San Luis Valley is also the most solarized community in the United States, with 3,000 of its 13,000 households heating their hot water, their houses, or both by direct use of the sun's energy. This has all happened in the space of about eight years, with very little outside funding, but much community participation. There are now one hundred people working full-time on renewable energy installation, under the aegis of twenty different contracting businesses. A recent study by Akira Kawanabe shows $4.5 million being spent annually in the county on renewable energy materials, resulting in an immediate annual saving of $4.5 million in utility costs! All these factors have combined to improve the quality of residents' lives by reducing money spent for energy and keeping the energy money spent in the valley.

The importance of this has not been lost on San Luis Valley's banks.

Now they won't consider a mortgage loan without an explanation of why solar utilities are *not* being installed! One bank even offers a 1 percent interest rate discount for solar-supplied buildings.

The solar age began in San Luis Valley in 1975 when a traditional building contractor, Bill North, started working with farmers to help them reduce their energy costs. North and others designed a solar collector—now in its "100th modification since 1975"—that is efficient and easy to build. The materials for a collector sufficient to retrofit an average, insulated, four-room house with solar heat and hot water now cost around $800 (though a badly designed house may be impossible to retrofit for 100 percent solar). A recently constructed commercial building of 3,000 square feet, with rock, underfloor heat storage, and a supplemental $900 solar collector, is 100 percent solar heated, as are fifteen to twenty new homes that use this method. The rock takes a full month of cloudy weather to lose its accumulated heat entirely.

Under the auspices of the San Luis Valley Energy Center, over one hundred workshops have been given since 1976 to demonstrate weatherization and solar collector building techniques. Almost every household that has decided to build its own solar system has the help of friends and neighbors, who may hear about the project through the Energy Center and come to get experience they can use in building their own. Bob Dunsmore, president of the Energy Center, observed that often people install their first solar collector and then become really interested in tightening up their houses to make the system work—when they see the possibility of becoming truly energy self-sufficient. Another bonus of solar development has been three large, adobe-foundationed community greenhouses, which have been built by the combined labor of hundreds of people. One greenhouse, in La Jara, starts vegetables for twelve hundred valley gardens every spring and then provides areas for families to grow warm-weather crops, such as tomatoes during the summer. Food is also now being grown throughout winter in the greenhouses.

San Luis Valley is anxious to share its knowledge with other communities. They have distributed twenty thousand copies of a manual that shows you how to build their solar collector (see Bibliography). The Energy Center has supervised workshops sponsored by the San Luis Valley Christian Community Services, bringing around seven hundred junior high and high school students from all over the United States to work on solar and weatherization projects. Perhaps the best news for interested communities is that Bob Dunsmore, the center's president, will give an evening presentation followed by an all-day, how-to-do-it workshop for $200 plus the expense of getting him to and from your community (which can be considerably reduced by coordinating with nearby communities).

San Luis Valley provides a message broader than that of renewable energy for those who wonder whether taking charge in one area can lead to other changes. Dunsmore observes that he has seen important changes in his community since people first became involved with energy activities:

I now see the same people sitting on committees for an emergency foodbank, working on providing shelter for battered women, focusing on the needs of the elderly, providing staff for a local hospice, working on putting together farmers' markets. There is an amazing feeling of empowerment here—there's a lot going on without a lot of financial resources.

SOLAR JOBS

Because solar jobs are relatively new, there are more entry-level possibilities for minorities who have had difficulty breaking into the construction trades. The Westside Development Corporation in San Bernardino, California, has tried to combine this possibility with its program for providing services to benefit its 90 percent minority, low- and middle-income community.

Over the years, the organization has trained around two thousand neighborhood residents in housing construction, electronics, and solar industry skills: about two to three hundred in the solar area. Their overall direct placement rate in the private sector is well over 50 percent. Most of the solar training has been in the form of manufacture and installation of systems in low-income homes. Recently, the organization built an 18,000-square-foot industrial facility, part of a larger industrial park that, it is hoped, will bring jobs to the depressed neighborhood. They outfitted the building with a 35kW photovoltaic system, designed to provide 40 percent of the building's electrical needs and to provide data for research. It is the largest photovoltaic industrial installation west of the Mississippi.

Due to federal budget cuts, the organization lost 65 percent of its staff and program in 1981—but it is still doing its best to further its twin goals.

PORTLAND, OREGON

In 1979, Portland developed and enacted a comprehensive energy policy with the goal of cutting the city's energy use by one-third by the year 1995—thus saving residents and employers $1 billion per year on energy bills. Portland, a sizeable city of 350,000, shows the potential open to American communities that act with strong local government support for innovative energy policies.

Portland's government started by looking at its own energy use. They have so far invested $700,000 in energy efficiency, in every area from heat pumps to building insulation to smaller city cars (experimentally powered by a variety of fuels), to a computerized energy-efficiency tracking system that helps them decide where their next investment should go. They have even purchased devices that allow a police officer to turn off the car engine while keeping the car warm. So far, the city government is saving at least $300,000 per year on its energy bills. A possible next step, according to Senior Energy Analyst Mike Philips, is an incentive system to encourage city employees to find further ways to save energy in their bureaus.

A major goal was to "fully weatherize" (as defined by an energy audit) every residence in Portland within five years. By mid-1983, 42 percent of single-family homes had been fully weatherized, and only 7 percent had had no weatherization done. Philips explains that rental units are a more difficult problem, since the often-absentee landlord of an individually metered apartment gains no personal financial benefit from energy conservation. The Energy Office plans to try a number of options in cooperation with landlords before requesting a city vote on mandatory weatherization.

A major factor in Portland's success with weatherization and solar installations has been the efforts made by the city and local utilities to provide low-interest loans. For homes heated with electricity, Pacific Power and Light first financed a zero percent loan program that didn't have to be repaid until one's house was sold. The loans are still available at zero percent, but with a five-year payback period. The gas utility also offers weatherization loans at 10 percentage points below the current market interest rate.

The majority of Portlanders heat with oil, however, and the city stepped in to finance loans through Portland Energy Conservation, Inc., a nonprofit financing and energy counseling center with a staff of eleven. Through a storefront Energy Savings Center, the city offers 4.75 percent loans to low- and moderate-income householders. The money is voluntarily obtained from local banks at below-market, tax-exempt rates and is further subsidized from a federal Urban Development Action Grant (UDAC)—the first community to use such grants for energy conservation. The city also provides landlords and higher income householders with 8 percent loans—very popular the first two years of the program, until the state of Oregon enacted a 6.5 percent energy loan program!

Portland Energy Conservation has made further innovative use of UDAC funds to subsidize zero percent loans to local businesses for energy audits. Although a householder can obtain a free audit, commercial prices begin at $2,000 for an audit of a neighborhood restaurant. If the business agrees to institute all energy saving recommendations shown by the audit to pay for themselves within one year, the loan is forgiven. So far, every business that has made use of this service has also instituted the necessary changes, investing approximately six dollars for every dollar spent on the audit. Philips explained that finding more below-market-rate money to help businesses make more expensive energy investments is now a priority: "The less money our businesses have to spend on energy and the more money they have to keep their operations afloat, the more jobs we can keep in the city."

In mid-September 1983, Portland passed a zoning code exception ordinance that will make solar installations easier, and a comprehensive solar access code is being drafted, which will cover everything from guaranteeing that solar construction will not be shaded by new, neighboring construction to identifying the type of deciduous street trees that will ensure the best solar exposure in winter. The same loans financed by the city for weatherization are also available for solar installations.

In the area of transit, the three-county area that includes Portland has successfully encouraged a larger bus ridership through a number of means, including bus-only streets downtown and an innovative fare system that doesn't charge at all for short trips within the downtown area. Carpools and vanpools have also become commonplace.

To save energy through recycling, a Portland resident can call for a free, curbside pickup of recyclable materials, in addition to the bottles and cans already recycled under Oregon's five-cent deposit law.

In the future, Portland will be showing the way to its neighbors as part of the four-state region covered by the Pacific Northwest Electric Power Planning and Conservation Act, passed by Congress in 1981. In the summer of 1983, the Northwest Power Planning Council, an administrative agency established by the act, issued a plan specifying that no new power plants can be built in the Pacific Northwest until feasible conservation has been done and renewable resources have been utilized. Watching the Pacific Northwest as it explores a renewable energy future will be interesting for all of us.

KEEPING OUR OPTIONS

As can be seen from the facts and figures above, less fantastic sums of money are necessary to develop renewable energy sources than non-renewable ones—but we still don't have the money, as individuals or as a society, for both. And many of the nonmonetary costs will be difficult to reverse. In addition to focusing on the development of renewable energy sources, it is also necessary to ensure our option and right to do so by blocking some of the more drastic actions being taken today by large energy companies and utilities.

Every state has an agency that regulates energy utility prices, and in many places ratepayers have joined together to protest rate increases that have resulted from damaging choices to rely on nonrenewable fuels. One such group is the Kansas Electric Shock Coalition, a coalition of two hundred and fifty organizations that successfully opposed Kansas Gas and Electric' 1983 $48 billion rate increase request. Coalition members thoroughly educated themselves and staged the largest public hearing in Kansas history. Wichita Gray Panther Convener Pat Moore, an active member of the coalition, described that hearing: "One of my greatest joys was to watch the faces of the utility's attorneys and officials as reel after reel of their figures were thrown back at them and shown to be incorrect by the people testifying." After the hearing, KG&E voluntarily reduced its rate increase request by two-thirds! The group hopes to stop further rate increases, as well as the scheduled 1985 opening of Wolf Creek Nuclear Power Plant, since the utility already is capable of generating considerably more electricity than is being used in Kansas.

Another urgent subject of conflict is the "National Sacrifice Area"—this is the label placed by the Carter Administration on lands "necessary" for uranium mining, coal strip-mining, and oil shale production. Most of these lands were previously thought to be "worthless"—and were left for Native Americans to eke out a living on. Now, the Black Hills, the Dakotas, Montana, and the Four Corners area of Arizona, Colorado, New Mexico, and Utah are the scenes of struggles between energy companies and the Native Americans and other local farmers and ranchers who are trying to preserve their land from destruction and their water from poisoning.

A third serious area of concern is nuclear power. On the balance, energy activists have been winning this fight in the United States, but there is still a long way to go. No active orders for nuclear power plants have been placed in the United States since 1974; since 1964, ninety-eight plants have been cancelled, fifty-four delayed, and fifteen indefinitely deferred.[48] Opposition, however, to some of the most dangerous reactors has necessitated massive civil disobedience—as was the case with Diablo Canyon Nuclear Power Plant, which is built near an earthquake fault near San Luis Obispo, California. Following the arrest of hundreds of protesters at Diablo Canyon in 1981, "design errors" were suddenly revealed by at least one company engineer, such as the fact that a structural component of one reactor had been designed and built in mirror-image. This resulted in the revocation of Diablo's safety certification for low-power testing. However, in September of 1983, the Nuclear Regulatory Commission again declared Diablo "safe," and the ultimate outcome of the struggle remains open.

The nuclear industry is still making money maintaining existing U.S. plants, as well as in selling plants overseas. Nuclear expert Mark Hertsgaard believes that "their basic strategy is to outwait the opposition."[49] They may be surprised when their opposition ultimately wins by converting to renewable energy.

WHAT YOU CAN DO

1. Alone or together with your family or a group, list the ways that more community could mean less energy use. What ways could you start on this variety of energy conservation?
2. Using the chart, try to figure out who really controls the energy you use. Identify the areas where you have some control and those where

WHO EXERTS CONTROL OVER MY ENERGY CONSUMPTION?

Categories	Subcategories	I control	I do or might have some influence	Control exerted by others				
				Industry	Local gov.	State gov.	Federal gov.	Other
My home	a. heating/cooling b. food used c. food storage and preparation d. lighting e. clothing f. garden g. other							
My transpor-tation	a. walking b. bicycle c. public d. auto e. other							
My work	a. machine use b. temperature c. facilities d. cafeteria e. stairs/elevator f. other							
My recreation	a. transportation b. items consumed c. other							
Regional and national systems	a. food preparation and delivery b. transportation c. consumer items d. communication e. military							

you have little or none. Can you think of ways in which you and your community could increase your share of control?

3. Try playing the Energy Game. To play the game, make a list of the things you use each day that consume energy. Consider the energy needed in the original production of the item as well as the energy needed for its continued use. Next, cross out the items on your list that you could do without fairly easily. Then go through the list again and circle all the things you could do without only if you were to simplify your life drastically. Next to the circled items write down something that could be substituted. For example, if you circled "automobile," you might replace it with a bicycle or public transportation. Try this process in a small group; have everyone share their lists. Perhaps you can also decide whether this has helped you see some changes you can make in real life.

4. Perhaps you would like to have a more exact idea of how much energy is used by different machinery and processes. A number of books have charts that help you do this. One such book is *Home Energy Guide: How to Cut Your Utility Bills* by John Rothchild and Frank Tenney.

5. Every county in the United States has at least one person who likes to play with windmills, photovoltaics, and/or solar collectors. Ask this person to share some of that excitement with your neighborhood group or class—preferably at the location of the windmill workshop.

6. Find out how energy decisions are being made in your community and how the administrative structures and decisions compare to those in Davis, Portland, or the San Luis Valley. Consider ways that interest could be generated to make the needed changes.

7. Are there already energy facilities in or near your community that pose some of the grave dangers discussed in this chapter? Consider how your community might eliminate its energy dependence on them— gradually or very quickly. How might your group assist that process?

NOTES

1. Amory B. Lovins, "Energy Strategy, the Road Not Taken?" *Not Man Apart,* November 1976.
2. *The Good News About Energy,* a report prepared by the Council on Environmental Quality, Executive Office of the President (1979), p. 6.
3. Calculation by Lee Shipper (Staff Scientist, Lawrence Berkeley Laboratory), personal communication, January 1984.
4. Eric Hirst, "Food-Related Energy Requirements," *Science* 184, no. 4134 (April 19, 1974).
5. Barry Commoner, "A Reporter at Large: Energy," *The New Yorker,* February 2, 9, 16, 1976.
6. Amory B. Lovins, *Soft Energy Paths: Toward a Durable Peace* (Cambridge, Mass.: Ballinger Publishing Company, 1977), pp. 27–28.
7. "A Time to Choose: Synthetic Fuels and the American Future," published by Sierra Club, 530 Bush Street, San Francisco, Calif. 94108.

8. Lovins, *Soft Energy Paths*, p. 40.
9. Robert Stobaugh and Daniel Yergin, *Energy Future, Report of the Energy Project at Harvard Business School* (New York: Random House, 1979), p. 136. The comparison of fourteen hundred nuclear power plants was made by Jim Harding, Friends of the Earth, San Francisco.
10. Lovins, *Soft Energy Paths*, p. 43.
11. Larry Strain, "In Choosing Solar, Solar Lets Us Make the Choice What We Can Do At Home," *Simple Living*, 1977, no. 12, p. 14.
12. Ibid.
13. Commoner, "A Reporter at Large: Energy."
14. William Heronemus, "Offshore Wind Power Systems," paper given at the 8th Annual Conference of the Marine Technology Society in Washington, D.C. (contact author through Department of Civil Engineering, University of Massachusetts, Amherst, Mass.).
15. Barry Commoner, *The Politics of Energy* (New York: Knopf, 1979), pp. 42–43.
16. J. Baldwin, "Alcohol," *The Next Whole Earth Catalog*, rev. 2nd ed. (Sausalito, Calif.: Point, 1982), p. 203.
17. Wilson Clark, "Power from Waste," *Asia 2000* 1 (1981) 1, pp. 12–13.
18. Lovins, *Soft Energy Paths*, p. 96.
19. Stewart Brand, ed., *The Next Whole Earth Catalog*, 1st ed., p. 204.
20. David Morris, *Self Reliant Cities* (San Francisco: Sierra Club Books, 1982), p. 160.
21. P. W. McCracken et al., "Industrial Energy Center Study," Dow Chemical Company report, discussed by Lovins, *Soft Energy Paths*, p. 34.
22. Morris, *Self Reliant Cities*, p. 157.
23. *Yoedler* (San Francisco Bay Area Sierra Club), 1982.
24. Douglas Steinberg, "The Garbage Dilemma: To Recycle or Burn?", *Not Man Apart*, January 1982, p. 9.
25. Lovins, *Soft Energy Paths*, p. 8.
26. Commoner, *Politics of Energy*, pp. 24–31.
27. Adapted from Lovins, *Soft Energy Paths*, p. 134.
28. John Rothchild and Frank Tenney, *Home Energy Guide: How to Cut Your Utility Bills* (New York: Balantine Books, 1978), p. 114.
29. Lovins, *Soft Energy Paths*, p. 20.
30. James J. Lueck, "Synthetic Fuels' Appeal Fades," *New York Times* (business section), July 1983, p. 1.
31. Statement made in "We've Got the Power," AFSC slide show.
32. Robert deGrasse et al., *Creating Solar Jobs: Options for Military Workers and Communities*, a report of the Mid-Peninsula Conversion Project, Mountain View, Calif., November, 1978.
33. Ivan Illich, *Energy and Equity* (London: Marion Boyers, 1974), pp. 30–31.
34. Lovins, *Soft Energy Paths*, p. 139.
35. Ibid., p. 93.
36. Richard Munson, "Ripping off the Sun," *The Progressive*, September 1979.
37. John Barton (Stanford Law School), "Intensified Nuclear Safeguards and Civil Liberties," report commissioned by the Nuclear Regulatory Commission (1975).
38. Richard Barnet, *The Lean Years—Politics in the Age of Scarcity* (New York: Simon & Schuster, 1980); "We've Got the Power," AFSC slide show.
39. American Friends Service Committee, "Atoms for Peace, Atoms for War" (NARMIC, 1979).
40. Lovins, *Soft Energy Paths*, pp. 209–210.
41. Morris, *Self Reliant Cities*, p. 121.
42. Ibid.
43. Judy Corbett, in "We've Got the Power," AFSC slide show.
44. Thomas Dietz and Edward L. Vine, summary of report in Project #79-74-3963, *University of California Appropriate Technology News & Views* 6 (June 1983) no. 2.
45. U.S. Department of Energy Region I, *Groundwork*, Energy Planning in Franklin County, p. 28.
46. Morris, *Self Reliant Cities*, p. 129.

47. U.S. Department of Energy, *Groundwork,* p. 28.
48. Jeff Bentoff, "Conference Targets Limping Nuclear Industry," *Multinational Monitor,* April 1983, p. 5.
49. Ibid., p. 6.

SOURCES OF FURTHER INFORMATION

Groups Mentioned in Chapter

Abalone Alliance. 2940 16th Street, San Francisco, Calif. 94103.

Franklin County Extension Service, Energy Agent. Court House, Greenfield, Mass. 01301.

Friends of the Earth. 1045 Sansome Street, San Francisco, Calif. 94111.

Kansas Electric Shock Coalition. c/o Gray Panthers of Wichita, 147 North Segwick, Wichita, Kans. 67203.

Portland Energy Conservation, Inc. 2755 Northeast Broadway, Portland, Oreg. 97232.

San Bernardino West Side Community Development Corporation. 1736 West Highland Avenue, San Bernardino, Calif. 92411.

San Luis Valley Energy Center. 512 Ross Avenue, Alamosa, Colo. 81101.

Solar Center. 1115 Indiana Street, San Francisco, Calif. 94107.

Additional Resource Groups

Black Hills Alliance. Box 2508, Rapid City, S. Dak. 57709.

Blacks Against Nukes. 3728 New Hampshire Avenue, N.W., Suite 202, Washington, D.C. 20001. Seminars, workshops, slideshow, war toys boycott, solar energy.

Center for Renewable Resources. 1001 Connecticut Avenue, N.W., Washington, D.C. 20026.

Citizen/Labor Energy Coalition. 606 West Fullerton Parkway, Chicago, Ill. 60614.

Critical Mass Energy Project. 133 C Street, S.E., Washington, D.C. 20003.

Domestic Technology Institute. Box 2043, Evergreen, Colo. 80439. Designs renewable energy alternatives for rural, Third World countries.

Integral Urban House. 1516 5th Street, Berkeley, Calif. 94710. Demonstration, research, and consultation on ecologically integrated houses and gardens.

Labor Committee for Safe Energy and Full Employment. 1536 16th Street, N.W., Washington, D.C. 20035.

Natural Resources Defense Council. 122 East 42 Street, New York, N.Y. 10168.

Solar Lobby. 1001 Connecticut Avenue, N.W., Washington, D.C. 20036.

Southwest Research and Information Center. Box 4524, Albuquerque, N. Mex. 87106. Information on National Sacrifice Area struggles and alternatives.

World Information Service on Energy (WISE). 1536 16th Street, N.W., Washington, D.C. 20036.

Bibliography

Community Energy

Benson, Jim, and Alan Okagaki. *County Energy Plan Guidebook: Creating a Renewable Energy Future.* 1979. Available from: Institute for Ecological Policies,

9208 Christopher Street, Fairfax, Va. 22031. $7.50 individuals; $15 all
others.

Franklin County Energy Goals and Policy Document, 1980–1985. Available from: Franklin County Extension Service, address above.

Illich, Ivan. *Energy and Equity.* London: Marion Boyers, 1974.

Portland's Energy Conservation Policy. Available from: Energy Department, Office of Planning and Development, 620 Southwest 5th Avenue, Portland, Oreg. 97104.

Ridgeway, James, *Energy-Efficient Community Planning: A Guide to Saving Energy and Producing Power at the Local Level.* Emmaus, Pa.: JB Press, 1979.

Schaefer, E., and J. Benson. *Energy and Power in Your Community.* 1980. Available from: Institute for Ecological Policies, 9208 Christopher Street, Fairfax, Va. 22031. $6.

We've Got the Power. Slideshow/filmstrip that explores our energy choices and features communities that have chosen alternatives. Available from: AFSC, 2160 Lake Street, San Francisco, Calif. 94121. $70/$50; or rental from AFSC regional offices.

Renewable Energy

Anderson, Bruce, and Malcolm Wells. *Passive Solar Energy: The Homeowners Guide to Natural Heating and Cooling.* Andover, Mass.: Brick House Publishing, 1981.

Butti, K., and J. Perlin. *A Golden Thread: 2500 Years of Solar Architecture and Technology.* New York: Van Nostrand Reinhold, 1980.

Coe, Gigi. *Present Value.* San Francisco: Friends of the Earth, 1980. Twenty farms, factories, homes, and offices that use solar energy.

DeGrasse, Robert, et al. *Creating Solar Jobs: Options for Military Workers and Communities.* 1978. Available from: Mid-Peninsula Conversion Project, 867 West Dana, Suite 203, Mountain View, Calif. 94041. $4 ppd.

Fisher, Rick, and Bill Yanda. *The Food and Heat Producing Solar Greenhouse—Design, Construction and Operation,* 2nd ed. Santa Fe, N. Mex.: John Muir Publishers, 1980.

Grossman, Richard, and Gail Daneker. *Energy, Jobs and the Economy.* Boston: Alyson Publications, 1979.

Hibshman, Dan. *Your Affordable Solar Home: Featuring Designs for Six Solar Homes that Can Be Built for $20,000 or Less.* San Francisco: Sierra Club, 1983.

Hudson, Mike. *The Bike Planning Book.* England. Distributed by Friends of the Earth, San Francisco, address above. $4.95.

Hudson, Mike. *Way Ahead: The Bicycle Warrior's Handbook.* England. Distributed by Friends of the Earth, San Francisco, address above. $2.50.

International Project for Soft Energy Paths. *Tools for the Soft Path.* San Francisco: Friends of the Earth, 1982.

Leckie, Jim, et al. *More Other Homes and Garbage: Designs for Self-Sufficient Living,* rev. ed. San Francisco: Sierra Club, 1981.

Lovins, Amory. *Soft Energy Paths: Toward a Durable Peace.* New York: Harper & Row, 1979.

Mazria, Edward. *The Passive Solar Energy Book: A Complete Guide to Passive Solar Home, Greenhouse and Building Design.* Emmaus Pa.: Rodale Books, 1979. Also, an expanded professional edition, 1979.

Massachusetts Audubon Society. *The Energy Saver's Handbook for Town and City People.* Emmaus, Pa.: Rodale Press, 1982.

Olkowski, Helga, et al. *The Integral Urban House: Self-Reliant Living in the City.* San Francisco: Sierra Club, 1979.

Olsen, Christine, ed. *Recycling: The State of the Art.* 1978. Available from: Community Environmental Council, Box 448, Santa Barbara, Calif. 93102. $11.-25.

Rain: Journal of Appropriate Technology. Available from: 2270 Northwest Irving, Portland, Oreg. 97210.

Robinson, Steven and Fred S. Dubin. *The Energy Efficient Home: A Manual for Saving Fuel and Using Solar, Wood and Wind Power.* New York: New American Library, 1978.

Scully Dan et al. *The Fuel Savers: A Kit of Solar Ideas for Existing Homes.* Andover, Mass: Brick House Publishing, 1978.

Soft Energy Notes. Periodical. Available from: Friends of the Earth, 1045 Sansome Street, San Francisco, Calif. 94111.

Solar Collector Manual. San Luis Valley Energy Center, address above. p. 4.

Stobaugh, Robert, and Daniel Yergin. *Energy Future: Report of the Energy Project of the Harvard Business School.* New York: Random House, 1979.

Stoner, Carol. *Producing Your Own Power: How to Make Nature's Energy Sources Work for You.* Emmaus, Pa.: Rodale Press, 1974.

Thompson, Bob, ed. *Do-It-Yourself Energy Saving Projects.* Menlo Park, Calif.: Lane Publishing, 1981.

U.S. Department of Housing and Urban Development. *How to Insulate Your Home and Save Fuel.* New York: Dover Books, 1977.

Warren, Betty. *The Energy and Environment Checklist,* rev. ed. San Francisco: Friends of the Earth, 1980.

Wilson, Tom, ed. *Home Remedies.* Available from: Mid-Atlantic Solar Energy Association, 2233 Gray's Ferry Avenue, Philadelphia, Pa. 19146. $10.

Wing, Charles. *From the Walls In.* Waltham, Mass.: Little, Brown, 1979. On energy retrofit.

Nuclear Power

Acceptable Risk? Slideshow/filmstrip that examines connections between nuclear power and nuclear weapons. Available from: AFSC National Office, 1501 Cherry Street, Phila., Pa. 19102. $60/$50; or rental from regional offices.

Berger, John. *Nuclear Power: The Unviable Option.* Palo Alto, Calif.: Ramparts Press, 1976.

Citizen's Energy Project. *Nuclear Power and Civil Liberties: Can We Have Both?* 1979. Available from: Citizen's Energy Project, 1110 6th Street, N.W., Suite 300, Washington, D.C. 20001. $7.

Gyorgy, Ana, et al. *No Nukes: Everybody's Guide to Nuclear Power.* Trumansburg, N.Y.: Crossing Press, 1979.

I Have Three Children of My Own. Dr. Helen Caldicott's slideshow/filmstrip statement on the medical implications of nuclear technology. Available from: Packard Manse/Media Project, Box 450, Staughton, Mass. 02072. Purchase or rental (also, rental from many other organizations).

Lovins, Amory, and L. Hunter Lovins. *Energy/War: Breaking the Nuclear Link.* New York: Harper & Row, 1981.

Non-Renewable Energy

Barney, Gerald O., study director. *Global 2000 Report to the President.* New York: Viking/Penguin, 1979.

Clark, Wilson, and Jake Page. *Energy, Vulnerability and War: Alternatives for America.* New York: W. W. Norton, 1981.

Crabbe, David, and Richard McBride, eds. *The World Energy Book: An A–Z Atlas and Statistical Source Book.* Cambridge, Mass: MIT Press, 1979. Also contains information about renewable energy.

Four Corners. Film about the National Sacrifice Area struggle in the Four Corners area of the Southwest. Available from: Bullfrog Films, Inc., Oley, Pa. 19547. $100 rental.

Sampson, Anthony. *The Seven Sisters: The Great Oil Companies and the World They Shaped.* New York: Bantam, 1976.

CHAPTER X

Consuming the World

QUERIES

1. Do American consumption patterns provide a good example for other nations?
2. Do I think the "American way of life" can be maintained at its present level of resource consumption indefinitely? Who would benefit? Who would suffer?
3. What relationship does militarism and military spending have to global resource use and distribution?
4. Are the principles for sustainable and ecologically balanced development different for "more developed" societies and "less developed" societies?
5. What burdens do overall American consumption patterns place on poorer people at home and abroad?
6. Are we individually responsible for injustice that is built into the world economy?
7. How can living more simply affect global economic conditions?

The patterns of consumption largely taken for granted by the majority of the U.S. population bear a heavy responsibility for the perpetuation of poverty. This occurs directly through our own impact on global resources through consumerism, military spending, and the corporate investment that supplies and profits from these. It occurs indirectly through the spread of a consumer culture based on American and European patterns, as popularized through movies and advertising. The stores that serve the small élites of Buenos Aires, Seoul, and Jeddah are as richly stocked with the latest consumer goodies as those of New York, London, and Paris.

Americans comprise 5 percent of the world's population, but in order to support the way of life to which we have become accustomed, we consume nearly 28 percent of the total energy used in the world. The average American uses nearly five and a half times as much energy as the average world citizen. We use fifty-four times as much energy as the average resident of India. These rather remarkable figures represent marked improvements over the situation fourteen years ago, when each American consumed well over six times the world average and over seventy-five times what each Indian consumed.[1] From 1970 to 1980, however, world energy consumption grew by 13.5 percent, putting increasing pressure on reserves and increasing levels of pollution in the atmosphere.[2]

We ate around 177 pounds of beef and pork per person and 62 pounds of poultry in 1981.[3] Raising these animals uses enough vegetable protein annually to end world hunger.

We spent $167 billion for military purposes in fiscal year 1981—a figure that with congressional approval is scheduled to grow to around $240 billion in fiscal year 1984.[4]

We take billions more in profits out of Third World countries than is returned in foreign aid. In 1979 and 1980, U.S.-based corporations made over $30 billion a year in pretax profits abroad, and in 1981, $22.8 billion (with the economic downturn)—about 11 percent of total corporate profits. By comparison, U.S. foreign economic assistance averaged around $4 billion for those years, over $650 million of which financed U.S. exports.[5]

The problem with U.S. and European multinationals is not simply that they take cash profits from poorer nations. Due to their sheer size and scope of operations, the multinationals exert a tremendous amount of control over the policy decisions of the governments of the nations where they operate. In a combined asset ranking of the 130 largest multinationals and nations, 65 are countries and 65 are companies. Exxon is number 23, Shell (Dutch and British) is number 31, General Motors is number 24. Chile is number 69, the Philippines is number 49, and Bangladesh is number 103. The rest of the world's approximately 130 nations don't even make the list.[6]

Policies advocated by the multinationals and carried out by those in power are often in direct conflict with what is in the interest of a majority of a nation's people. Some areas where this difference can manifest itself are: allocation, distribution, and usage rate of natural resources; centralization versus decentralization of decision-making; rural-centered versus urban-centered development policies; tax levels; and wage rates and labor policies.

In order to find peaceful solutions to the world's problems, we must create a world where people can interact in dignity as equals, both within each country and between countries. Instead of this nonviolent alternative, the dominant policies of many of the world's governments today support massive armament, international war, domestic repression, and a widening of the gap between rich and poor.

Despite rhetoric concerning "human rights," United States foreign policy has consistently supported dictatorships and other corrupt governments to keep the way open for the profit-making activities of the multina-

tionals. Such policies have often prevented the establishment and maintenance of a way of life based on sustainable agriculture and fair access to
local resources for most of a country's population. Instead, the majority
must live lives of constant want and risk. Many are condemned to death
by the present international economic system.

WAR AND RESOURCES

The world's governments now spend collectively over $600 billion
annually for military purposes. The United States is well in the lead with
a third of this total to be spent for military purposes in fiscal year 1984.

The international arms trade amounts to over $21 billion per year,
$17.7 billion of it to the Third World.[7] By comparison, in 1980, foreign
economic aid from industrialized to Third World countries amounted to
$29.5 billion, and aid from richer Third World countries added another
$8.6 billion.[8] Thus, almost half of the economic aid is wiped out by direct
military purchases from other nations, completely apart from internal
military manufacturing and support of military forces. The international
debt situation, discussed below, has certainly been magnified by this
degree of military spending.

A recent United Nations study points out that "in the case of aluminum, copper, nickel and platinum, estimated global consumption for
military purposes is greater than the demand for all of these minerals for
all purposes in Africa, Asia (including China) and Latin America combined."[9] Added to the damage caused by this misuse of mineral and
financial resources is the direct and tragic impact of war on human populations and the actual destruction of farmlands, villages, and cities. The
United Nations also estimates that around 20 percent of the world's
scientific and technological talent is included among the approximately
40 million people employed in military or military-related work worldwide.[10] How much could these human and material resources contribute
to self-reliant development if they were redirected?

Redirection of even a relatively small portion of these funds could go
a long way toward meeting the needs of the poor of the world. Two
billion people are exposed to disease because they do not have access to
clean water.[11] There are around one billion people who lack access to
most other basic needs.[12] Many of these are in India, Pakistan, Bangladesh, and Indonesia—countries that spent over $6.75 billion for mili-
tary purposes in 1979.[13]

U Thant, former U.N. Secretary General, pointed out that the amounts
spent for one day of the Indochina War in 1971 were equivalent to the
United Nations' entire annual budget.[14] Even this is a relatively large
amount of money. OXFAM, the British development and emergency
relief agency, and OXFAM America have together aided over one thousand projects annually throughout the world. Assistance given is usually

in the range of $50 (to purchase, for example, a bicycle for a village health worker) to $25,000, at an average rate of $10,000 per project. One hundred and sixty-four thousand projects could be funded on what global military forces spend in a day. That's almost two projects per second.

The Trickle Up Program, Inc., has funded 735 projects in 54 countries with $100 incentive grants.[15] These incentive grants generally fund the beginning of cottage industries run by the unemployed and underemployed in countries such as Costa Rica, Belize, Antigua, and Cameroon: poultry raising, broom-making, children's pajama sewing, a women's union "bake sale." The returns from the initial efforts—often ranging from 100 percent to 900 percent on the $100 combined with large amounts of volunteer labor—are used to expand operations from a one-time project to an ongoing cottage industry, if possible.

Does all the military spending described above give the world's people peace and security? In 1983, people were dying in wars in Chad, Central America, Afghanistan, Cambodia, Lebanon, Angola, Iran, Iraq, Grenada, and elsewhere.

Some of these wars involve direct control of natural resources, such as the Iraq-Iran conflict over oil fields, refineries, and access to shipping channels for their products. The Biafra War in the late 1960s, which killed over 500,000 people, was fought in part over Nigeria's reluctance to give up control over oil resources in Biafra. The Indochina War was the biggest of the sixty-five major wars occuring between 1960 and 1982. It was fought in large part by the United States in an attempt to guarantee access to Asia's material resources, labor market, and trade for the "free world" following the collapse of French colonial dominance. Because we are so dependent on large and disproportionate quantities of imported resources to sustain both our consumer and military way of life, Americans are vulnerable to being enticed into military conflict to maintain continued supply. In 1982, the United States imported, for example, 94 percent of its aluminum ores, 90 percent of its chromium, 85 percent of its platinum and related metals, 80 percent of its tin, 98 percent of its manganese, 34 percent of its petroleum, 72 percent of its nickel, and 28 percent of its iron ore.[17]

There are also the wars fought by the elites of poor nations to keep hold of an unequal share of their country's resources. Many of these wars are fought with the overt or covert aid of multinational corporations and their home governments. This has occurred in such countries as the Philippines, El Salvador, and Indonesia (whose civil war of 1965 cost over half a million lives).

The most frightening potential for war in the world today is in the Middle East. To protect its access to oil in the region, the United States now has substantial naval and Rapid Deployment Force capabilities in Kenya, ready to intervene if anyone tries to block the Persian Gulf oil routes. And in Comiso, Sicily, U.S. deployment of highly accurate, first-strike Cruise missiles is scheduled for December 1983. These missiles can reach every important oil country in the Middle East and Northern Africa.

DEVELOPMENT FOR WHOM?

Brazil is a "rich" Third World country. It is the fifth largest country in the world, larger than the contiguous forty-eight U.S. states. It has local supplies of many important resources, including one-third of the world's iron ore reserve.

In October 1983, Brazil stood on the brink of national bankruptcy with $90 billion in international debt.[18] From 1964 to 1976, Brazil had a high rate of economic growth, measured by the GNP. Yet the real income of Brazilian workers fell during that period.

In October 1983, Brazil had 20 percent unemployment and 40 percent underemployment, 160 percent annual inflation, and hundreds of thousands of people squatting on the outskirts of the cities with little or no shelter.[19] Eighty-four out of every one thousand children die in infancy; only 54 percent of the children are in school; 25 percent of the adults are illiterate.[20] So what did the development mean?

Much of the development meant attracting foreign investment, which drove out and replaced local ownership in many sectors of the economy. Huge areas of the country were auctioned off to foreign firms for mineral exploration and exploitation.[21] Brazil has also systematically destroyed large portions of its tropical rainforests, which support a tremendously delicate and complex ecosystem. Rainforests

have not only been the main centers for living species on earth, but have held the lands together, moderated and modified world climates, and helped to maintain a desirable balance of atmospheric gasses. . . . [Now] there has been a 40 percent reduction in total area. They are disappearing at a rate of 16 million hectares per year.[22]

What has the forest been destroyed for? Aside from mineral exploration, for example, Volkswagen of Brazil is cattle ranching on 140,000 acres in the interior. One foreign industrialist has cleared an area the size of Connecticut for rice-growing and timber monocropping. Small farmers have first been settled in the interior by the government and then thrown off that land at the request of larger enterprises. The lives and ways of life of native tribal people have been destroyed as a result. These measures have been encouraged and enforced by a military dictatorship that has not hesitated to use torture to suppress political dissent and labor organizing.[23]

The International Monetary Fund and creditor banks are demanding a great deal from Brazil in exchange for putting off the day of reckoning, but no more than they have demanded of many smaller countries in the same predicament: no wage hikes, cuts in aid for food, transportation, housing, and other basic needs, cuts in public employment, continued currency devaluation. (Mexico, which owes almost as much as Brazil, had the peso reduced to one-sixth of its 1981 value by mid-1983.) There's a lot at stake. Nine of the biggest U.S. banks have an average of 57 percent of their collective capital on loan to Brazil.[24]

There's also a lot at stake for the Brazilian people. Can we truly call what has happened in Brazil development? Or is it systematic mal-development?

IS THERE ANOTHER WAY?

At a conference of development experts (largely from poorer countries) held in Algeria in 1975, the following definitions of development emerged:[25]

- Development is a human-centered process. Technology and organization must serve the concrete needs of people rather than vice versa.
- Participation in making and carrying out decisions is not simply a means to development; it is in itself development.
- Self-reliance and cooperation rather than rigid division of labor and dependence are the basis of true development.
- To succeed, development strategies must give highest priority to meeting the basic needs of the poor rather than providing more luxuries for the rich and comfortably off.
- High levels of consumption are inconsistent with development because they are unattainable by the vast majority of the population. They also breed passivity among the consumers, or are otherwise undesirable in themselves.
- All countries need development, rich as well as poor.

By these standards, the United States is in many ways not a developed country. It is overdeveloped in some ways, with technologies and institutions which defy understanding and control by average human beings. It is underdeveloped in many others, including the self-reliance of its citizens, their level of personal and economic autonomy, and their knowledge and use of emotional, spiritual, creative and cooperative abilities. Alternatives to this sort of "underdevelopment" have been the topic of much of the rest of this book.

If we agree that poorer nations deserve a greater share of the world's resources, one of the most effective things we can do to assist their development is to get out of the way by lessening our overconsumption. However, growing our own vegetables, by itself, is not going to get Del Monte off Mexican and Namibian backs. We must seek legal limits in the size and foreign operations of the multinationals and restrict the tax advantages they enjoy. We must look at where our banks are putting our money and the money of our pension funds, our neighborhood organizations, and our churches: is the money supporting apartheid in South Africa or runaway shops in South Korea? We must also seek to change U.S. foreign policy to curtail government support for multinational dominance of other countries.

PEOPLE TAKING CHARGE OF THEIR LIVES

The idea of "intermediate" or "appropriate" technology, first discussed by E. F. Schumacher in 1962, has greatly assisted people in taking charge of their lives. There is no one definition of appropriate technology, but it usually refers to technology of a scale, price, and ease of manufacture usable at decentralized settings and controllable by the people it serves. Multinational corporations are not generally interested in appropriate technology, even when it may seem to us to be of quite a large scale. One of E. F. Schumacher's projects was to assist Zambia with obtaining the design for an egg-carton manufacturing plant small enough to serve the entire nation! The multinational that does such manufacturing was uninterested in investing in so small a plant and instead wished the country to import its egg cartons. The plant Zambia built has 2 percent of the capacity of the next smallest plant at 2 percent of the capital cost.[26]

Often, alternative technology and simplicity are advocated for the poor while Westernization and modernization remain the goals of the better-off. While the government of Zambia was interested in alternative technology, the Chiko (hugging trees) movement in the Himalayas had to struggle nonviolently against a combination of government dishonesty, corporate profits, and lack of knowledge among the people. The movement was formed to deal with the fact that forests in India and Nepal have been destroyed in order to satisfy needs for wood fuel and exports. Lowered rainfall, increased flooding, and severe losses of topsoil and agricultural land have been among the results. To stop this, villagers would literally hug the trees in order to prevent them from being cut to provide tennis racket frames for export rather than wood for locally needed plows and ox-yokes. Through this action they learned to protect the trees for their own sake and began a number of reforestation projects.

In India, the Anand Niketan Ashram works with tribal peoples in Gujarat. In addition to agricultural and reforestation projects, a "people's court" was established, which resolves conflicts over land and personal matters that used to be matters for violent resolution. The people's court influence has grown to the point where many landlords feel compelled to abide by its decision in landlord-tenant disputes brought before it.

Where the government has a policy of simplicity, it is possible for people to live reasonably well without riches. The poor of China, prior to their revolution, were as vulnerable to famine, disease, and exploita-

tion as those of India. But since 1949, famine and many of the diseases
of underdevelopment have been virtually wiped out. Alternative technology (small-scale steel mills, hand-run rice hullers, biogas generators,
barefoot doctors, and the use cf traditional herbal medicine) is widespread throughout China alongside modern complex industrial technology. Though China remains in the bottom third of the world's nations
in GNP per capita, her people's basic material needs are largely met.

The implementation of biogas technology provides an interesting contrast between China and India. (For an explanation of biogas, see Chapter
IX.) It is reported that China installed around 600,000 biogas generators
in one period of one and one-half years, 200,000 in Szechuan province
alone. By contrast, India in 1977 had only 45,000 units functioning, with
a 1980 target of 100,000. Amory Lovins comments:

> The stakes are high; a full-scale biogas program could by 2000 supply almost 90
> percent of India's rural household needs (now about 45 percent of India's total
> energy use). . . . [T]he tendency of local elites to use energy systems (or food or
> land or water systems) to reinforce their own power, and the disparity between
> distribution of private capital and of energy needs . . . have some striking parallels
> in industrial countries such as the United States.[27]

The Catholic Church has been among the groups in the forefront of
promoting development from poverty to simplicity and justice in Latin
America. Church-sponsored, base Christian community groups study the
relevance of the Gospel to the lives of the poor. Their implementation
of literacy campaigns and sponsorship of local development projects have
played a major role in helping people at the local level to begin a process
of transformation. In Nicaragua, the Base Christian Community Movement had a good deal to do with the success of the Sandinista Revolution,
which overthrew a tyrannical government of over forty years' standing.
The literacy campaign that followed raised literacy levels from 50 percent
to 90 percent in less than a year. Much other progress has been made in
meeting food, land, and medical needs of the general population, despite
the U.S. government's support of forces seeking to overthrow the Nicaraguan government.

In Sri Lanka, the Sarvodaya Shramadana Movement has helped people
to see how they can benefit by a shared gift of labor. The program helps
villages decide on a project (such as a new road or irrigation system),
helps them design the project, and gets everyone in the village (even
small children) to help in the construction. So far, four thousand of the
island's fourteen thousand villages have participated. In villages where
the organization is especially active, it sets up a men's council, a women's
council, an older people's council, and a children's council for consultation, innovation, and decision-making. A typical shared workday includes
a noon break for a potluck meal, which promotes interaction and understanding among people of different occupations and religions who may
not ordinarily talk with one another.

Instead of growth for its own sake, Sarvodaya's orientation is a synthesis of the Gandhian ideal of village self-reliance and Buddhist principles of right action and right livelihood. The Sarvodaya movement is exemplary in that it holds that social, economic, political, moral, cultural, and spiritual development are all necessary and are mutually reinforcing. The movement's founder and president, A. T. Ariya-ratne and his followers believe that through following the principles of the movement, Sri Lanka can become a "land of plenty and isle of righteousness."

What can we do to help? We can give our financial support to such organizations as the American Friends Service Committee, OXFAM America, Intermediate Technology, Church World Service, many Catholic Relief Service programs, the Mennonite Central Committee, the Unitarian Universalist Service Committee, Trickle Up Programs, Inc., and Save the Children (which sponsors a variety of integrated community development programs as part of its work on behalf of sponsored children).

We can also offer whatever intellectual resources may be available to develop appropriate technology. In the egg-carton incident described above, the multinational's basic egg-carton design produced wobbly stacks. Students at the Royal College of Art in London were able to produce a stable design in six weeks.[28]

Even as we offer both financial and intellectual assistance, we need to continue to overcome mal-development at home by creating an economic system that is no longer dependent on consuming the world.

NOTES

1. Author's calculations from data provided in U.S. Department of Commerce, Bureau of the Census, *Statistical Abstract of the United States,* 1982–83, Washington, D.C. (U.S. Government Printing Office, 1982), table 1542, pp. 876–877 (energy use).
2. Author's calculations, based on ibid.
3. *Statistical Abstract,* table 203, p. 127 (per capita consumption of major food commodities).
4. Stockholm International Peace Research Institute, *World Armaments and Disarmament: SIPRI Yearbook,* 1982.
5. U.S. Department of Commerce, Bureau of the Census, *Statistical Abstract,* table 918, p. 545 (corporate profits before taxes); tables 1480–1481, p. 832 (foreign aid).
6. Holly Sklar, *Trilateralism: The Trilateral Commission and Elite Planning for World Management* (Boston: South End Press, 1980).
7. U.S. Department of Commerce, Bureau of the Census, *Statistical Abstract,* table 584, p. 355 (value of arms exports and imports—1979 data).
8. Ibid., table 1554, p. 898.
9. United Nations Disarmament Division, *The Relationship Between Disarmament and Development,* Study Series No. 5 (New York: United Nations, 1982), p. 51.
10. Ibid., p. 55.
11. Ruth L. Sivard, *World Military and Social Expenditures,* 1981 (Leesburg, Va.: World Priorities, 1981).
12. Ruth L. Sivard, *World Military and Social Expenditures,* 1982 (Leesburg, Va.: World Priorities, 1982), p. 18.
13. Author's calculations based on ibid., table 2, p. 28.

14. Willem L. Oltmans, ed., *On Growth,* (New York: Capricorn Books, 1974).
15. Trickle Up Program, Inc., *Newsletter* 3, no. 2 (July 1983), p. 1.
16. Ibid., throughout.
17. *Statistical Abstract,* table 1298, p. 724 (net U.S. mineral imports).
18. R. C. Longworth, "Failing Nation That Could Bust World's Banks," *San Francisco Examiner,* October 2, 1983, p. 1.
19. Ibid., p. A18.
20. Sivard, *World Military and Social Expenditures,* 1982, table 3, pp. 30–31.
21. Sue Carroll and George Lakey et al., *Revolution: A Quaker Prescription for a Sick Society* (Philadelphia: New Society Press, 1972), pp. VI–12, VI–24.
22. Susan Gowan and George Lakey et al., *Moving Toward a New Society,* (Philadelphia: New Society Press, 1976), pp. 45–48, 61.
23. Carroll and Lakey et al., *Revolution.*
24. Longworth, "Failing Nation."
25. Denis Goulet, *The Cruel Choice.* Johan Galtung (rapporteur), *Resolution,* Commission A of the First Conference of the U.N. International Development Center, Algiers, 1975. The Dag Hammarskjöld Trust, *What Now,* Special edition of *Development Dialogue,* spring 1975.
26. E. F. Schumacher, *Good Work,* (New York: Harper & Row, 1979), pp. 58–60.
27. Amory B. Lovins, *Soft Energy Paths* (Cambridge, Mass.: Ballinger Publishing Company, 1977), pp. 96–97.
28. Schumacher, *Good Work,* p. 60.

SOURCES OF FURTHER INFORMATION

Groups Mentioned in Chapter

American Friends Service Committee, International Division. 1501 Cherry Street, Philadelphia, Pa. 19102. Programs in Africa, Asia, Latin America, East-West, Middle East, United Nations Office.

Catholic Relief Service. 1011 First Avenue, New York, N.Y. 10022.

Church World Service. 475 Riverside Drive, New York, N.Y. 10115.

Intermediate Technology. 556 Santa Cruz Avenue, Menlo Park, Calif. 94025. U.S. branch of Schumacher's organization.

Mennonite Central Committee. 21 South 12th Street, Akron, Pa. 17501.

OXFAM America. 115 Broadway, Boston, Mass. 02116.

Save the Children Federation. 54 Wilton Road, Westport, Conn. 06880.

Trickle Up Program, Inc. 54 Riverside Drive, New York, N.Y. 10024.

Unitarian Universalist Service Committee. 78 Beacon Street, Boston, Mass. 02108.

Additional Resource Groups

Aprovecho Institute. 442 Monroe Street, Eugene, Oreg. 97402. Designs, disseminates, and trains in the use of appropriate technologies in the United States and Third World.

Coalition for Priorities for a New Foreign and Military Policy. 120 Maryland Avenue, N.E., Washington, D.C. 20002.

Interfaith Center on Corporate Responsibility. 475 Riverside Drive, Room 566, New York, N.Y. 10115.

Mexico-U.S. Border Program. C/o American Friends Service Committee, Pacific Southwest Regional Office, 980 North Fair Oaks Avenue, Pasadena, Calif. 91103.

Transnational Network for Appropriate/Alternative Technologies (TRANET).
Box 567, Rangeley, Maine 04970.

Bibliography

American Friends Service Committee. *South Africa: Challenge and Hope.* 1982.
Available from: AFSC National Office, address above. $5.95 ppd.; 10 or
more copies, $2.50/copy + 20 percent postage.

Appropriate Technology. Published by Schumacher's co-workers. Available from:
I.T. Publications Ltd., 9 King Street, London WC2E 8HN England.

Barnet, Richard J. *The Lean Years: Politics in the Age of Scarcity.* New York: Simon
and Schuster, 1980.

Barney, Gerald O., study director. *Global 2000 Report to the President.* New York:
Viking/Penguin, 1979.

Bello, Walden, et al. *Development Debacle: The World Bank in the Philippines.* Available
from: Institute for Food and Development Policy, 1885 Mission Street,
San Francisco, Calif. 94110. $6.95.

Brandt, Willy, and Anthony Sampson, eds. *North-South: A Programme for Survival.*
Cambridge, Mass.: MIT Press, 1980.

Congdon, R. J., ed. *Introduction to Appropriate Technology: Toward a Simpler Lifestyle.*
Emmaus, Pa.: Rodale Press, 1977.

The Corporate Examiner. Newsletter. Available from: Interfaith Center on Corporate Responsibility, 475 Riverside Drive, Room 566, New York, N.Y.
10115.

Corson-Finnerty, Adam. *World Citizen: Today's Context for the Role of Church People
in Social Action.* Maryknoll, N.Y.: Orbis Books, 1982.

Development Dialogue. Quarterly development journal. Available from: Dag Ham-
marskjold Memorial Foundation, Ovre Slottsgatan 2, Uppsala, Sweden.

Finnerty, Adam D. *No More Plastic Jesus: Global Justice and Christian Lifestyle.* Maryknoll, N.Y.: Orbis Books, 1977.

Goulet, Denis. *The Cruel Choice: A New Concept in the Theory of Development.* New
York: Athenum, 1971.

Heilbroner, Robert. *The Great Ascent: The Struggle for Economic Development in Our
Time.* New York: Harper & Row, 1963.

Korea: Time for a Change. Slideshow/filmstrip. Available from: AFSC, address
above, $50/$40; or rental from regional offices.

McRobie, George. *Small Is Possible.* New York: Harper/Colophon, 1981.

Meadows, Donella, et al. *The Limits to Growth,* 2nd ed. New York: Universe, 1974.

Mesarovic, Mihajilo, and Eduard Pestel. *Mankind at the Turning Point: The Second
Report to the Club of Rome.* New York: New American Library, 1976.

Multinational Monitor. Available from: Box 19405, Washington, D.C. 20036.
$15/year.

National Action/Research on the Military Industrial Complex (NARMIC). *Auto-
mating Apartheid.* Available from: AFSC National Office, address above,
$4.50 ppd.

North American Committee on Latin America (NACLA). *NACLA Report on the
Americas.* Available from: 151 West 19 Street, New York, N.Y. 10011.

Oxford Economic Atlas of the World, 4th ed. Oxford: Oxford University Press, 1972.

Pacific Studies Center. *Pacific Research.* Asian focus. Available from: 867 West
Dana Street, #204, Mountain View, Calif. 94041.

Polner, Murray, ed. *The Disarmament Catalogue.* New York: Pilgrim Press, 1982.

Ridgeway, James. *Who Owns the Earth?* Riverside, N.J.: Macmillan, 1980.

Roots of the Crisis. Slideshow on Central America, rev. 1983. Available from: AFSC, address above. $60 purchase; or rental from regional offices.

Seeking Safe Haven. Resource packet for religious groups and congregations working with and for refugees. Available from: AFSC National Office, address above. $5 ppd.; 10 or more copies, $3/copy + 20 percent postage.

Shannon-Thornberry, Milo, ed. *The Alternate Celebrations Catalogue.* New York: Pilgrim Press, 1982. Includes descriptions of self-help projects that welcome support and donations.

Stokes, Bruce. *Helping Ourselves; Local Solutions to Global Problems.* New York: Norton and Company, 1981.

Volunteers in Technical Assistance, eds. *Village Technology Handbook.* 1978. Available from: 3707 Rhode Island Avenue, Mt. Ranier, Md. 20822.

Women in Development: A Resource Guide for Organization and Action. Produced by Women's International Information and Communication Service. Available from: AFSC National Office, address above. $14.40 ppd.

CHAPTER XI

Taking Charge of Our Lives

QUERIES

1. What beliefs or visions govern my personal and political actions?
2. How can I best contribute to the process of taking charge, given my present roles and obligations? What changes might I want to make in these roles and obligations? How far am I willing to go in changing my personal life and activities?
3. Where and to what degree am I already taking charge of my life and helping to create a more sustainable world? In what ways has that empowered me and helped to transform my situation positively? In what ways has it created new obstacles and challenges for me?
4. How do I measure value?
5. What would an economic system be like that promoted harmony with the environment and the rest of the world family?
6. What institutions, organizations, and services exist in my area that support me in taking charge? What ones are needed? What can I do to support the ones that we now have or to bring new ones into being?

This book has looked at many separate aspects of taking charge of our lives, such as growing a garden, keeping housing affordable, cleaning up poisons from our waters, ending discrimination in our workplaces. But how might all of this fit together to build new kinds of lives for all of us? In this concluding chapter, we will look at the overall picture from three perspectives—the individual, the local community, and the broader regional, national, and world community.

THE INDIVIDUAL TAKING CHARGE

A personal decision to take charge must begin with a decision to engage oneself with basic problems, instead of relying on a strategy for just putting up with what one doesn't like in the world—whether that strategy be fantasizing it away or ignoring it, hoping a co-worker will risk getting fired to protest an unsafe machine or that a great world leader will at last bring peace. This is said with the awareness that to change some things may take decades, and we may not see our dreams realized in our lifetimes.

What can we do to help us find the will and perspective to work for a better world? Lucy Anderson suggests that

even if we are not formally religious, we need time for renewal and strengthening of our physical and spiritual energy. . . . [F]or me, setting aside places and times as sacred spaces reminds me that all the world is sacred.[1]

Most of the solutions discussed in this book are in the long-term economic, social, and/or political self-interest of the people engaged in them and, we feel, of most of our readers. Beyond this type of "self-interest," however, our solutions can reach for the sacred, for the sacred in every person, for the sacredness of the earth. What are we working for if not justice, peace, dignity, respect for the land, air, and water and for all life?

Each of us must begin to decide how our lives can be lived in accordance with these principles—to make the choices, rather than letting the choices be made for us. What would lives look like that we can be proud of? That our great-grandchildren can be proud of? What will our lives, as personal examples, say to others who are also searching?

One question that has been asked or implied many times in this book is one of value. What is the value of cancer-causing chemicals? What is the value of a big, solid, old house? What is the value of a ten-year-old barter network of friends and neighbors? What is the value of Lake Erie? What is the value of some basic information about your body's health? Is your first impulse to answer any of these questions in terms of dollars?

In our struggle to define value in terms other than money, we must look to intrinsic value. Julius Nyerere, president of Tanzania and theoritician of "African socialism" (or "familyhood"), speaks of this sense of value:

There are bound to be certain groups which, by virtue of the "market value" of their particular industry's products, *will* contribute more to the nation's income than others. But the others may actually be producing goods or services which are of equal, or greater, *intrinsic* value although they do not happen to command such a high *artificial* value. For example, the food produced by the peasant farmer is of greater social value than the diamonds mined at Mwadui.[2]

To put this concept of value into practice in our daily lives can be difficult—but it can help if we are able to seek out others who have a similar understanding of value. Wally and Juanita Nelson, a black couple who left the city for rural Massachusetts and survive on their gardening, which produces a cash income of $2,000 per year, speak of this method of exchange when they barter:

Our arrangement recognizes that the hours we spend hoeing carrots are judged equivalent to whatever time the dentist devotes to a root canal. A root for a root, an hour for an hour. When I have a toothache I go see the dentist. When raspberries come in, we ask how many the dentist can use.[3]

A mention of this sort of arrangement, however, raises the question of how far each of us is willing to go. Does this dentist really live at a similar economic level to the Nelsons? Or is this a special arrangement, aside from which she or he lives life pretty much the same as do other dentists? And how many of us would not secretly wish to change places with that dentist and have the *option* to barter for raspberries or to buy porterhouse steak?

Most people reading this book have probably experimented already with some of the things discussed here and have, or are thinking of, experimenting with more. But the number of changes can overwhelm and tire us. When we decide we are interested in food changes, do we forget about energy use? When we decide to fight for rent control, do we ignore the basics of our body's health? We can really only concentrate on a couple of new things at once, but it is important to try to keep the process of change going once we have adjusted to the new parts of our lives.

Another essential is recognizing the political tie of many of our personal choices. For example, deciding where you shop for food is a personal choice. In Chapter II, we encouraged consideration of shopping at a food buying club, a community food cooperative, or an independent community food store. Most of the time, for most items, it is cheaper to shop this way, so you've got short-term economic interest on the side of that choice, too.

When you and other people in your community realize this, the co-op's volume grows and the chain supermarket's volume starts to shrink. So the supermarket drops prices—for a while—and if you were to add up your grocery bill this week, this month, this six months, it might be lower if you shopped in the chain store. So people start drifting back to the chain store's "good deals," until the co-op can't afford to survive.

Our "personal" choices must become more sophisticated if we are to bring about fundamental change in our system. They must have the sophistication of the choices of workers who strike for weeks or months, at the expense of a lower income this year, to gain decent wages long-term, a healthy workplace, and dignity on the job. We have been conditioned to look for the "good deal" rather than the intrinsic value of a particular choice to the society most of us would deeply prefer to live in. And we need to coordinate some of our personal choices with others' personal choices to get long-term change.

GETTING TOGETHER

One man fights the KKK, but he hates the queers
One woman works for ecology, it's equal rights she fears
Some folks know that war is hell, but they put down the blind
I think there must be a common ground, but it's mighty hard to find. . . .

—*Holly Near, in her song "Unity"*[4]

So many of the projects and communities discussed in this book provide living proof against "can't be done" arguments that small means impossible. But sometimes our small groups have to get together to bring about broader changes.

When the change is economic, communities have tried different methods of supporting each other. Where financial resources are needed, community credit unions such as the one mentioned in Philadelphia (see Chapter IV) have tried to keep a community's money circulating within it to make needed changes. Another approach, in areas with many "alternative businesses," has been a voluntary community tax, with the proceeds going to assist member groups or to support nonincome-generating alternative community services. Yet another approach used by alternative businesses is networking, where financial information and business experience is shared in an attempt to help all survive. On a national scale, the Industrial Cooperative Association, drawing its support from several foundations and religious organizations, gives technical assistance to worker cooperatives as well as administering a $1 million revolving loan fund to provide the "down payment" necessary to attract additional government and commercial financing for worker cooperatives.

When the change is political, this means a coalition, such as the Survival Services Coalition to which the Country Doctor Medical Clinic in Seattle belongs. (see Chapter IX) Building and nourishing an effective coalition is hard work. The very term tells us that people are coming together from different geographic areas, different personal, political, economic, racial, ethnic, and religious backgrounds. How these differences are handled can not only make the difference in the outcome of today's issue; it can determine whether and how this diversity of people can work together in the future. When a group sets out to bring together a coalition to support or protest something, these are some of the questions it might look at:

- What do we need to agree to in order to work together in a principled way on *this* issue?
- Is there an existing coalition that might be interested in acting on this issue?
- What do we have in common with other groups on *their* main issue? Have we ever offered them our help?
- Has the coalition sought out groups that are not automatically identified with this issue, who may not realize the long-term effects on their main issue?
- What are potential areas of prejudice or misunderstanding among group members?
- How would we plan a shared social event—such as a picnic or a dance—so that the diversity of the groups is enjoyed and respected?

- What have we done to share our dreams with members of other groups? What have we done informally to share information about our problems? Would any of the other groups be interested in a program at their meeting about our issue? Would our group be interested in a program about "someone else's" issue?
- What alternative proposals might the coalition make that take important concerns of some members or potential members into consideration? (Example: If low- and moderate-income housing construction is opposed at one location for ecological reasons, how and where is the community to get needed housing? Will the coalition work to see that it gets built at a more suitable location?)
- Is is appropriate or possible to put together a coalition now that might address the root causes and overall solutions to the present problem, rather than dealing piecemeal with each incident?

Under "What You Can Do," an imagined fact situation is given to start you thinking about these questions concretely. Building a peaceful world where conflict is worked out nonviolently is a skill that can only start at home.

ON THE BIGGEST SCALE

Such a movement ought to lead to a situation where the government will be in control of empty shops but not the market; employment but not the means of livelihood; the state press but not information; printing houses but not the publishing movement; telephones and post but not communication; schooling but not education.

—Wiktor Kulerski, Warsaw, 1983
(underground debate of violent versus
nonviolent methods of change)[5]

When we begin to think about regional, national, or international confrontation with basic issues of peace and justice, it can be frightening to see how far we have to go. Marie Simirenko speaks of her discussion group's reaction when they first started to confront these issues:

We were not surprised to learn that Americans use more food, energy, and resources per capita than people of any other nation. But it was a sobering shock to most of us to learn just how much more we used, and that there isn't enough for everyone in the world to do the same. Our sense of helplessness grew when it became clear that the economies of both this country and the world are dominated by large corporations whose concerns and priorities often run counter to our own.[6]

In their "Ethical Reflections on the Economic Crisis," the Canadian Conference of Catholic Bishops observes that:

As a country, we have the resources, the capital, the technology and above all else, the aspirations and skills of working men and women required to build an alternative economic future. An alternative economic vision, for example, could place priority on serving the basic needs of all people in this country, on the value of human labor, and an equitable distribution of wealth and power among people and regions. What would it mean to develop an alternative economic model that would place emphasis on—socially-useful forms of production; labor-intensive industries; the use of appropriate forms of technology; self-reliant models of economic development; community ownership and control of industries; new forms of worker management and ownership; and greater use of the renewable energy sources in industrial production? *Yet, the people of this country have seldom been challenged to envision and develop alternatives to the dominant economic model that governs our society.* [7]

Consideration and debate of such alternative visions must become widespread. As we develop our ideas, we are also challenged to use new methods and new tools for achieving our visions. This book hasn't made much mention of writing to our representatives in Congress, although that is one important avenue of influence and protest. But we've been trained by our political system to act *only* by trying to influence one person who is "representing us," instead of representing ourselves by using other methods of nonviolent change. Every individual act and group project discussed in this book is a method of nonviolent change:

- Organizing a food cooperative that purchases from small, local farmers is a nonviolent challenge to agribusiness and a method of bringing about a sustainable food system.
- Blocking morning rush-hour traffic to publicize a city's withdrawal of a neighborhood's fire protection is a nonviolent challenge to neighborhood destruction and a method of community preservation.
- Removing food from supermarket dumpsters to feed the hungry is a nonviolent challenge to the waste of human lives and a method of sustaining those lives.
- Walking a picket line through two Minnesota winters is a nonviolent method of building a new community consciousness of sex discrimination.
- Entering an air force base and being arrested while writing peace messages on nuclear missile silos is a nonviolent challenge to find new forms of international conflict resolution and to the concept of "military security."
- Participating in an intergenerational study of personal, community, and world problems is a nonviolent method of building understanding and communication.
- Supporting an affirmative action training program is a nonviolent method of creating the skills that remove the economic basis of racist divisions in our society.
- Working in a cooperative or collective that makes decisions by con-

sensus is a nonviolent challenge to the economic, political, and social dominance of one group of people by another group of people.

- Sharing and planning at family meetings is a nonviolent alternative to the feeling of being alone and out-of-control of the basics of one's life.
- Helping a doctor learn to work with a patient and to treat her or him as a whole person is a nonviolent challenge to the hierarchical system of medical treatment.
- Building solar collectors together in weekend workshops is a nonviolent method of attaining a sustainable, decentralized energy future.
- Hugging trees in the Himalayas to prevent their being cut down is a nonviolent challenge to the system that removes a country's vital resources for the profit of a few.

"Nonviolence training" is one way in which people are learning to reach for alternatives together. The training is usually an all-day session of preparation for a particular nonviolent action. In addition to exploring strategic details, emphasis is placed on learning how to keep a commitment to nonviolence in the face of one's own anger or of provocation to violence. Many groups of trainers also give workshops in long-term strategy development, organizing skills, internal group process, coalition building, and other important subjects.

A few years ago, there were few nonviolence trainers; now there are hundreds, in every section of the United States and throughout Western Europe. The training is currently used primarily in the movements against nuclear weapons, militarism, and nuclear power, although its roots are in many sources, including the Civil Rights Movement of the 1950s and 1960s and in Quaker traditions. Additionally, its use is slowly spreading to such movements as environmental preservation, housing rights, and Native American land rights.

A special focus of nonviolence training has been the exploration of new ways for large numbers of people to act powerfully together, while maintaining many locally based, active groups. One example of a way to do this is a month-long peace vigil carried out at the gates of a nuclear weapons facility, with a different church or neighborhood group responsible for each day of the vigil. Another is the many civil disobedience actions that have taken place at nuclear weapons or nuclear power facilities, in a number of cases with as many as one thousand arrests in a single action. One thousand arrests represents at least *160 separate affinity groups* (see pages 96–97 for definition) coordinating their actions, since only five to seven people are typically arrested from any one affinity group in a particular action.

Nonviolence trainer Liz Walker explains that:

often, people have made up their minds that they want to act on a particular issue, but do not feel they have a full understanding of how to go about putting their beliefs into motion. Nonviolence training incorporates emotional, physical, and spiritual preparation, drawing the participants together into a community of people who can act in concert.

Each act helps build the momentum for broader change, though this can be hard to see at the time. One example is the financial aspect of the anti-apartheid movement in the United States. In the early 1970s, student activists and others were successful at persuading only individuals and several universities to withdraw investments in companies that did business in South Africa. There is still a long way to go, but in 1980 Michigan became the first state to bar deposit of public funds in banks that continue to lend to South Africa. In 1983, the First National Bank of Chicago stopped selling Krugerrands—a one-ounce South African gold coin—in the face of declarations by both mayoral candidates that they would seek withdrawal of city funds from any bank that continued such sales.[8]

Each alternative also creates a "lifeboat"—as Schumacher argued to big farmers (pp. 39–40)—an experiment and an example that can be reached for by the wider community as the necessity for change becomes clearer and clearer. And we can take encouragement from the fact that it *is* possible to "reach for" such alternatives, because we know about them. As the multinational corporations have developed increased ease at transferring capital and investments from country to country, the "lifeboat" movement benefits from modern methods of communication and information exchange. Regional, national, and international networks, linked by newsletters, home-sized computers, and late-night phone calls, have sprung up in almost every major area of alternative work to share strategies, information, encouragement, and support. The tool of information-sharing is as powerful on the group level as on the personal level for promoting growth and turning around despair.

Should we try to take charge of our lives? Perhaps E. F. Schumacher put it best:

Can we rely on it that a "turning around" will be accomplished by enough people quickly enough to save the modern world? This question is often asked, but no matter what the answer, it will mislead. The answer "Yes" would lead to complacency, the answer "No" to despair. It is desirable to leave these perplexities behind us and get down to work.[9]

WHAT YOU CAN DO

1. Some individuals and groups find taking a pledge of their intentions for change to be a useful way of clarifying their commitments. Here is one example that was taken by hundreds of people. It was written by a group that was religiously oriented and who felt they had re-

sources to share. We encourage you to draft your own pledge in whatever wording may be most meaningful to you:

The Shakertown Pledge

Recognizing that the earth and the fulness thereof is a gift from our gracious God, and that we are called to cherish, nurture, and provide loving stewardship for the earth's resources.

And recognizing that life itself is a gift, and a call to responsibility, joy, and celebration.

I make the following declarations:

1. I declare myself to be a world citizen.
2. I commit myself to lead an ecologically sound life.
3. I commit myself to lead a life of creative simplicity and to share my personal wealth with the world's poor.
4. I commit myself to join with others in reshaping institutions in order to bring about a more just global society in which each person has full access to the needed resources for their physical, emotional, intellectual, and spiritual growth.
5. I commit myself to occupational accountability, and in so doing I will seek to avoid the creation of products which cause harm to others.
6. I affirm the gift of my body, and commit myself to its proper nourishment and physical well-being.
7. I commit myself to examine continually my relations with others, and to attempt to relate honestly, morally, and lovingly to those around me.
8. I commit myself to personal renewal through prayer, meditation, and study.
9. I commit myself to responsible participation in a community of faith.

2. Practice building coalitions together by using real situations from your own community and asking the questions on pages 244 and 245. Here is one imaginary situation to get you started:

A developer announces plans to drain and fill a marshland (the feeding ground for many birds and fish) to build low- and moderate-income, integrated housing in conjunction with an industrial park that will make the entire project profitable. The industrial park's major tenant will be a company that builds missile guidance systems. The project is on the outskirts of a medium-sized city with a large Spanish-speaking, immigrant population. A local peace group wishes to build a coalition to stop the construction.

3. Discuss with your family and friends where you shop and where you invest any money you may have. What is the investment and loan policy of the bank, pension fund, or insurance company of which you are a client? To what extent is your money supporting multinational corporations, military contractors, or companies operating in countries with racist or oppressive military regimes? What could you do to change these companys' policies? What else could you do with your money? In addition to local banks and credit unions that directly invest in your community, there are a number of national "socially responsi-

ble" investment funds. You can get information on them in the following publications: *Audubon,* January 1984, "What to Read and Where to Go for Socially Responsible Investing"; *Sierra,* November–December, 1983, page 110; *Changing Times,* December 1983; *New York Times,* August 7, 1983 (Business Section), "Doing Well While Doing Good"; *Forbes,* November 21, 1983, "Faces."

4. Give to the Future. Jonathan Schell has written, "We do not inherit the earth from our parents. We borrow it from our children." How can we, as individuals use our gifts and abilities to enhance the future? Each person, if possible with a partner or a group, should examine her or his own abilities. Do your talents and interests lie primarily in creating new institutions, maintaining existing ones, or helping them to undergo needed changes? Are you better at criticizing and confronting existing situations and practices, or at formulating and bringing into being visions of a better future?

After doing this analysis, try to write a newspaper headline from sometime within the foreseeable future (five, ten, twenty years hence) about future improvements that might come about as a result of your activities. A person with a gift for organizing and management might write: "First Nationwide Network of Co-operatively Owned Auto-Repair Shops Celebrates Tenth Anniversary." Another whose gift is in the area of interpersonal conflict resolution might write: "Court Calendars Reduced Again: Community Arbitration Boards Now Handling 75 Percent of Former Civil Suits." Then, try to work backward at one- or five-year intervals to think about how you would get there.

This is also an exercise that could be done by an entire group, or by a coalition, with members looking not only at their own group's goals, but at the future of "the peace movement" or "the alternative economic movement."

NOTES

1. Lucy Anderson was a first-edition author of *Taking Charge.*
2. Julius K. Nyerere, "Communitarian Socialism," Institute for the Study of Nonviolence, Santa Cruz, Calif.
3. Juanita Nelson, "Bypassing the Buck," *New Roots,* spring 1982, p. 25.
4. Holly Near, "Unity," Hereford Music, 1981. The song is on the record *Journeys* (1983), Redwood Records, Oakland, Calif.
5. Quoted in Lawrence Weschler, "A Reporter At Large: Poland, Part II," *New Yorker,* April 18, 1983, p. 68.
6. Marie Simirenko was a first-edition author of *Taking Charge.*
7. Excerpts from "Ethical Reflections on the Economic Crisis," January 1983, Episcopal Commission for Social Affairs, Canadian Conference of Catholic Bishops, 90 Parent Avenue, Ottawa, Canada K1N7B1. Quoted in *The Interreligious Economic Crisis Organizing Network Newsletter,* vol. 1, no. 1 (April 1983).
8. Carole Collins, "Banking on Apartheid—An Expanding Business," *Multinational Monitor,* vol. 4, no. 4 (April 1983), p. 5.
9. E. F. Schumacher, *A Guide for the Perplexed* (San Francisco: Harper & Row, 1977), p. 140.

SOURCES OF FURTHER INFORMATION

Groups Mentioned in Chapter

Industrial Cooperative Association. 249 Elm Street, Somerville, Mass. 02144.

Additional Resource Groups

American Friends Service Committee, Peace Education Division. 1501 Cherry Street, Philadelphia, Pa. 19102. Wide variety of programs centered in both national and ten regional offices, including: human rights and Central America; antidraft and militarism; youth and militarism; disarmament and economic conversion; creative responses to conflict; nuclear weapons facilities network; human rights in the Philippines; the Middle East; Southern Africa.

The Barter Project. 1214 16th Street, N.W., Washington, D.C. 20036. Technical assistance to groups.

Friends Committee on National Legislation. 245 2nd Avenue, N.E., Washington, D.C. 20002.

Institute for Policy Studies. 1901 Q Street, N.W., Washington, D.C. 20009. Studies global politics of natural resources and national issues such as housing.

Institute for World Order. 777 United Nations Plaza, New York, N.Y. 10036. Conducts peace education and peace studies.

The Integral Urban House. 1516 5th Street, Berkeley, Calif. 94710. Demonstration, research, and consultation on ecologically integrated urban houses and gardens.

Interfaith Center on Corporate Responsibility. 475 Riverside Drive, Room 566, New York, N.Y. 10115.

National Coalition Against Domestic Violence. 1728 N Street, N.W., Washington, D.C. 20007.

National Consumer Cooperative Bank. 2001 S Street, N.W., Washington, D.C. 20009.

National Lawyers Guild. 853 Broadway, Suite 1705, New York, N.Y. 10003. A multichapter organization of lawyers, law students and legal workers who offer individual and group assistance in many struggles.

National Peace Academy. 110 Maryland Avenue, N.E., Washington, D.C. 20002. Campaign for congressionally funded, U.S. Academy of Peace and Conflict Resolution.

Nonviolent Movement Building Program, American Friends Service Committee, Northern California Regional Office. 2160 Lake Street, San Francisco, Calif. 94121.

Physicians for Social Responsibility. Box 144, Watertown, Mass. 02172.

Public Interest Research Group. Box 19367, N.W., Washington, D.C. 20036. A Nader organization with many chapters.

Public Media Center. 25 Scotland Street, San Francisco, Calif. 94133. Assists groups with all aspects of media work.

Resource Center for Non-Violence. Box 2324, Santa Cruz, Calif. 95063. Workshops, seminars, newsletter.

Urban Action, American Friends Service Committee, New England Regional Office. 2161 Massachusetts Avenue, Cambridge, Mass. 02140. Works in communities where groups are pitted against each other in struggles over resources and space; seeks to create communication between groups and to develop understanding of the common oppression generated from sources outside the strife-torn communities.

Bibliography

Alternative, Responsible, Simple Way of Life

Eller, Vernard. *The Simple Life; The Christian Stance Toward Possessions.* Grand Rapids, Mich.: Eerdmans, 1973.

Gibson, William E., and the Eco-Justice Task Force. *A Covenant Group for Lifestyle Assessment.* Available from: Alternatives, Box 1707, Forest Park, Ga. 30051, $4.

Gish, Arthur. *Beyond the Rat Race,* rev. ed. Scottdale, Pa: Herald Press, 1981.

Henderson, Hazel. *The Politics of the Solar Age: Alternatives to Economics.* New York: Anchor/Doubleday, 1981.

Johnson, Warren. *Muddling Toward Frugality.* Boulder, Colo.: Shambhala, 1978.

Jurgenson, Barbara. *How to Live Better on Less: A Guide for Waste Watchers.* Minneapolis, Minn.: Augsburg, 1974.

Leopold, Aldo. *Sand County Almanac.* New York: Oxford Univ. Press, 1949.

Nearing, Helen, and Scott Nearing. *Living the Good Life: How to Live Sanely and Simply in a Troubled World.* New York: Schocken, 1971.

Nearing, Helen, and Scott Nearing. *Continuing the Good Life: Half a Century of Homesteading.* New York: Schocken, 1979.

Sine, Tom. *The Mustard Seed Conspiracy.* Waco, Texas: Word Books, 1981.

Nonviolent Social Change

Allen, Herb, ed. *The Bread Game: The Realities of Foundation Fundraising,* 3rd ed. 1981. Available from: New Glide Publications, 330 Ellis Street, San Francisco, Calif. 94102. $7.70.

American Friends Service Committee. *A Compassionate Peace: A Future for the Middle East.* 1982. Available from: AFSC National Office, address above. $6.95 ppd.; 10 or more copies, $5/copy + 20 percent postage.

American Friends Service Committee. *South Africa: Challenge and Hope.* 1982. Available from: AFSC National Office, address above. $5.95 ppd.; 10 or more copies, $2.50/copy + 20 percent postage.

Borremans, Valentine. *Guide to Convivial Tools.* New York: Bowker, 1979. A special edition of *Library Journal;* bibliography of nearly one thousand items.

Brigham, Nancy, and Steve Bagson. *How to Do Leaflets, Newsletters, and Newspapers.* New York; Hastings, 1982.

Brinton, Howard. *The Peace Testimony of the Society of Friends.* Available from: AFSC, address above. $.50.

Brown, Robert McAfee. *Making Peace in the Global Village.* Philadelphia, Pa.: Westminster Press, 1981.

Choice or Chance. Slideshow on the draft and enlistment; Spanish or English. Available from: AFSC, address above. $80 for slideshow; $80 for film strip; $110 for video cassette; or rental from AFSC regional office.

Coover, Virginia, et al. *Resource Manual for a Living Revolution,* rev. ed. Philadelphia: New Society, 1981.

Desai, Narayan. *Handbook for Satyagrahis: A Manual for Volunteers of Total Revolution.* Philadelphia: New Society, 1982.

Durland, William. *People Pay for Peace.* Published by Center on Law and Pacifism. Available from: Alternatives, Box 1707, Forest Park, Ga. 30051. $4/copy + 15 percent postage.

Gandhi, M. K. *All Men Are Brothers.* Chicago: World Without War Publications, 1972.

Gordon, Robbie. *We Interrupt This Program . . . A Citizen's Guide to Using the Media for Social Change.* 1978. Available from: Citizen Involvement Training Project, c/o Univ. of Mass., Amherst, Mass. 01003.

Gowan, Susanne, et al. *Moving Toward a New Society.* Philadelphia: New Society.

Kahn, Si. *Organizing, A Guide for Grassroots Leaders.* New York: McGraw-Hill, 1982.

Lakein, Alan. *How to Get Control of Your Time and Your Life.* New York: New American Library, 1973.

Lipnack, J., and J. Stamps. *Networking; The First Report and Directory.* New York: Doubleday/Dolphin, 1982.

Macy, Joanna. *Despairwork: Awakening to the Peril and Promise of Our Time.* Philadelphia: New Society, 1983.

Macy, Joanna Rogers. *Despair and Personal Power in the Nuclear Age.* Philadelphia: New Society, 1983.

McAllister, Pam, ed. *Rewaeving the Web of Life: Feminism and Nonviolence.* Philadelphia: New Society, 1982.

McFadden, Dave, and Jim Wake. *The Freeze Economy.* 1983. Available from: Mid-Peninsula Conversion Project, 222 C View Street, Menlo Park, Calif. 94041. $2.50.

Mitiguy, Nancy. *The Rich Get Richer and the Poor Write Proposals.* 1978. Available from: Citizen Involvement Training Project, c/o Univ. of Mass., Amherst, Mass. 01003.

Sharp, Gene. *The Politics of Nonviolent Action.* 3 vols. Boston: Porter Sargent Publishers, 1973. Vol. 2 details hundreds of examples of nonviolent change tactics.

Sider, Ronald J., and R. K. Taylor. *Nuclear Holocaust and Christain Hope: A Book for Christian Peacemakers.* Ramsey, N.J.: Paulist Press, 1982.

Stokes, Bruce. *Helping Ourselves; Local Solutions to Global Problems.* New York: Norton and Company, 1981.

Taylor, Richard K. *Blockade! Guide to Nonviolent Intervention.* Maryknoll, N.Y.: Orbis Books, 1977.

Vanguard Public Foundation. *Robin Hood Was Right: A Guide to Giving Your Money for Social Change.* 1977. Available from: Vanguard, 4111 24th Street, San Francisco, Calif. 94114. $5.

Villarejo, Don. *Research for Action.* 1980. Available from: California Institute for Rural Studies, Box 530, Davis, Calif. $8.75.

Wagner, P., and L. Smith. *The Networking Game.* Available from: Network Research, Box 18666, Denver, Colo. 80218. $2 ppd.

Wallis, Jim. *Waging Peace: A Handbook for the Struggle to Abolish Nuclear Weapons.* San Francisco: Harper & Row, 1982.

References Concerning Many Topics Discussed in This Book

Boyle, Godfrey, and Peter Harper, eds. *Radical Technology.* New York: Pantheon, 1976.

Brand, Stuart, ed. *The Next Whole Earth Catalog: Access to Tools,* 2nd ed. Sausalito, Calif.: Point, 1982.

Callenbach, Ernest. *The Ecotopian Encyclopedia for the Eighties.* Berkeley, Calif.: And/Or Press, 1981.

Center for Renewable Resources. *Shining Examples: Model Projects Using Renewable Resources.* Available from: 641 South Pickett Street, Alexandria, Va. 22304. $6.95 + 15 percent postage.

Co-Evolution. Quarterly journal by the Whole Earth Catalog people. Available from: Box 428, Sausalito, Calif. 94965.

Community Publications Cooperative. *A Guide to Cooperative Alternatives.* 1979. Available from: Box 426, Louisa, Va. 23093. $5.95.

Corporate Examiner. Newsletter. Available from: Interfaith Center on Corporate Responsibility, 475 Riverside Drive, Room 566, New York, N.Y. 10115.

Daly, Herman. *Steady-State Economics; The Economics of Biophysical Equilibrium and Moral Growth.* San Francisco: W. H. Freeman, 1977.

Daly, Herman. *Toward a Steady State Economy.* San Francisco: W. H. Freeman, 1973.

Daly, Herman, ed. *Economics, Ecology, Ethics: Essays Toward a Steady-State Economy.* San Francisco: W. H. Freeman, 1980.

deMoll, Lane, and Gigi Coe, eds. *Stepping Stones.* New York: Schocken, 1978.

Rainbook: Resources for Appropriate Technology. New York: Schocken, 1977.

Rain: Journal of Appropriate Technology. Available from: 2270 Northwest Irving, Portland, Oreg. 97210.

Raise the Stakes. Periodical concerning bioregionalism and global change. Available from: Planet Drum Foundation, Box 31251, San Francisco, Calif. 94131. $15/year membership in foundation includes subscription.

Schumacher, Ernest F. *Small Is Beautiful: Economics as If People Mattered.* New York: Harper & Row, 1973.

The Work Book. Periodical. Available from: Southwest Research and Information Center, Box 4524, Albuquerque, N.Mex. 87106.